MASTERS

HOW TWO GUYS CREATED AN EMPIRE
AND TRANSFORMED POP CULTURE

OF DOOM

MASTERS

HOW TWO GUYS CREATED AN EMPIRE
AND TRANSFORMED POP CULTURE

OF DOOM

DAVID KUSHNER

piatkus

PIATKUS

First published in the US in 2003 by Random House, Inc.
First published in Great Britain in 2003 by Judy Piatkus
This paperback edition published in 2004
Reprinted 2011, 2012 (twice), 2013 (twice), 2014

A CIP catalogue record for this book
is available from the British Library.

ISBN 978-0-7499-2489-8

Book design by Jennifer Ann Daddio

Printed and bound by CPI Group (UK) Ltd, Croydon, CR0 4YY

Papers used by Piatkus are from well-managed forests
and other responsible sources.

MIX
Paper from
responsible sources
FSC® C104740

Piatkus
An imprint of
Little, Brown Book Group
100 Victoria Embankment
London EC4Y 0DY

An Hachette UK Company
www.hachette.co.uk

www.piatkus.co.uk

FOR MY FAMILY

CONTENTS

INTRODUCTION

The Two Johns

There were two games. One was played in life. The other was lived in play. Naturally these worlds collided, and so did the Two Johns.

It happened one afternoon in April 2000 in the bowels of downtown Dallas. The occasion was a $100,000 prize tournament of the computer game Quake III Arena. Hosted by the Cyberathlete Professional League, an organization that hoped to become the NFL of the medium, the gathering was BYOC—bring your own computer. Hundreds of machines were networked together in the basement of the Hyatt hotel for seventy-two hours of nonstop action. On a large video screen that displayed the games being played, rockets soared across digital arenas. Cigar-chomping space marines, busty dominatrix warriors, maniacal bloodstained clowns, hunted each other with rocket launchers and plasma guns. The object was simple: The player with the most kills wins.

The gamers at the event were as hard-core as they came. More than one thousand had road-tripped from as far as Florida and even Finland with their monitors, keyboards, and mice. They competed until they passed out at their computers or crawled under their tables to sleep on pizza box pillows. A proud couple carried a newborn baby in home-made Quake pajamas. Two jocks paraded with their hair freshly shaved into the shape of Quake's clawlike logo; their girlfriends made their way around the convention hall, brandishing razors for anyone else who wanted the ultimate in devotional trims.

Such passion was hardly uncommon in Dallas, the capital of ultra-violent games like Quake and Doom. Paintball-like contests played from a first-person point of view, the games have pioneered a genre known as first-person shooters. They are among the bestselling franchises in this $10.8 billion industry and a sizable reason why Americans spend more money on video games than on movie tickets. They have driven the evolution of computing, pushing the edge of 3-D graphics and forging a standard for online play and community. They have created enough sociopolitical heat to get banned in some countries and, in the United States, blamed for inciting a killing spree by two fans at Columbine High School in 1999.

As a result, they have spawned their own unique outlaw community, a high-stakes, high-tech mecca for skilled and driven young gamers. In this world, no gamers were more skilled and driven than the co-creators of Doom and Quake, John Carmack and John Romero, or, as they were known, the Two Johns.

For a new generation, Carmack and Romero personified an American dream: they were self-made individuals who had transformed their personal passions into a big business, a new art form, and a cultural phenomenon. Their story made them the unlikeliest of antiheroes, esteemed by both Fortune 500 executives and computer hackers alike, and heralded as the Lennon and McCartney of video games (though they probably preferred being compared to Metallica). The Two Johns had escaped the broken homes of their youth to make some of the most influential games in history, until the very games they made tore them apart. Now in minutes, years after they had split, they were coming back together before their fans.

Carmack and Romero had each agreed to speak to their minions about their latest projects: Carmack's Quake III Arena, which he'd programmed at the company they cofounded, id Software, and Romero's Daikatana, the long-awaited epic he had been developing at his new and competing start-up, Ion Storm. The games embodied the polar differences that had once made the Two Johns such a dynamic duo and now made them seemingly irreparable rivals. Their relationship was a study of human alchemy.

The twenty-nine-year-old Carmack was a monkish and philanthropic programmer who built high-powered rockets in his spare time (and made Bill Gates's short list of geniuses); his game and life aspired to the elegant discipline of computer code. The thirty-two-year-old Romero was a brash designer whose bad-boy image made him the industry's rock star; he would risk everything, including his reputation, to realize his wildest visions. As Carmack put it shortly after their breakup: "Romero wants an empire, I just want to create good programs."

When the hour of the Two Johns' arrival at the hotel finally approached, the gamers turned their attention from the skirmish on screen to the real-life one between the ex-partners. Out in the parking lot, Carmack and Romero pulled up one shortly after the other in the Ferraris they had bought together at the height of their collaboration. Carmack walked quickly past the crowd; he had short, sandy blond hair, square glasses, and a T-shirt of a walking hairball with two big eyes and legs. Romero sauntered in with his girlfriend, the sharpshooting gamer and *Playboy* model Stevie Case; he wore tight black jeans and matching shirt, and his infamous dark mane hung down near his waist. As they passed each other in the hall, the Two Johns nodded obligatorily, then continued to their posts.

It was time for this game to begin.

MASTERS OF DOOM

ONE

The Rock Star

Eleven-year-old John Romero jumped onto his dirt bike, heading for trouble again. A scrawny kid with thick glasses, he pedaled past the modest homes of Rocklin, California, to the Roundtable Pizza Parlor. He knew he wasn't supposed to be going there this summer afternoon in 1979, but he couldn't help himself. That was where the games were.

Specifically, what was there was Asteroids, or, as Romero put it, "the coolest game planet Earth has ever seen!" There was nothing else like the feeling he got tapping the control buttons as the rocks hurled toward his triangular ship and the *Jaws*-style theme music blipped in suspense, *dum dum dum dum dum dum;* Romero mimicked these video game sounds the way other kids did celebrities. Fun like this was worth risking everything: the crush of the meteors, the theft of the paper route money, the wrath of his stepfather. Because no matter what Romero suffered, he could always escape back into the games.

At the moment, what he expected to suffer was a legendary whipping. His stepfather, John Schuneman—a former drill sergeant—had commanded Romero to steer clear of arcades. Arcades bred games. Games bred delinquents. Delinquency bred failure in school and in life.

3

As his stepfather was fond of reminding him, his mother had enough problems trying to provide for Romero and his younger brother, Ralph, since her first husband left the family five years earlier. His stepfather was under stress of his own with a top-secret government job retrieving black boxes of classified information from downed U.S. spy planes across the world. "Hey, little man," he had said just a few days before, "consider yourself warned."

Romero did heed the warning—sort of. He usually played games at Timothy's, a little pizza joint in town; this time he and his friends headed into a less traveled spot, the Roundtable. He still had his initials, AJR for his full name, Alfonso John Romero, next to the high score here, just like he did on all the Asteroids machines in town. He didn't have only the number-one score, he owned the entire top ten. "Watch this," Romero told his friends, as he slipped in the quarter and started to play.

The action didn't last long. As he was about to complete a round, he felt a heavy palm grip his shoulder. "What the fuck, dude?" he said, assuming one of his friends was trying to spoil his game. Then his face smashed into the machine.

Romero's stepfather dragged him past his friends to his pickup truck, throwing the dirt bike in the back. Romero had done a poor job of hiding his bike, and his stepfather had seen it while driving home from work. "You really screwed up this time, little man," his stepfather said. He led Romero into the house, where Romero's mother and his visiting grandmother stood in the kitchen. "Johnny was at the arcade again," his stepfather said. "You know what that's like? That's like telling your mother 'Fuck you.' "

He beat Romero until the boy had a fat lip and a black eye. Romero was grounded for two weeks. The next day he snuck back to the arcade.

Romero was born resilient, his mother, Ginny, said, a four-and-one-half-pound baby delivered on October 28, 1967, six weeks premature. His parents, married only a few months before, had been living long in hard times. Ginny, good-humored and easygoing, met Alfonso Antonio

Romero when they were teenagers in Tucson, Arizona. Alfonso, a first-generation Mexican American, was a maintenance man at an air force base, spending his days fixing air conditioners and heating systems. After Alfonso and Ginny got married, they headed in a 1948 Chrysler with three hundred dollars to Colorado, hoping their interracial relationship would thrive in more tolerant surroundings.

Though the situation improved there, the couple returned to Tucson after Romero was born so his dad could take a job in the copper mines. The work was hard, the effect sour. Alfonso would frequently come home drunk if he came home at all. There was soon a second child, Ralph. John Romero savored the good times: the barbecues, the horsing around. Once his dad stumbled in at 10:00 P.M. and woke him. "Come on," he slurred, "we're going camping." They drove into the hills of saguaro cacti to sleep under the stars. One afternoon his father left to pick up groceries. Romero wouldn't see him again for two years.

Within that time his mother remarried. John Schuneman, fourteen years her senior, tried to befriend him. One afternoon he found the six-year-old boy sketching a Lamborghini sports car at the kitchen table. The drawing was so good that his stepfather assumed it had been traced. As a test, he put a Hot Wheels toy car on the table and watched as Romero drew. This sketch too was perfect. Schuneman asked Johnny what he wanted to be when he grew up. The boy said, "A rich bachelor."

For a while, this relationship flourished. Recognizing Romero's love of arcade games, his stepfather would drive him to local competitions—all of which Romero won. Romero was so good at Pac-Man that he could maneuver the round yellow character through a maze of fruit and dots with his eyes shut. But soon his stepfather noticed that Romero's hobby was taking a more obsessive turn.

It started one summer day in 1979, when Romero's brother, Ralph, and a friend came rushing through the front door. They had just biked up to Sierra College, they told him, and made a discovery. "There are games up there!" they said. "Games that you don't have to pay for!" Games that some sympathetic students let them play. Games on these strange big *computers*.

Romero grabbed his bike and raced with them to the college's computer lab. There was no problem for them to hang out at the lab. This was not uncommon at the time. The computer underground did not discriminate by age; a geek was a geek was a geek. And since the students often held the keys to the labs, there weren't professors to tell the kids to scram. Romero had never seen anything like what he found inside. Cold air gushed from the air-conditioning vents as students milled around computer terminals. Everyone was playing a game that consisted only of words on the terminal screen: "You are standing at the end of a road before a small brick building. Around you is a forest. A small stream flows out of the building towards a gully. In the distance there is a gleaming white tower."

This was Colossal Cave Adventure, the hottest thing going. Romero knew why: it was like a computer-game version of Dungeons and Dragons. D&D, as it was commonly known, was a pen-and-paper role-playing game that cast players in a *Lord of the Rings*–like adventure of imagination. Many adults lazily dismissed it as geekish escapism. But to understand a boy like Romero, an avid D&D player, was to understand the game.

Created in 1972 by Gary Gygax and Dave Arneson, two friends in their early twenties, Dungeons and Dragons was an underground phenomenon, particularly on college campuses, thanks to word of mouth and controversy. It achieved urban legend status when a student named James Dallas Egbert III disappeared in the steam tunnels underneath Michigan State University while reportedly reenacting the game; a Tom Hanks movie called *Mazes and Monsters* was loosely based on the event. D&D would grow into an international cottage industry, accounting for $25 million in annual sales from novels, games, T-shirts, and rule books.

The appeal was primal. "In Dungeons and Dragons," Gygax said, "the average person gets a call to glory and becomes a hero and undergoes change. In the real world, children, especially, have no power; they must answer to everyone, they don't direct their own lives, but in this game, they become super powerful and affect everything." In D&D, there was no winning in the traditional sense. It was more akin to interactive fiction. The participants consisted of at least two or three players and a Dungeon Master, the person who would invent and direct the adventures. All they needed was the D&D rule book, some special polyhedral dice, and a pencil and paper. To begin, players chose and developed characters they would become in the game, from dwarves to elves, gnomes to humans.

Gathered around a table, they would listen as the Dungeon Master cracked open the D&D rule book—which contained descriptions of monsters, magic, and characters—and fabricated a scene: down by a river, perhaps, a castle shrouded in mist, the distant growl of a beast. *Which way shall you go?* If the players chose to pursue the screams, the Dungeon Master would select just what ogre or chimera they would face. His roll of the die determined how they fared; no matter how wild the imaginings, a random burst of data ruled one's fate. It was not surprising that computer programmers liked the game or that one of the first games they created, Colossal Cave Adventure, was inspired by D&D.

The object of Colossal Cave was to fight battles while trying to retrieve treasures within a magical cave. By typing in a direction, say "north" or "south," or a command, "hit" or "attack," Romero could explore what felt like a novel in which he was the protagonist. As he chose his actions, he'd go deeper into the woods until the walls of the lab seemed to become trees, the air-conditioning flow a river. It was another world. Imbued with his imagination, it was real.

Even more impressively, it was an alternate reality that he could *create*. Since the seventies, the electronic gaming industry had been dominated by arcade machines like Asteroids and home consoles like the Atari 2600. Writing software for these platforms required expensive development systems and corporate backing. But computer games were different. They were accessible. They came with their own tools, their own portals—a way inside. And the people who had the keys were not authoritarian monsters, they were *dudes*. Romero was young, but he was a dude in the making, he figured. The Wizard of this Oz could be him.

Every Saturday at 7:30 A.M., Romero would bike to the college, where the students—charmed by his gumption—showed him how to program on refrigerator-size Hewlett-Packard mainframe computers. Developed in the fifties, these were the early giants of the computer industry, monolithic machines that were programmed by inserting series of hole-punched cards that fed the code. IBM, which produced both the computers and the punch card machines, dominated the market, with sales reaching over $7 billion in the 1960s. By the seventies, mainframes and their smaller cousins, the minicomputers, had infiltrated corporations, government offices, and universities. But they were not yet in homes.

For this reason, budding computer enthusiasts like Romero trolled university computer labs, where they could have hands-on access to the machines. Late at night, after the professors went home, students gathered to explore, play, and hack. The computer felt like a revolutionary tool: a means of self-empowerment and fantasy fulfillment. Programmers skipped classes, dates, baths. And as soon as they had the knowledge, they made games.

The first one came in 1958 from the most unlikely of places: a U.S. government nuclear research lab. The head of the Brookhaven Nation Laboratory's instrumentation division, Willy Higinbotham, was planning a public relations tour of the facility for some concerned local farmers, and needed something to win them over. So, with the help of his colleagues, he programmed a rudimentary tennis simulation using a computer and a small, round oscilloscope screen. The game, which he called "Tennis for 2," consisted merely of a white dot ball hopping back and forth over a small white line. It thrilled the crowds. Then it was dismantled and put away.

Three years later, in 1961, Steve "Slug" Russell and a group of other students at the Massachusetts Institute of Technology created Spacewar on the first minicomputer, the PDP-1. In this game, two players shot up each other's rocket ships while drifting around a black hole. Ten years later, a programmer and amateur cave explorer in Boston, Will Crowther, created text-based spelunking simulation. When a hacker at Stanford named Don Woods saw the game, he contacted Crowther to see if it was okay for him to modify the game to include more fantasy elements. The result was Colossal Cave Adventure. This gave rise to the text-adventure craze, as students and hackers in computer labs across the country began playing and modifying games of their own—often based on Dungeons and Dragons or *Star Trek.*

Romero was growing up in the eighties as a fourth-generation game hacker: the first having been the students who worked on the minicomputers in the fifties and sixties at MIT; the second, the ones who picked up the ball in Silicon Valley and at Stanford University in the seventies; the third being the dawning game companies of the early eighties. To belong, Romero just had to learn the language of the priests, the game developers: a programming language called HP-BASIC. He was a swift and persistent student, cornering anyone who could answer his increasingly complex questions.

His parents were less than impressed by his new passion. At issue were Romero's grades, which had plummeted from A's and B's to C's and D's. He was bright but too easily distracted, they thought, too consumed by games and computers. Despite this being the golden age of video games—with arcade games bringing in $5 billion a year and even home systems earning $1 billion—his stepfather did not believe game development to be a proper vocation. "You'll never make any money making games," he often said. "You need to make something people really need, like business applications."

As the fights with his stepfather escalated, so did Romero's imagination. He began exorcising the backwash of emotional and physical violence through his illustrations. For years he had been raised on comics—the B-movie horror of E.C. Comics, the scatological satire of *MAD*, the heroic adventures of Spider-Man and the Fantastic Four. By age eleven, he churned out his own. In one, a dog named Chewy was invited to play ball with his owner. With a strong throw, the owner hurled the ball into Chewy's eye, causing the dog's head to split open and spill out green brains. "The End," Romero scrawled at the bottom, adding the epitaph "Poor Ol' Chewy."

At school, Romero turned in a homemade comic book called *Weird* for an art class assignment. In one section he described and illustrated "10 Different Ways to Torture Someone," including "Poke a needle all over the victim's body and in a few days . . . watch him turn into a giant scab" and "Burn the victim's feet while victim is strapped in a chair." Another, titled "How to Drive the Babysitter Mad!," illustrated suggestions including "Get out a very sharp dagger and pretend that you stabbed yourself" and "Stick electric cord into your ears and pretend that you are a radio." The teacher returned the assignment with a note that read, "This was awfully gross. I don't think it needs to be that way." Romero got a B+ for his artistic efforts. But he saved his hardest work for his code.

Within weeks of his first trip to Sierra College, he had programmed his first computer game: a text adventure. Because the mainframes couldn't save data, the programming had to be punched on waxy paper cards; each card represented a line of code—a typical game would take thousands. After every day at the school, Romero would wrap the stack of cards in bungee cord around the back of his bike and pedal home. When he'd return to the lab the next time, he'd have to feed the cards into the computer again to get the game to run. One day on the way home from the college, Romero's bike hit a bump in the road. Two hundred cards went flying into the air and scattered across the wet ground. Romero decided it was time to move on.

He soon found his next love: the Apple II computer. Apple had become the darling of the indie hacker set ever since the machine was introduced at a 1976 meeting of the Homebrew Computer Club, a ragtag group of California techies. As the first accessible home computers, Apples were ideally suited for making and playing games. This was thanks in no small part to the roots of the company's cofounders, Steve Jobs and Stephen Wozniak—or, as they became known, the Two Steves.

Jobs, a college dropout with a passion for Buddhism and philosophy, took his first job at a start-up video game company called Atari in the mid-seventies. Atari was legendary because its founder, Nolan Bushnell, had produced the 1972 arcade hit, Pong, a tennislike game that challenged players to maneuver white strip paddles on either side of the screen while hitting a dot back and forth. Jobs would share the confidence and brashness of his boss, who had hacked Spacewar to create his first arcade game, Computer Space. But Jobs had larger plans to realize with his childhood friend Wozniak, a.k.a. Woz, a math whiz who could spend hours playing a video game.

Woz was equal parts programming genius and mischievous

prankster, known around the San Francisco Bay Area for running his own dial-a-joke phone number. In computers, Woz found the perfect place to combine his humor and his math skills, creating a game that flashed the message "Oh Shit" on the screen when the player lost a round. Jobs recruited Woz to design Breakout, a new game for Atari. This alchemy of Jobs's entrepreneurial vision and Woz's programming ingenuity gave birth to their company, Apple. Created in 1976, the first Apple computer was essentially a prototype for the Homebrew crowd, priced devilishly at $666.66. But the Apple II, made the following year, was mass market, with a keyboard, BASIC compatibility, and, best of all, color graphics. There was no hard drive, but it came with two game paddles. It was *made* for games.

Romero had first seen the stylish beige Apple II computers up at Sierra College. While a mainframe's graphics were capable of, at best, spitting out white blocks and lines, the Apple II's monitor burst with color and high-resolution dots. Romero had spent the rest of the day running around the lab trying to find out all he could about this magical new box. Whenever he was at the school, Romero played the increasingly diverse lineup of Apple II games.

Many were rip-offs of arcade hits like Asteroids and Space Invaders. Others showed signs of true innovation. For instance, Ultima. Richard Garriott, a.k.a. Lord British, the son of an astronaut in Texas, spoke in Middle English and created the massively successful graphical role-playing series of Ultima games. As in Dungeons and Dragons, players chose to be wizards or elves, fighting dragons and building characters. The graphics were crude, with landscapes represented by blocky colored squares; a green block, ostensibly, a tree; a brown one, a mountain. Players never saw their smudgy stick figure characters attacking monsters, they would just walk up to a dragon blip and wait for a text explanation of the results. But gamers overlooked the crudeness for what the games *implied:* a novelistic and participatory experience, a world.

Ultima also showed off the latent entrepreneurship of this new breed of hackers. Garriott came to fame in the early eighties through his own initiative. Like many other Apple II programmers, he would hand-distribute his games on floppy disks sealed in clear plastic Ziploc bags to local computer stores. Ken and Roberta Williams, a young married couple in Northern California, also pioneered the Ziploc distribution method, turning their homemade graphical role-playing games into a $10 million–a–year company, Sierra On-Line—a haven of hippie digerati with hot tub parties to boot. Silas Warner, a six-foot, nine-inch, 320-pound legend, cofounded his own company, Muse Software, and put out another of Romero's favorite games, the darkly suspenseful Castle Wolfenstein, in which players ran their stick figure characters through a series of plain mazes while battling Nazis and, ultimately, Hitler himself.

Romero spent so much time on the games that his stepfather decided it was best for the family to have a computer at home, where they could better keep an eye on him. The day the Apple II arrived, he found his wife standing at the door. "Promise you won't get angry," she pleaded. An empty Apple II box sat in the living room. "Johnny put it all together already," she said cautiously. A few ill-sounding beeps could be heard. Enraged, Schuneman stomped down the hall and flung open the door, expecting to encounter a savage pile of plastic and wires. Instead he found Romero at the functioning machine, typing. His stepfather stood for a minute quietly, then went in and let the boy show him some games.

For Christmas that year, 1982, Romero had two requests: a book called *Apple Graphics Arcade Tutorial* and another called *Assembly Lines*, which explained assembly language, a faster and more cryptic code. These books became his lifeblood when his stepfather took the family on a job reassignment to the Royal Air Force base in Alconbury, a small town in central England. There Romero wrote games that could exploit his refined assembly language skills. He drew his own packages and created his own artwork. Selling his games at school, Romero became known for his skills.

Romero's stepfather knew something was up when an officer working on a classified Russian dogfight simulation asked him if his stepson was interested in a part-time job. The next day an officer led the boy into an icy room filled with large computers. A black drape blocked Romero's view of the classified maps, documents, and machines. He was told they needed help translating a program from a mainframe to a minicomputer. On the monitor he saw a crudely drawn flight simulation. "No problem," he said. "I know everything about games."

Romero was ready for the big time. The computer was now a cultural icon. *Time* magazine even put a computer on its cover in place of its usual Man of the Year as 1982's "Machine of the Year." Games for the computer were becoming all the more enticing as video games — made for systems or "consoles" that hooked up to television sets — collapsed with a resounding crash. A surplus of games and hardware had led to $536 million in losses for Atari alone in 1983. Meanwhile, home computers were gaining speed. Commodore's VIC-20 and 64 computers helped it surpass Apple with $1 billion in sales. And these computers needed games.

For a kid working with an Apple II, there were two ways to get published in the nascent industry. The big publishers, like Sierra and Electronic Arts, Romero found, were fairly inaccessible. More within his reach were the enthusiast magazines, which, to save costs, printed games as code on their pages. To play, the reader would have to type the program laboriously into a computer.

While in England, Romero spent every spare moment in front of the Apple, working on games to send away for publication. The resulting slip in his grades angered his stepfather, reviving old battles and inspiring, for Romero, new comics he called "Melvin." The action was always the same: Melvin, a boy, would do something his father, a bald guy with sunglasses, like his stepdad, had told him not to do — then suffer the creatively grisly consequences. In one strip, Melvin agrees to do the dishes but instead disappears to play computer games. After discovering this, his dad waits until Melvin is sleeping, runs into his room screaming, "You little fucker!" then punches his face into a bloody, eye-popping pulp. Romero wasn't the only one who found a release in the violent comics. Kids at school would sneak him ideas for how Melvin should meet his doom. Romero drew them all, exaggerating every opportunity for scatological gore. He was much admired.

The attention changed him. He was listening to heavy metal — Judas Priest, Metallica, Mötley Crüe. He dated a half dozen girls. The one he liked best soon became his girlfriend, a popular, intelligent, and outgoing daughter of a respected officer. She had him buy button-down shirts, wear nice jeans and contacts. After years of being beaten down by his father and his stepfather, Romero was finally getting recognition.

At sixteen, Romero was just as eager to have success with his games. After eight months of rejections, the good news came on March 5, 1984, from an Apple magazine called *InCider*. An editor, weary from a recent trip to Mardi Gras, wrote that the magazine had decided to publish the code for Romero's Scout Search, a low-resolution maze game in which the player—represented by a single dot—had to gather all his scouts—more dots—before being attacked by a grizzly bear—another dot. It didn't look great, but it was fun to play. Romero would be paid $100. And the magazine might be interested in publishing some of the other games Romero had sent in. "I'll get around to them as soon as my hangover clears up," the editor wrote.

Romero put all his energy into making more games, for which he did all the programming and art. He could program one game in a half hour. He arrived at a naming convention: every game title was a two-word alliteration, like Alien Attack or Cavern Crusader. He grew increasingly brash. "When I win this month's [programming] contest," he wrote to one magazine, "(I *will* win; my program's awesome!), instead of a $500 prize, could I just take the $500? The same goes for the annual prize of $1000 (which I'll get also)." He signed this letter, like all of them, "John Romero, Ace Programmer." And he won the cash.

The success inspired him to get back in touch with his biological dad, who was living in Utah. In a letter he wrote on makeshift letterhead for his company, Capitol Ideas Software, he was eager to show how far he'd come, telling about all the contests and publications. "I've been learning computers for $4^{1}/_{2}$ years now," Romero wrote. "My programming has just undergone another revolution." This time he signed his letter "John Romero, Ace Programmer, Contest Winner, Future Rich Person." He was already on his way, he could *feel* it. But to make it big, Future Rich Person big, he had to leave England and get back to America.

Romero got his wish in 1986, when he returned with his family to California. He signed up for classes at Sierra College, which he started just before finishing his senior year of high school. His publishing rolled; almost everything he churned out found its way into a computer magazine. His games made magazine covers. And, during a shift at Burger King, he fell in love.

Kelly Mitchell came into the restaurant one day and caught Romero's eye from behind the cash register. The two began dating. Kelly was the daughter of an upper-middle-class Mormon family. Best of all, she lived in a cool house high on a hill in town. Though Romero had dated other girls, no one was as fun and compatible as Kelly—even if she didn't care about games. For nineteen-year-old Romero, it seemed like the chance to start the family he'd never really had. He proposed, and the two were married in 1987.

He decided it was time to go for his dream job. He had published ten games. He was about to graduate from high school. He was taking on a family. He needed a gig. The opportunity came on September 15, 1987, with a gathering for Apple computer enthusiasts called the Applefest. Romero had read about it in a computer magazine and knew that *everyone* would be there: the big game publishers, Origin and Sierra, as well as the magazines that were keeping him gainfully published, *Uptime, Nibble,* and *InCider.* He arrived at the convention center in San Francisco as hackers and gamers lugged monitors, printouts, and disks inside. A table overflowed with *Nibble* magazines that featured one of Romero's games on the cover. In the booth for *Uptime,* a computer magazine published on floppy disk, another of his games played on the monitors. Oh yeah, Romero thought, I'm gonna do well here.

At the *Uptime* booth, Romero met Jay Wilbur, the editor who had been buying up his work. Jay, a strapping twenty-seven-year-old former bartender at T.G.I. Friday's, looked like a kid pumped up with air and peppered with facial hair. Jay had a soft spot for Romero: an irreverent but reliable programmer who understood the magic formula of a great game—easy to learn, difficult to master. Jay offered him a job. With typical bravado, Romero told him he'd have think about it.

Buzzed on his *Uptime* meeting, Romero headed right for the Origin booth, where a banner read, "Ultima V: Coming October 31!" Oh my God, Romero thought, the next Ultima! He sat down in front of a machine and popped in his disk. "What do you think you're doing?" a woman in marketing from Origin asked him. "You're taking our game out of our machine! You're not supposed to do that!"

Romero tapped a few keys. "Look at this!" he said. On the screen appeared a maze chase. He had written it using a complicated program that doubled the resolution of the graphics, making it look, essentially, twice as colorful and pristine. So-called double-res graphics were considered the high art of programming, and here was this skinny kid showing off some game that looked even better than the Ultima version on screen. The woman had only one question: "Are you looking for a job?"

Two months later, in November 1987, Romero was driving across the country, heading for his first day of work at Origin's office in New Hampshire. Eager but broke, he wrote hot checks to pay for tollbooth fees. He was driving with Kelly, his pregnant wife—their first baby was due in February. Kelly was less than thrilled about heading off into the snow, but Romero had convinced her in his charming and enthusiastic way. His life as an Ace Programmer and Rich Person was on its way, he promised.

The promise fell through. Despite his immediate success at Origin, Romero took the gamble of joining his boss, who was leaving to start a new company. It was a bad bet. The start-up couldn't drum up the requisite business. Before long Romero—now twenty-one years old with a wife, a baby boy, Michael, and another child on the way—was out of a job. The strain was beginning to wear on Kelly. Romero's hyperbole seemed to have no payoff, and she had returned to California to have her second baby near her parents. Romero had to call and tell her that there was nothing: no job, no apartment. He was sleeping on a friend's couch.

But Romero wasn't going to lie down and die. He had a dream to pursue, a family he loved. He could be the dad he'd never had himself, the kind of dad who would not just support his kids' games but *play* them. Romero phoned Jay Wilbur to see about a job at *Uptime*. Jay told him he was leaving *Uptime* to join his competitor Softdisk in Shreveport, Louisiana. Maybe, Jay suggested, Romero could get a job there too. Romero didn't hesitate. Sure, he'd go to Shreveport. The weather was there. The games were there. And so, he hoped, were the most hard-core of gamers.

TWO

The Rocket Scientist

John Carmack was a late talker. His parents were concerned until one day in 1971, when the fifteen-month-old boy waddled into the living room holding a sponge and uttered not just a single word but a complete sentence: "Here's your loofah, Daddy." It was as if he didn't want to mince words until he had something sensible to say. "Inga," the boy's father, Stan, told his wife, "perhaps we might have something a bit extraordinary on our hands."

The Carmacks were already a self-taught family. John Carmack's paternal grandfather and namesake was an electrician with a second-grade education, taught to read and write by his wife, a homemaker who had reached only the eighth grade. They raised their boy Stan in the poorest part of eastern Kentucky; Stan studied hard enough to earn a scholarship to a university, where he excelled at engineering, math, and eventually broadcast journalism and became the family's first college graduate. His wife was the daughter of a chemist and a physiotherapist. She inherited the interest in science, pursuing both nuclear medicine and a doctorate in microbiology. Inga and Stan, attractive college sweethearts, would pass their love of learning on to their first son.

Born on August 20, 1970, John D. Carmack II — or Jondi as he was nicknamed—grew amid the fruits of his parents' hard work. After his father became the nightly news anchor for one of the big three television stations in Kansas City, Missouri, the family moved to an upper-class suburb, where his younger brother, Peter, was born. There, Carmack went for the best education in town at a Catholic elementary school called Notre Dame. Skinny, short, with unruly blond hair and large glasses he had worn since before he was one year old, Carmack quickly distinguished himself. In second grade, only seven years old, he scored nearly perfect on every standardized test, placing himself at a ninth-grade comprehension level. He developed a unique speech impediment, adding a short, robotic humming sound to the end of his sentences, like a computer processing data: "12 times 12 equals 144 . . . mmm."

At home, he grew into a voracious reader like his parents, favoring fantasy novels such as Tolkien's *The Lord of the Rings*. He read comic books by the dozen, watched science fiction movies, and, most enjoyably, played Dungeons and Dragons. Carmack, more interested in creating D&D than playing, immediately gravitated to the role of Dungeon Master. He proved himself to be a unique and formidable inventor. While most Dungeon Masters relied on the rule book's explicitly charted styles of game play, Carmack abandoned the structure to devise elaborate campaigns of his own. After school, he would disappear into his room with a stack of graph paper and chart out his game world. He was in the third grade.

Despite his industriousness, there were some things Carmack couldn't escape. When assigned to write about his top five problems in life, he listed his parents' high expectations—twice. He found himself at particular odds with his mother, the disciplinarian of the family. In another assignment, he wrote about how one day, when he refused to do extracredit homework, his mother padlocked his comic book collection in a closet; unable to pick the lock, he removed the hinges and took off the door.

Carmack began lashing out more at school—he hated the structure and dogma. Religion, he thought, was irrational. He began challenging his classmates' beliefs after mass on Wednesdays. On at least one occasion, the other kid left the interrogation in tears. Carmack found a more productive way to exercise his analytical skills when a teacher wheeled in an Apple II. He had never worked on a computer before but took to the device as if it were an extension of his own body. It spoke the language of mathematics; it responded to his commands; and, he realized after seeing some games on the monitor, it contained worlds.

Until this point Carmack had been entranced by arcade games. He wasn't the best player around, but he loved the fast action and quick payback of Space Invaders, Asteroids, and Battlezone. Battlezone was unique in its point of view: it was first-person. Instead of looking down on the action from the side or from overhead, Carmack was in the action, looking out from inside a tank. Though the graphics were crude, made up of green geometric lines, they had the illusion of being three-dimensional. The game was so compelling that the U.S. government took notice, requesting a customized version for military training. It didn't take long for Carmack to want to customize games of his own. With a computer, it was possible.

When Carmack was in the fifth grade, his mother drove him to a local Radio Shack, where he took a course on the TRS-80 computer. He returned to school with the programming book in hand and set about teaching himself everything he needed to know. He read the passage about computers in the encyclopedia a dozen times. With his grades on the rise, he wrote a letter to his teacher explaining that "the logical thing to do would be to send me to the sixth grade," where he could learn more. The next year Carmack was transferred to the "gifted and talented" program of the Shawnee Mission East public school, among the first in the area to have a computer lab.

During and after school, Carmack found other gifted kids who shared his enthusiasm for the Apple II. They taught themselves BASIC programming. They played games. Soon enough they hacked the games. Once Carmack figured out where his character in Ultima resided in the code, he reprogrammed it to give himself extra capabilities. He relished this ability to create things out of thin air. As a programmer, he didn't have to rely on anyone else. If his code followed the logical progression of the rules established, it would work. Everything made sense.

Everything, he thought, except for his parents. When Carmack was twelve, they suddenly got divorced. Tensions between Stan and Inga over how to rear their children had become too great. The aftermath for Carmack was traumatic, Inga felt. Just as he was finding himself in school, he was pulled out and separated from his brother. They alternated years between parents, switching schools in turn. Carmack hated being separated from his father. Worse, when he was living with his mother, he had to fend for himself alone.

Despite his growing interest in computers, Inga didn't see the point of all his *games*. In her mind, if a boy was interested in computers, he didn't sit around playing Ultima; instead he worked hard in school, got good grades, then went to the Massachusetts Institute of Technology—just the recipe for a job at IBM. She loved him and only wanted what she thought was best. But Carmack didn't want any of it. All he wanted was his own computer with which to pursue his worlds. He became increasingly obstinate. Inga took him to psychologists to see why her once compliant boy was becoming so uncontrollable and dark.

Carmack found reprieve when his mother decided to move to Seattle soon after to pursue a new relationship. His father took the teenage boys to live with him, his new wife, and her two kids. Though Stan was still making a decent living as a news anchor, the sudden doubling of family size was too great to maintain his former lifestyle. So he ventured into the nearby blue-collar neighborhood of Raytown, where he found an old farmhouse on two acres of land within city limits. Overnight, it seemed, Carmack was in a strange house, with a strange family, and going to a strange school, a junior high with no gifted program or computers. He'd never felt so alone. Then one day he realized he wasn't.

The book *Hackers: Heroes of the Computer Revolution* was a revelation. Carmack had heard about hackers: In 1982 a Disney movie called *Tron* told the story of a video game designer, played by Jeff Bridges, who hacked *himself* into a video game world; in a 1983 movie called *WarGames*, Matthew Broderick played a young gamer who hacked into a government computer system and nearly triggered Armageddon. But this book's story was different—it was real. Written by Steven Levy in 1984, it explored the uncharted history and culture of the "Whiz Kids Who Changed Our World." The book traced the rise of renegade computer enthusiasts over twenty-five rollicking years, from the mainframe experimentalists at MIT in the fifties and sixties to the Homebrew epoch of Silicon Valley in the seventies and up through the computer game start-ups of the eighties.

These were not people who fit neatly into the stereotypes of outlaws or geeks. They came from and evolved into all walks of life: Bill Gates, a Harvard dropout who would write the first BASIC programming code for the pioneering Altair personal computer and form the most powerful software company in the world; game makers like Slug Russell, Ken and Roberta Williams, Richard "Ultima" Garriott; the Two Steves—Jobs and Wozniak—who turned their passion for gaming into the Apple II. They were all hackers.

"Though some in the field used the term *hacker* as a form of a derision," Levy wrote in the preface, "implying that hackers were either nerdy social outcasts or 'unprofessional' programmers who wrote dirty, 'nonstandard' computer code, I found them quite different. Beneath their often unimposing exteriors, they were adventurers, visionaries, risk-takers, artists . . . and the ones who most clearly saw why the computer was a truly revolutionary tool."

This Hacker Ethic read like a manifesto. When Carmack finished the book one night in bed, he had one thought: *I'm supposed to be in there!* He was a Whiz Kid. But he was in a nowhere house, in a nowhere school, with no good computers, no hacker culture at all. He soon found others who sympathized with his anger.

The kids from Raytown he liked were different from the ones he had left behind in Kansas City—edgier and more rebellious. Carmack fell into a group who shared his enthusiasm for games and computers. Together they discovered an underworld: an uncharted world on the emerging online communities of bulletin board systems, or BBSs. While an international network of computers known as the Internet had been around since the seventies, it was still largely the domain of government defense scientists and university researchers. By contrast, BBSs were computer clubhouses for the people—people just like Carmack.

Bulletin board systems came about in 1978, when two hackers named Ward Christensen and Randy Seuss wrote the first software to transmit data between microcomputers over telephone lines. The result was that people could "call" up each other's computers and swap information. In the eighties the systems quickly spawned what were essentially the first online communities, places where people with the will and skills could trade software and "talk" by posting text messages in forums. Anyone with a powerful enough computer system and a setup of phone lines and modems could start a BBS. They spread across the world, starting in dorm rooms, apartment buildings, computer labs. Systems such as the Whole Earth 'Lectronic Link, a.k.a. the WELL, in San Francisco and Software Creations in Massachusetts became hotbeds for hackers, Deadheads, and gamers.

Carmack didn't go on BBSs only for games. Here, he could research the most thrilling and illicit strains of hacker culture. He learned about phone phreaking: a means of hijacking free long-distance telephone service. He learned about MUDs: multiuser dungeons, text-based role-playing games that allowed players to act out D&D-type characters in a kind of real-time masquerade adventure. And he learned about bombs.

For Carmack, bombs were less about cheap thrills than about chemical engineering—a neat way to play scientist and, for good measure, make things go boom. Before long he and his friends were mixing the recipes they found online. They cut off match heads and mixed them with ammonium nitrate, made smoke bombs from potassium nitrate and sugar. Using ingredients from their high school science class, they brewed thermite, a malleable and powerful explosive. After school, they'd blow up concrete blocks under a bridge. One day they decided to use explosives for a more practical purpose: getting themselves computers.

Late one night Carmack and his friends snuck up to a nearby school where they knew there were Apple II machines. Carmack had read about how a thermite paste could be used to melt through glass, but he needed some kind of adhesive material, like Vaseline. He mixed the concoction and applied it to the window, dissolving the glass so they could pop out holes to crawl through. A fat friend, however, had more than a little trouble squeezing inside; he reached through the hole instead and opened the window to let himself in. Doing so, he triggered the silent alarm. The cops came in no time.

The fourteen-year-old Carmack was sent for psychiatric evaluation to help determine his sentence. He came into the room with a sizable chip on his shoulder. The interview didn't go well. Carmack was later told the contents of his evaluation: "Boy behaves like a walking brain with legs . . . no empathy for other human beings." At one point the man twiddled his pencil and asked Carmack, "If you hadn't been caught, do you think you would have done something like this again?"

"If I hadn't been caught," Carmack replied honestly, "yes, I probably would have done that again."

Later he ran into the psychiatrist, who told him, "You know, it's not very smart to tell someone you're going to go do a crime again."

"I said, 'if I hadn't been caught,' goddamn it!" Carmack replied. He was sentenced to one year in a small juvenile detention home in town. Most of the kids were in for drugs. Carmack was in for an Apple II.

If life felt structured and unyielding when Carmack lived with his mother, it was nothing compared with the life he found in the juvenile home. Everything took place during its allotted time: meals, showers, recreation, sleep. For every chore completed, he would receive a point toward good behavior. Each morning he was herded into a van with the other kids and carted off to his old school for classes. The van would pick him up at the end of the day and return him to the home.

Carmack emerged hardened, cynical, and burning to hack. His parents agreed to get him an Apple II (though they didn't know he used the money to buy a hot one from a kid he had met in the juvenile home). He found he most liked programming the graphics, inventing something in a binary code that came to life on screen. It gave him a kind of feedback and immediate gratification that other kinds of programming lacked.

Carmack read up on 3-D graphics and cobbled together a wireframe version of the MTV logo, which he managed to spin around on his screen. The real way to explore the world of graphics, he knew, was to make a game. Carmack didn't believe in waiting for the muse. He decided it was more efficient to use other people's ideas. Shadowforge, his first game, resembled Ultima in many ways but featured a couple of inventive programming tricks, such as characters who attacked in arbitrary directions as opposed to the ordinary cardinal ones. It also became his first sale: earning a thousand dollars from a company called Nite Owl Productions, a mom 'n' pop publisher that made most of its income from manufacturing camera batteries. Carmack used the money to buy himself an Apple II GS, the next step up in the Apple's line.

He strengthened his body to keep up with his mind. He began lifting weights, practicing judo, and wrestling. One day after school, a bully tried to pick on Carmack's neighbor, only to become a victim of Carmack's judo skills. Other times Carmack fought back with his intellect. After being partnered with him for an earth science project, a bully demanded that Carmack do all the work himself. Carmack agreed. They ended up getting an F. "How could you get an F?" the bully said. "You're the smartest guy around." Carmack had purposely failed the project, sacrificing his own grade rather than let the oaf prevail.

Carmack's increasingly cocksure attitude was not going over well at home. After he became more combative with his stepmother—whose vegetarianism and mystical beliefs incensed the young pragmatic—his father rented an apartment where Carmack and his younger brother, Peter, could live while they finished high school. The first day there, Carmack plugged in his Apple II, tacked a magazine ad for a new hard drive to his wall, and got to work. There were games to make.

One night in 1987, Carmack saw the ultimate game. It occurred in the opening episode of a new television series, *Star Trek: The Next Generation*, when the captain visited the ship's Holodeck, a futuristic device that could simulate immersive environments for relaxation and entertainment. In this case, the door opened to reveal a tropical paradise. Carmack was intrigued. This was *the* virtual world. It was just a matter of finding the technology to make it happen.

In the meantime, Carmack had his own games to pursue. Having graduated high school, he was ready to cash in the trust fund that his father, years before, had told him would be available when he turned eighteen. But when he went to retrieve the money, he found that his mother had transferred it to her account in Seattle. She had no intention of letting her son use the fund for some ridiculous endeavor like trying to go into business making computer games. Her philosophy had not wavered: if you want to go into computers, then you need to go to college, preferably MIT, get a degree, and get a job with a good company like IBM.

Carmack fired off a vitriolic letter: "Why can't you realise [*sic*] that it isn't your job to direct me anymore?" But there was no swaying his mother, who argued that her son had yet to balance his checkbook, let alone manage his finances. If Carmack wanted the money, he would have to sign up for college, pay for the courses himself, and then, if he earned grades that she deemed worthy, he would be reimbursed.

In the fall of 1988, the eighteen-year-old Carmack reluctantly enrolled at the University of Kansas, where he signed up for an entire schedule of computer classes. It was a miserable time. He couldn't relate to the students, didn't care about keg parties and frat houses. Worse were the classes, based on memorizing information from textbooks. There was no challenge, no creativity. The tests weren't just dull, they were insulting. "Why can't you just give us a project and let us perform it?" Carmack scrawled on the back of one of his exams. "I can perform anything you want me to!" After enduring two semesters, he dropped out.

Much to his mother's chagrin, Carmack took a part-time job at a pizza parlor and immersed himself in his second game, Wraith. It was an exhausting process that required him constantly to insert and eject floppy disks in order to save the data because his Apple II GS didn't come with a hard drive. He labored over a story included in the game's "about" file:

WRAITH
"THE DEVIL'S DEMISE"

For a long while all was peaceful on the island of Arathia. Your duties as protector of the temple of Metiria at Tarot were simple and uneventful. Recently things have changed. An unknown influence has caused the once devout followers of the true god Metiria to waver in their faith.

Corruption has spread through the island, with whispers of an undead being of great might granting power to those who would serve. The lords of the realms fell to him one by one, and monsters now roam the land. The temple at Tarot is the last outpost of true faith, and you may be Arathia's last hope for redemption.

Last night, as you prayed for strength and guidance, Metiria came to you in a vision, bestowing upon you the quest to destroy the Wraith. She spoke solemnly, alerting you to the dangers which lay ahead. The only way to reach the hell that the Wraith rules from is by way of an interplanar gate somewhere in Castle Strafire, stronghold of his most powerful earthly minions.

Although the castle is only a short distance away from Tarot, on an island to the northeast, a terrible reef prevents it from being reached by conventional means. You only know that monsters have come from the castle and turned up on the mainland. Remember, although many have been seduced by the power of the Wraith, greed still rules their hearts, and some may even aid your quest if paid enough gold. As the vision fades, Metiria smiles and says, "Fear not, brave one, my blessing is upon you."

You have begun preparing yourself for your quest, but even the towns-people seem unwilling to help you. They insist on gold for equipment and spells. Gold you do not have. Gold that the servants of the Wraith do have . . .

Carmack sent the game to Nite Owl, the publisher of Shadowforge, which snapped it up. Though the graphics were not breakthrough—they had the chunky stick figures of most games—the game was huge in scope compared with most titles, offerings hours more of play. He earned twice as much this time, two thousand dollars, despite the fact that the game, like Shadowforge, was not a big seller. Carmack used the cash to finance his other hobby: modifying his car, a brown MGB.

Though he was barely getting by, Carmack relished the freelance lifestyle. He was in control of his time, slept as late as he wanted, and, even better, answered to no one. If he could simply program the computer, fix up his car, and play D&D for the rest of his life, he would be happy. All he needed to do was churn out more games. It didn't take long for him to find another buyer listed in the back of a computer magazine: a small company in Shreveport, Louisiana, called Softdisk. After buying his first submission — a Tennis game with impressive physics of the rise and fall of balls over a net — they immediately wanted more. Taking a cue from the Ultima series, Carmack, already a shrewd businessman, suggested selling not just one game but a trilogy: why not triple his earnings? Softdisk accepted the offer, contracting him to do a trilogy of role-playing games called Dark Designs.

Carmack learned another way to cash in: converting his Apple II games for a new breed of computer called the IBM PC. He knew next to nothing about this system but was not one to turn down a programming challenge. So he drove to a store and rented a PC. Within a month he sent Softdisk not only an Apple II version of Dark Designs but a version converted, or "ported," for a PC as well. Working long into the night, Carmack got his process so down pat he could create one game and port three versions: one for the Apple, one for the Apple II GS, and one for the PC. Softdisk would buy each and every one.

With every new game, the company begged Carmack to come down for an interview. *Who was this kid who'd taught himself an entirely new programming language in half the time it would take a normal person?* Carmack declined at first — why screw up his life by going to work for a company? But eventually their persistence won him over. He had just put some nice new parts in his MGB and could use an excuse for a long drive. After all those years on his own, he hardly expected to meet someone who had something to teach him.

THREE

Dangerous Dave in Copyright Infringement

Shreveport was renowned in the art of simulation long before the gamers arrived. In 1864, Confederate soldiers at Fort Turnbull duped invaders by positioning charred tree trunks on mounted wagons as if they were cannons. Spotting the apparent artillery, Union soldiers fled in fear. When a Confederate general came to inspect the site, he told the fort's commander that his defenses were "nothing but a bunch of humbug." The site became known as Fort Humbug.

One hundred and twenty-seven years later, there were new simulated weapons in town—inside the computer games of Softdisk. The company was helmed by Al Vekovius, a former math professor at Louisiana State University at Shreveport. Though only in his forties, Al had a receding hairline with strands sticking up as if he had just taken his hands off one of those static electricity spheres found at state fairs. He dressed in muted ties and sweaters but possessed the eccentric streak shared by the students and faculty he would visit in the university computer lab during his job there in seventies. At the time the Hacker Ethic was reverberating from MIT to Silicon Valley. As head of the academic computing section at the school, Al, by vocation and passion, was plugged in from the start. He wasn't tall or fat, but the kids affectionately called him Big Al.

Energized by this emerging zeitgeist, in 1981 Al and another LSUS mathematician, Jim Mangham, hatched a business scheme: a computer software subscription club. For a small fee, a subscriber would receive a new disk every month filled with a variety of utility and entertainment programs, from checkbook balancing software to solitaire. The plan filled what to Al and his partner seemed like an obvious niche: the computer hobbyist.

At the time the big software publishers largely neglected individual consumers, focusing instead on reaching businesses through retail. Though hobbyists congregated on BBSs, the computer bulletin board services online, early modems were still too slow to provide a viable distribution means. A monthly disk seemed like a perfect way to distribute wares to the underground. It also seemed like a great way to give exposure to young coders, who did not have another means through which to distribute their programs; it was like an independent record label, putting unsigned bands on compilation albums.

In 1981 Softdisk's first disk went out for users of the Apple II. Business went well, and the company soon expanded with programs for both Apple and Commodore computers. In 1986 the company launched a subscription disk for the IBM personal computer and its burgeoning clones, machines that could run the same operating systems. Personal computers at long last were plummeting into affordability. As a result, a world of new computer users—sometimes called "newbies"—opened up. By 1987 Softdisk had 100,000 subscribers who were paying $9.95 per month to get the disks. Al was voted Shreveport's businessman of the year.

The good times brought challenges. Al was soon running a $12 million company with 120 employees and feeling overwhelmed. Competition followed, including a company in New Hampshire called Uptime. In the winter of 1989, Al phoned Jay Wilbur, an Uptime editor he had met at a gaming convention, and asked him if he wanted to come down and help. Jay, who was growing tired of the cold and feeling underappreciated by the Uptime owner, agreed to run Softdisk's Apple II department. He also mentioned that he knew two game programmers, John Romero and Lane Roathe—a former Uptime programmer—who were looking for work too.

Al was thrilled. Though he had occasionally been including games on his disks, he sensed an opportunity to expand into the emerging PC entertainment marketplace. He could see other successful companies like Sierra On-Line, Broderbund, and Origin doing well in games. There was no reason that Softdisk couldn't have a larger piece of that pie as well. He told Jay to bring the gamers down too.

For Romero, the stakes couldn't have been higher. He had just been through a series of disappointments, from the unrelenting winters of New Hampshire to his faulty gamble to leave his dream job at Origin for his boss's ill-fated start-up. His wife and kids were clear across the country, waiting to see how his fortune would turn. Despite his early successes, a family life was once again slipping to the wayside. He hoped a new life down south would turn things around.

The road trip from New Hampshire to Shreveport that summer of 1989 was just the prescription. Along the way, he bonded with his fellow gamers, Lane and Jay. Lane, with whom Romero had lived for a month, was very much a kindred spirit. Five years older than Romero, Lane came from a similar background. He'd grown up in Colorado, not far from where Romero was born, raised on heavy metal, underground comics, and computer games. Easygoing, with long hair wrapped in a bandanna, Lane got along perfectly with Romero. Though he didn't share Romero's insurmountable energy or ambition, he too loved the nuances, tricks, and thrills of Apple II programming. And, like Romero, all he wanted to do was make games. While in New Hampshire, the two even decided to merge their one-man-band companies—Romero's Capitol Ideas and Lane's Blue Mountain Micro—under one roof as Ideas from the Deep.

Jay was an Apple II guy as well, but of a different nature. By his own admission, he wasn't much of a programmer. But he had two important qualities that Romero respected: a genuine understanding of

Apple II code and an intense passion for games. Seven years older than Romero, the thirty-year-old Jay grew up in Rhode Island as the son of an insurance adjuster and a gift card saleswoman. In high school Jay was tall but not skilled in sports. Instead he had a way with machines, whether racking up high scores in Asteroids or dismantling his motorcycle. He used the money he received from insurance after a motorcycle accident in his early twenties to buy his first Apple II.

It didn't take long for Jay to realize that his predisposition was not for the solitary lifestyle of code. He was much more suited for the world of schmoozing and good times, a world he excelled in as a bartender at a neighborhood T.G.I. Friday's restaurant. He became beloved in his bar and was even selected to teach Tom Cruise how to mix drinks in preparation for the bartender film *Cocktail.* Jay's people skills led to him into restaurant management. Later at Uptime he was able to combine his skills: as a manager and as a game enthusiast. Now, at Softdisk, he was ready to soar even higher.

By the time they hit Shreveport, Lane, Romero, and Jay felt like old friends. They had made an adventure of the trip down, stopping for a few days at Disney World. As they pulled up in Shreveport, however, they had no sense of their future or, for that matter, if they had even arrived. Baked into the northwest corner of Louisiana just a tobacco spit from Texas, Shreveport was in rough shape in 1989. A busted oil boom had left the area deflated and depressed. The air was thick with humidity, made thicker by the overgrown patches of swamps. Downtown crawled with homeless people escaping the heat in the shadows of run-down brick buildings—including the offices of Softdisk.

Softdisk occupied two buildings in the downtown area. The administration office was built under a blacktop parking lot; the passing street sloped down a hill near the door. It was like working in an ant farm. As the gamers arrived, Al burst through the door with sparkling eyes, gushing about how quickly the company was growing and how eagerly he wanted their help. Romero and Lane showed him an Asteroids knockoff they'd made called Zappa Roids. Al was impressed, not only by their obvious programming abilities but by their youthful zeal.

Romero made his ambition clear from the start—he had no interest in working on utility programs; he wanted only to make big commercial games. That was fine with Al, who explained how excited he was to get into the gaming world. Romero and Lane would be the first two employees in a new Special Projects division devoted solely to making games. On the way out, Al patted Romero on the back and said, "By the way, let me know if you boys need an apartment to rent. I've got some places in town; I'm a landlord too."

Romero, Lane, and Jay left Softdisk's business office for the building where the programmers and "talent" worked. For a software company, it sure didn't seem like fun. Squeezed between floors of insurance brokers, each programmer worked in a separate quiet office under bright fluorescent lights. There was no music, no revelry, no game playing. Life at Softdisk had become something of a pressure cooker, with several programs to get out the door every month.

Romero introduced himself to a group of programmers. They asked whether Big Al had offered him a place to rent. When Romero said yes, they snickered. "Don't do it," one of the guys said. He told Romero how when he got hired he took Al up on the offer, only to find the apartment in a desperate state of squalor—a wooden shack in a bad part of town. When the guy lay on the couch, he saw a long worm poke its head up out of a patch of dirt on the floor.

But nothing could get Romero down. He was back on track. The sun was shining. He had a job making games. His wife, Kelly, and toddlers, Michael and Steven, would be happy in the new environment. Now they could have a fresh start. He called and told Kelly to pack her bags; they were moving to Shreveport.

Romero and Lane spent their first weeks living out their dream, working on games in the Special Projects division. Romero had another agenda too: to pull himself away from the Apple II and convert to the PC. Early on he told Al that he thought the Apple II was on the way out, especially because of the rise of clones of the IBM PC. By refusing to incorporate the new IBM software standard, Apple was rapidly diminishing as the personal computer of choice. What Romero didn't tell Al was that he felt like he was missing the boat. His unbridled devotion to the Apple II, he thought, had put him about a year behind the curve.

If he was going to be a Future Rich Person and Ace Programmer, he was going to have to master the PC before it was too late.

"You can't keep programming into the future on the same machines," Romero told Al. "I want you to know that I do not know the PC but I'll learn it really fast."

"That's fine by me," Al said. "Do whatever you want."

What Romero wanted to do was learn a hot new programming language called C. But he was told he couldn't pursue it because the other programmers in the department didn't know it. Romero felt limited by the others' lack of skills. Instead, while polishing his game Zappa Roids, he hit the books, consuming everything he could about the PC programming languages Pascal and 8086 assembly. He soon knew enough to port one of his old Apple II games called Pyramids of Egypt to the PC. Within the first month, he had published something on Softdisk's main PC software product, the Big Blue Disk.

The problem was that his work on the Big Blue Disk started going *too* well. The PC department, overtaxed and unenergetic, started to rely more and more heavily on Romero's skills. By the end of his first month, he was spending more time rewriting other people's PC programs than working on his own games. Before he knew it, the Special Projects division was kaput.

Al needed Romero instead to work on utility programs on the PC disk. Though Lane had the option to join Romero at Softdisk, he stuck with the Apple II division. It was the first sign, Romero thought, that his friend didn't share his vision of the future, the sense of opportunity that awaited in PC, not Apple, games. Since Romero still wanted to learn the PC, he agreed to join that team for the time being. But, he told Al, he wanted to make games when the time was right.

That time began to feel like it was never going to come. Romero grew unhappy. He spent nearly a year working on PC utilities programs. He did manage to refine his skills on the PC by porting more of his old Apple II games over to this platform. But PCs were still largely thought of as having only business applications. After all, they displayed just a handful of colors and squeaked out sounds through tiny, tinny speakers. Romero was nowhere near making games full-time.

To make matters worse, Romero's home life was bearing down. In order to save money, he moved his wife and kids into a house with Lane and Jay in nearby Haughton, Louisiana. It was tense, with the kids running around and Romero's wife growing frustrated by his long hours and her lack of a social life. He would try to assure her, but she would just sit on the couch and mope. She was starting to lose hope that anything would become more important to him than his games.

The bad vibes didn't let up at work either. Romero's initial impression of the beaten-down Softdisk crew only turned worse. Al was feeling the pains of running an increasingly big business and, to keep things in order, began to crack down. Romero and Lane were reprimanded for turning off the fluorescent lights in their office, a move they pulled because they hated the glare on their machines. Romero was also chastised for playing his music too loud. Grudgingly, he wore headphones.

The employees were getting on his nerves too. No one seemed to be motivated. A narcoleptic technical support worker kept falling asleep on the job—even while being asked a question. Romero got in the habit of cranking up the heavy metal music in his office just to wake the guy up. Then there was Mountain Man, the guy running the Apple II department. He had been a buttoned-down engineer at Hewlett-Packard when one day he had something of a breakdown and went off to live in the mountains for a year. He came back in a cut-off denim jacket with a long, scraggly beard and took over the Apple II department at Softdisk. But his Zen-like philosophy of life didn't do much for the growth of the department, Romero thought.

Romero confronted Al. "You told me that I would make big commercial games, and all I'm doing is helping them out in the PC department. If things don't change, I'm going to leave and go work for LucasArts," he said, referring to the new gaming company launched by George Lucas, creator of *Star Wars*. Big Al didn't like what he was hearing. Romero had proven to be one of his most valuable employees. He admired the kid's ability to focus. Whenever Al came by to check up, Romero was sitting there with his big square glasses pressed up against the computer monitor, working for hours on end. He told Romero he didn't want him to go.

Romero said he had spent the last year studying all the PC games and felt they were glaringly under par. Because the PC was still not as robust as the Apple II, the games were lackluster—static little screens with crappy graphics, nothing approaching the sophistication of the games being done for the Apple II. Now was the time to strike. Al agreed and suggested they start a subscription disk dedicated to games, a monthly.

"Monthly?" Romero said, "No way, one month is nowhere near enough time."

"Well, our subscribers are already used to a monthly disk," Al said. "Maybe we could do it every other month, but that would be pushing it."

"I think we can do that. That's still not a great amount of time, but we could probably do something decent, but I'm going to need a team: an artist, a couple programmers, and a manager, because I don't want to sit there interfacing with management all day; I want to program."

Al told Romero he couldn't have an artist; he'd have to farm out the work to someone in the existing art department. But he *could* have a manager and another programmer; he just had to find them.

Romero ran back to the Apple II department to tell Lane and Jay the good news: "Dudes, we're fucking making games!" Lane would now be editor of Gamer's Edge, Softdisk's new bimonthly games disk for the PC. All that remained was to get another programmer, someone who knew the PC and, just as important, could fit in with Lane and Romero. Jay said there was someone he knew who was definitely hardcore. This kid was turning in great games. And he even knew how to port from the Apple II to the PC. Romero was impressed by the apparent similarities to himself. But there was a problem, Jay said. The Whiz Kid had already turned down a job offer three times because he liked working freelance. Romero pleaded with Jay to try him again. Jay wasn't optimistic but said okay. He picked up the phone and gave John Carmack one last pitch.

When Carmack pulled up to Softdisk in his brown MGB, he had no intention of taking the job. But, then again, times were getting rough.

Though he enjoyed the idea of the freelance lifestyle, he was having trouble making rent and would frequently find himself pestering editors like Jay to express him his checks so he could buy groceries. A little stability wouldn't be bad, but he wasn't eager to compromise his hard work and ideals to get there. It would take something significant to sway him.

When Al met Carmack, he was thrown off. *This* was the Whiz Kid he'd heard so much about? A nineteen-year-old in ripped jeans and a tattered T-shirt who, despite his muscles, seemed not to have reached puberty yet? But Carmack did pack plenty of attitude. When Al spelled out the plan for Gamer's Edge, Carmack brushed off the tight deadline as no problem at all. He was brutally honest in his criticism of the current crop of games, including those being put out by Softdisk. Al showed Carmack to the other building, where Romero and Lane were eagerly waiting. On the way, Carmack was impressed to see a stack of *Dr. Dobb's Journal*s, the magazine for hackers, which grew out of the Homebrew Computer Club. But the strongest impression came when he met Lane and Romero, a meeting that bordered on the kinetic.

Within moments the three programmers were discussing the spectrum of game programming, from the challenges of double resolution 16-bit graphics for the Apple II to the nuances of 8086 assembly language. They talked nonstop, not just about computers but about their other common interests: Dungeons and Dragons, Asteroids, *The Lord of the Rings*. Carmack told them about how he never had the computers he wanted when he was growing up. Romero said, "Man, I would have bought you those machines."

Carmack was unprepared to meet anyone who could keep up with him intellectually, particularly in programming. Not only could these two guys talk the talk but they actually knew *more* than Carmack himself. They weren't just good, they were better than he was, he thought. Romero was inspiring, not only in his knowledge of programming but in his all-around skills: his artistry, his design. Carmack was cocky, but if someone could teach him, he wasn't going to let his ego get in the way. On the contrary, he was going to listen and stick around. He was going to take the Softdisk job.

Before the Gamer's Edge crew could get started, they needed one vital machine: a fridge. Making computer games required an accessible mound of junk food, soda, and pizza. And to eat this stuff, they'd need someplace convenient to stash it. Romero, Carmack, and Lane agreed to kick in $180 of their own money to buy a used refrigerator for their new office, a small room in the back of Softdisk.

But as they carried the appliance through the door, they felt the icy stares of the jealous employees around them. All week they had been coming into the office with accessories: a microwave, a boom box, a Nintendo. *Fucking Romero even came in with a video game!* It was, Romero told them, research. The other employees weren't buying it. Worst of all was when they saw some workmen wheeling in a fleet of sparkling new 386 PCs—the fastest computers around—for the gamers. Everyone else in the company was stuck working on machines that were about one-fourth the power.

When the Gamer's Edge guys had everything set up, they plugged in the microwave and popped in some pizza. But the moment they hit cook, all the lights in the office fizzled out. This was grounds for a revolt, the other employees decided. They went to speak with Big Al. Al was quick to quiet the storm. The Gamer's Edge crew, he explained patiently, wasn't just out to have a good time, they were out to save the company. *Yes,* he said, *save the company.* The boom of the recent years, he told them, was coming to a close. The company had sunk tremendous resources into the ill-fated Apple II line. Al had recently been forced to lay off twenty-five people in one day.

"Look," he told the employees who were bemoaning the Gamer's Edge project, "don't complain. If these guys make a home run, we'll all benefit from it. It'll work. Don't worry." Truth was, Big Al was worried himself. He walked down to the Gamer's Edge office and opened the door. It was pitch-black, except for the glow of the computer monitors. He went to flip the light switch, but nothing happened.

"Oh," Romero said, "we took out the lights. They sucked."

"Fluorescent," Lane explained, squinting, "hard on the eyes."

Al looked up. The light sockets were gutted of their tubes. The team had clearly made itself at home. He saw the microwave, the fridge, the junk food. Metallica played from a boom box. A dart-strewn poster of the hair metal band Warrant hung on the wall. Carmack, Lane, and Romero each sat at his own fancy machine. "Look," Al said, "we can't take two months to get out this first disk. We have to get it out in four weeks. And you have to have two games on it so we can entice people to subscribe."

"One month!" they cried. Two months, the original deadline, was tight enough. There was no way they could come up with two games from scratch. They would have to port a couple of their existing Apple II games to PC—a specialty that both Carmack and Romero could handle. And they had just the titles: Dangerous Dave, an Apple II game of Romero's, and The Catacomb, a title of Carmack's. Romero had made his first Dangerous Dave back in 1988 for Uptime. It was a fairly straightforward adventure game, featuring a tiny little splotch of a guy with a purple bodysuit and green cap. The object was to run and jump through mazes and collect treasure without getting killed first. Donkey Kong, the arcade game from Nintendo, had a similar paradigm, one Romero admired.

Catacomb was Carmack's latest spin on the role-playing worlds he'd first explored with Shadowforge and Wraith. This one would show an even stronger influence from Gauntlet, the popular arcade game in which characters could run through mazes, shooting monsters along the way, casting spells. It was like Dungeons and Dragons with action. This was also a key point of communion for the Two Johns: their admiration for fast-action arcade games, their desire to emulate them, and, most important, their unbridled confidence in their abilities. They turned up the stereo. There was work to be done.

Romero gleefully referred to the ensuing experience as "crunch mode" or "the death schedule"—a masochistically pleasurable stretch of programming work involving sleep deprivation, caffeine gorging, and loud music. For pure sportsmanship, Carmack and Romero had a little contest to see who could port a game the fastest. It didn't take long for the Ace Programmer to see just how fast the Whiz Kid was, as Carmack fairly easily pulled ahead. It was all in good fun. And Romero was full of admiration for his new friend and colleague. They coded late into the nights.

There was a bitter reason for Romero's increased freedom. He was getting a divorce. Being a twenty-two-year-old Future Rich Person was challenging enough, without the demands of husbandry and parenthood. His wife didn't share his love for games and, in Romero's mind, was becoming even more depressed. She wanted family dinners, church, Saturday barbecues—things that Romero was feeling increasingly ill-equipped to provide.

For a while he had tried to make both worlds work, even leaving the office early while the others stayed behind. But it was never enough. The truth was, Romero didn't know if he had enough to give. Though part of him wanted to have the family he never had as a child, he sometimes felt that he wasn't programmed to be that kind of husband and dad. It would be best for everyone, they agreed, if they split up. But Kelly didn't just want this; she wanted to split to California to be closer to her family. Romero felt crushed. At the same time, he knew that he couldn't handle having the boys live with him. Instead, he convinced himself he could make long-distance fatherhood work. Even with several states between them, they would be closer than he ever was with his dad.

Rather than dwell on his family life, Romero immersed himself in Gamer's Edge. Working on the ports had helped Carmack and Romero realize how they could best work together given their strengths and weaknesses. Carmack was most interested in programming the guts of the game—what was called the engine. This integral code told the computer how to display graphics on the screen. Romero enjoyed making the software tools—essentially the palette they would use to create characters and environments or "maps" of the game—as well as the game design—how the game play would unfold, what action would take place, what would make it fun. It was like yin and yang. While Carmack was exceptionally talented in programming, Romero was multitalented in art, sound, and design. And while Carmack had played

video games as a kid, *no one* had played as many as Romero. The ultimate coder and the ultimate gamer—together they were a perfect fit.

But Lane wasn't fitting in at all. He was still serving as editor of the
Gamer's Edge project but becoming more distant. Unlike Romero,
Lane was not enthused about the PC. Romero could tell that his old
friend was not up to the task. And, as quickly as he had once decided to
befriend Lane, Romero shut him out. In Romero's eyes, Lane wasn't up
to the rigors of the death schedule. And Romero didn't want anything
standing in the way of the team's profitability. With Carmack, he had
everything he needed. One time when Lane left the room, Romero
spun around and told Carmack, "Let's get him out of here."

At the same time, there was someone Carmack and especially Romero
wanted in: Tom Hall. Tom was a twenty-five-year-old programmer
who had been working in the Apple II department since before Romero arrived. He was also, in Romero's mind, *fucking hysterical.* Tall and
witty, Tom existed in an accelerated state of absurdity, as though nothing could keep up with the creative output pouring from his mind. His
office was covered in yellow Post-it note reminders and doodles. Every
day he had a ridiculous new message on his computer screen, such
as "The Adventures of Squishy and the Amazing Blopmeister." When
Romero would pass him, Tom would frequently raise an eyebrow and
emit an alienlike chirping sound, then continue on his way. And: he was
a gamer.

Born and raised in Wisconsin, Tom didn't have to work nearly as
hard as Romero or Carmack to get into games. His father, an engineer,
and his mother, a journalist whom Tom described as "the Erma Bom-
beck of Milwaukee," provided their youngest son with all the ammunition he needed to pursue his early obsession: an Atari 2600 home
gaming system and, shortly thereafter, an Apple II.

Tom was charmingly odd. He would parade around the house in a
Green Bay Packers helmet and red Converse sneakers. At school, his
security blanket came in the form of a brown paper grocery sack filled
with all his drawings and eight-millimeter films. He carried it everywhere, keeping it beside his desk during class. Eventually he weaned

himself down to a satchel and then, in high school, a small bag. A *Star Wars* nut, he saw the film thirty-three times. He was just as passionate about quirky sports. He was the state Frisbee golf champion. He also loved origami and domino construction, building elaborate mazes around his parents' house. While other kids worshiped pop stars and athletes, Tom's hero was Bob Speca: the world domino toppling pro.

When Tom got his Apple II, it became an infinite world into which he could explode. Like Carmack and Romero, Tom taught himself to make games as quickly as he could. By the time he entered the University of Wisconsin to study computer science, he had made almost a hundred games, most of them imitations of arcade hits like Donkey Kong. Unlike Carmack and Romero, Tom *enjoyed* being a student. He immersed himself in cross-disciplinary studies, ranging from languages to physics and anthropology. The computer game, he believed, was a unique medium into which he could incorporate those disciplines. He could invent a language for aliens in a game. He could program realistic physics. He could write stories, invent characters.

He began volunteering around campus, eventually making games for learning-disabled kids. Tom relished their enjoyment of his work, the looks on their faces when they escaped into the worlds he created. He wasn't just making games for himself, he was making them for this audience. Though games were barely acknowledged as a legitimate form of expression, let alone a legitimate art form, Tom was convinced that they were almost sublime forms of communication, just as films or novels.

After graduating college, Tom found his dreams dashed. When his résumés to game companies went unanswered, he did what most college graduates did with their dreams—gave up and applied for "real jobs." Every time he put on his suit and went for an interview, the person on the other side of the desk would ask him the same exact question: "Is this really what you want to do?" Finally Tom listened to the answer he gave in his head and said no. Shortly thereafter, he got a job at Softdisk.

Tom took an instant liking to Romero, who came on more than a year after he had started. Romero loved one of the games Tom had recently made called Legend of the Star Axe. It was clearly descended from Tom's favorite book, *The Hitchhiker's Guide to the Galaxy*—a kind of Monty Python meets *Star Wars* romp by the British cult author Douglas Adams. The game featured an intergalactic '57 Chevy and a host of quirky characters like the Blehs—green creatures with two big eye sockets who went around trying to scare people by saying, "Bleh! Bleh! Bleh!"

As much as Romero and Carmack connected as programmers, Romero and Tom connected as comedians. They were always riffing off each other, transforming Tom's alien chirps into an elaborate language of blips and bleeps. They shared a love of dark comedy. Tom might say something like "go press your man-beef in a sheep's musky hollows" and Romero would respond by telling Tom to "go slice open a goat and tie the warm, wet intestines around you for a cock ring." They were never at a loss for sick jokes.

While Carmack and Romero were working on Catacomb and Dangerous Dave, Tom would frequently drop by to help. With Lane slipping, Romero decided to recruit Tom officially as the new managing editor of Gamer's Edge. Tom was as eager to work on games full-time as the other guys. Plus, he too realized that the days of the Apple II were numbered. Games for PCs were the future, *his* future. But Al Vekovius wasn't having any of it. Tom was already managing editor of the Apple II disk, and that was where he would stay.

Though disappointed, Romero and Carmack knew they could survive for the time being without Tom; what they couldn't survive without was an artist. Up until then the game programmer was responsible for doing his own artwork. But as Romero and Carmack envisioned making more ambitious games, they wanted to have someone who was as skilled in and focused on art as they were on programming and design. Though Romero was a more than competent artist—he had done the art for all his old Apple II games—he was ready to leave those responsibilities to someone else, specifically a twenty-one-year-old intern named Adrian Carmack.

Coincidentally, Adrian shared John Carmack's last name though they were not related. With dark hair down to his waist, Adrian stood out in the straitlaced art department from the moment he arrived. That department, Romero lamented, was as sluggish as the rest of the company. They weren't gamers, they didn't even think about games. All they did was churn out little blocks of graphics for check-balancing programs and clocked out at the end of the day. Adrian had a spark— plus, an awesome collection of heavy metal T-shirts.

But Adrian, unbeknownst to Romero, wasn't much of a gamer— not anymore, at least, though games had lured him to art. Growing up in Shreveport, Adrian went through the arcade phase, spending his afternoons playing Asteroids and Pac-Man with his friends. He so liked the artwork on the cabinets that he began copying the illustrations, along with Molly Hatchet album covers, in his notebooks during class. As an adolescent, Adrian found himself sinking more deeply into his art, leaving even video games in the past. There were other things weighing on his mind.

When Adrian was thirteen, his father—who sold sausages for a local food company—died suddenly of a heart attack. Adrian, already quiet and sensitive, fell deeper into withdrawal. While his mother, a loan officer, and two younger sisters tried to cope, Adrian spent more time illustrating. Not surprisingly for a teenage boy with a pet scorpion, the ideas and subject matter that most compelled him were dark. In college the inspiration turned grimly real.

To earn money for school, Adrian worked as an aide in the medical communications department of a local hospital. His job was to photocopy pictures taken of patients in the emergency room, the most graphic images of fatality and disease. He saw bedsores so terrible the skin was falling from the bone. He saw gunshot wounds, severed limbs. One time a farmer came in with a wooden fence post driven through his groin. The pictures took on an almost fetishistic quality, as Adrian traded them with his friends.

His artwork became not only darker but more skillful. His college art mentor, Lemoins Batan, recognized Adrian's talents, his ability to draw with precise and seemingly effortless detail. When Lemoins asked Adrian what he wanted to do, his student told him that he'd like to work in fine art. In the meantime, he was looking for experience. His teacher had heard through the grapevine of somewhere he might start: Softdisk.

When Adrian found out that the company was looking for people to do art for computer software, he was less than intrigued. He was partial to pencil and paper, not keyboard and printer. But the Softdisk internship paid better than the hospital, so he agreed, laboring at the innocuous work until one day he returned to find his boss arguing loudly with two young programmers. One of the other artists came over to Adrian and said, "You know what's going on?"

"No," Adrian replied quietly, "I have no idea."

"They're talking about you."

"Oh shit, man, I'm toast." Adrian assumed something was wrong, that he was being fired. The two young programmers came up to him when they were through and introduced themselves as Carmack and Romero, his partners at Gamer's Edge.

For the next Gamer's Edge disk, they were going to make only one game. Al agreed to that plan, letting Romero and Carmack pursue their vision of making one big commercial game from scratch every two months—still a considerable feat. But with their roles in place—Carmack doing the engine; Romero, the software tools and game design; Adrian, the art; Lane, the management and miscellaneous coding—it seemed within their reach.

The idea for the next game came from Carmack, who was experimenting with a breakthrough bit of programming that created an illusion of movement beyond the confines of the screen. It was called scrolling. Again, arcade games were the model. At first, the action of arcade games all took place within one static screen: in Pong, players controlled paddles that could move only from the bottom to the top of the screen as they hit a ball back and forth; in Pac-Man, the character would chomp dots as he cruised within a confined maze; in Space Invaders, players controlled a ship at the bottom of the screen that would shoot at descending alien ships. There was never a sense of broad movement, as though the players or enemies were actually progressing outside the box.

All this changed in 1980, when Williams Electronics released Defender, the first arcade game to popularize the idea of scrolling beyond the scope of the screen. In this sci-fi shoot-'em-up, players controlled a spaceship that moved horizontally above a planet surface, shooting down aliens and rescuing people along the way. A tiny map on the screen would show the player the entire scope of the world, which, if stretched out, would be the equivalent of about three and a half screens. Compared with the other games in the arcade, Defender felt big, as if the player was living and breathing in a more expansive virtual space. It became a phenomenal hit—filling almost as many arcades as Space Invaders and beating out Pac-Man as the industry's Game of the Year. Countless scrolling games would follow. By 1989 scrolling was the "it" technology, fueling in part the success of the bestselling home video game in history at the time: Super Mario Brothers 3 for the Nintendo Entertainment System.

But at this moment, in September 1990, no one had yet figured out how to scroll games for the PC; instead, they would use lame trickery to make the player feel like the action was larger than the screen. A player might get to the right edge of the screen and then, in one clunky movement, see the panel from the right shift over into place. The reason, in part, was the PCs' slow speed, which paled compared with those of arcade machines, the Apple II, or home consoles like the Nintendo. Carmack was determined to find a way to create a smooth scrolling effect, like the one in Defender or Super Mario.

The next Gamer's Edge game would be a step in that direction. When the crew discussed ideas for the game, Carmack demonstrated a technology he was working on that could scroll the action down the screen. Unlike the more sophisticated scrolling games, this one was set up like a treadmill—the graphics would descend the screen on a steady, set path. There was no sense that the player was willfully moving up through the action. It was more like standing on a stage and having a rolling landscape painting move behind the actor.

Romero, the erudite gamer who had played nearly every available title for the PC, had never seen anything like it; here was a chance at being the first. They called the game Slordax; it would be a straightforward shoot-the-spaceships descendant of arcade hits like Space Invaders and Galaga. They had four weeks.

From the start of the work on Slordax, the team gelled. Carmack would bang away at his code for the graphics engine while Romero developed the programming tools to create the actual characters and sections of the game. As Carmack engineered breakthrough code, Romero designed gripping game play. Tom Hall even managed to sneak into the Gamer's Edge office to create the creatures and backgrounds. Adrian, meanwhile, would sketch out the spaceships and asteroids on his screen. It was clear right away to Romero that the quiet intern was talented.

Though still new to computers, Adrian quickly assimilated with a palette on screen. Computer art at the time was almost like pointillism because game graphics were so limited. Most had only four colors, in what was known as Computer Graphics Adapter, or CGA; recently, games had evolved to allow sixteen colors in Enhanced Graphics Adapter, EGA. But that was still pretty tight for an artist. Adrian had only a few colors at his disposal. He couldn't even push them together; he just had to bring the worlds to life with what he had. People in the business called this craft "pushing pixels." And it was clear that Adrian could push pixels with ease.

It was also clear that Adrian liked to keep a profile so low it was almost subterranean. One reason he kept to himself was that he didn't know what to make of these gamers. Carmack was like a robot, the way he spoke in little clipped sentences with the strange "mmm" punctuation at the end. He could sit there all day and code, not saying anything but turning out amazing work. Romero was just plain *bizarre,* making all these sick jokes about disembowelment and dismemberment, and all those twisted Melvin cartoons he still drew. Adrian thought he was pretty funny too.

Tom Hall was another story. The first time Adrian met him was when Tom came leaping into the room in blue tights, a white undershirt, a cape, and a big plastic sword. He stood there, raised his eyebrow, and made a strange alien beep, to which Romero responded with almost debilitating laughter. It was Tom's costume for Halloween. Tom stayed, as he often did, helping out with the game design and tool creation. Adrian was thankful that he didn't stick around much longer.

One night shortly after that, however, Tom stuck around long after Adrian, Romero, and the rest of the Softdisk employees had gone home. The only people left were he and Carmack. Slordax was wrapping up nicely, and Carmack was on to something else. A born night owl, he remained at the office into the wee hours of the morning. He liked the solitude, the quiet, and the chance to immerse himself even more deeply in his work. He was doing what he had always wanted to do: code games. And he was happy, in the moment as always, not thinking at all about what would come next. If he could be here working on games with enough money for food and shelter, that was good enough for him. As he told the other guys on one of his very first days, put him in a closet with a computer, a pizza, and some Diet Cokes, and he would be fine.

As Tom settled into a chair late this night, Carmack showed him how he had figured out a way to create an animating block or tile of graphics on the screen. The screen consisted of thousands of pixels; a group of pixels make up a tile. When making a game, an artist would first use pixels to design a tile, then place the tiles together to create the entire environment. It was like laying down a tile floor in a kitchen. With Carmack's animation trick, a tile could have a little animating graphic on it too. "And," he explained, "I'll be able to make it so your guy can jump on the tile and something can happen."

"Would it be easy to do that?" Tom asked.

"Sure, mmm," Carmack said. He would just need to know what resulting action to program into the game when a player hit an animated tile. This was awesome, Tom understood, because games like Super Mario Brothers 3 were all about animated tiles; for instance, a player would jump up into a blinking block, which would then rain down a shower of golden coins. Tom was intrigued. But there was more.

Carmack punched a few buttons on his keyboard and showed Tom his other new feat: side scrolling. The effect, popularized by Defender and Mario, made it appear as if the game world continued when a character moved toward either edge of the screen. After a few nights of experimentation, Carmack had finally figured out how to simulate this movement on a PC. He had approached the problem, as always, in his own particular way. Too many people, he thought, went for the clever little shortcuts right away. That didn't make sense. First, he tried the obvious approach, writing a program that would attempt to draw out the graphics smoothly across the screen. It didn't work, because the PC, as everyone knew, was too slow. Then he tried the next step: optimization. Was there any way he could take greater advantage of the computer's memory so the images would draw more quickly? After a few attempts, he knew there wasn't a solution.

Finally then he thought to himself, Okay, what am I trying to achieve? I want the screen presented to move smoothly over as the user runs his character across the ground. He thought of his earlier game, The Catacomb. In that one, he'd created an effect that moved the screen over one big chunky strip at a time as a character ran toward the edge of a dungeon. It was a common trick called tile-based scrolling, moving the screen in the chunky way one set of tiles at a time. What he wanted now was to create an effect that would be much more subtle, if a character moved just a hair. The problem was that it simply took too much time and power for the computer to redraw the entire screen for every slight move. And that's when the leap came.

What if, Carmack thought, instead of redrawing everything, I could figure out a way to redraw only the things that actually change? That way, the scrolling effect could be rendered more quickly. He imagined looking at a computer screen that showed a character running to the right underneath a big blue sky. If that character ran far enough, a white puffy cloud would eventually pass from off screen over his head. The computer created this effect in a very crude way. It would redraw every little blue pixel on the entire screen, starting at the top left corner and making its way over and down, one pixel at a time, even though the only thing that was changing in the sky was the white puffy cloud. The computer couldn't intuit a shortcut to this drudgery just because a shortcut made sense. So Carmack did the next best thing. He tricked it into performing more efficiently. Carmack wrote some code that duped the computer into thinking that, for example, the seventh tile from the left was in fact the first tile on the screen. This way the computer would begin drawing right where Carmack wanted it to. Instead of spitting out dozens of little blue pixels on the way over to the cloud, the computer could *start* with the cloud itself. To make sure the player felt the effect of smooth movement, Carmack added one other touch, instructing the computer to draw an extra strip of blue tile outside the right edge of the screen and store it in its memory for when the player moved in that direction. Because the tiles were in memory, they could be quickly thrown up on the screen without having to be re-drawn. Carmack called the process "adaptive tile refresh."

In lay terms, as Tom immediately understood, this meant one thing: *They could do Super Mario Brothers 3 on a PC!* Nobody, no one, nowhere had made the PC do this. And now they could do it, right here, right now, take their all-time favorite video game and hack it together so it could work on the computer. It was almost a revolutionary act of sub-version, he thought, especially considering Nintendo's stronghold on its own platform. There was no way to, say, copy a Nintendo game onto a PC as one would tape an album. But now they could replicate it tile for tile, blip for blip. It was the ultimate hack.

"Let's do it!" Tom said. "Let's make the first level of Super Mario tonight!"

He fired up Super Mario on the TV in the Gamer's Edge office and started to play. Then he opened up the tile editor that they had running on their PCs. Like someone copying a famous painting, he re-created every little tile of the first level of Super Mario on the PC, hitting pause on the Nintendo machine to freeze the action. He included everything—the gold coins, the puffy white clouds; the only thing he changed was the character. Rather than re-create Mario, he used the stock graphics they had of Dangerous Dave. Meanwhile, Carmack was optimizing his side-scrolling code, implementing the features of the game that Tom barked out while he was pausing and playing. Dozens of Diet Cokes later, they finished the first level. It was 5:30 A.M. Carmack and Tom saved the level to a disk, set it on Romero's desk, and went home to sleep.

Romero came in the next morning at ten and found the floppy disk on his keyboard with a Post-it note that read merely, "Type DAVE2." It was in Tom's handwriting. Romero popped the disk into his PC and typed in the file location. The screen went black. Then it refreshed with the words

DANGEROUS

DAVE

IN

"COPYRIGHT INFRINGEMENT"

On one side of the words was a portrait of Dangerous Dave in his red baseball cap and green T-shirt. On the other was a dour looking judge with a white wig, brandishing a gavel. Romero hit the spacebar to see what would come next. There it was, the familiar milieu of Super Mario Brothers 3: pale blue sky, the puffy white clouds, the bushy green shrubs, the animated tiles with little question marks rolling over their sides and, strangely, his character Dangerous Dave standing ready on the bottom of the screen. Romero tapped his arrow key, moved Dave along the floor, and watched him scroll smoothly across the screen. That's when he lost it.

Romero could hardly breathe. He just sat in his chair with his fingers on the keys, scrolling Dave back and forth along the landscape, trying to see if anything was wrong, if somehow this wasn't really happening, if Carmack had not just figured out how to do *exactly what the fucking Nintendo could do*, if he had not done what every other gamer in the universe had wanted to do, to break through, to do for PCs what Mario was doing for consoles. On the strength of Mario, Nintendo was on the way to knocking down Toyota as Japan's most successful company, generating over $1 billion per year. Shigeru Miyamoto, the series's creator, had gone from being a poor country boy in Japan to being the gaming industry's equivalent of Walt Disney. Super Mario Brothers 3 sold 17 million copies, the equivalent of seventeen platinum records—something only artists like Michael Jackson had pulled off.

Romero saw it all come pouring down in front of him: his future, their future, scrolling across the room in brightly colored dreams. The PC was hot. It was heading into more homes each day. Pretty soon, it wouldn't be just a luxury item, it would be a home appliance. And what better to make it a friendly part of life than a killer game. With such a hit, people wouldn't even have to buy Nintendos; they could just invest in PCs. And here Romero was sitting in his crappy little office building in Shreveport looking at the technology that could make the first big league games for the PC. He saw their destiny, their Future Rich Personages. It was so devastating that he found he couldn't move, couldn't get up out of his seat. He was *destroyed*. And it wasn't until Carmack rolled back into the office a few hours later that Romero was able to muster the energy to speak. He had only one thing to tell his friend, his genius partner, his match made in gamer heaven.

"This is it," he said. "We're gone!"

FOUR

Pizza Money

An early and apparent difference between the Two Johns' internal human engines was the way they processed time. It was the kind of difference that made them perfect complements and the kind that could cause irreparable conflict.

Carmack was of the moment. His ruling force was focus. Time existed for him not in some promising future or sentimental past but in the present condition, the intricate web of problems and solutions, imagination and code. He kept nothing from the past—no pictures, no records, no games, no computer disks. He didn't even save copies of his first games, Wraith and Shadowforge. There was no yearbook to remind of his time at school, no magazine copies of his early publications. He kept nothing but what he needed at the time. His bedroom consisted of a lamp, a pillow, a blanket, and a stack of books. There was no mattress. All he brought with him from home was a cat named Mitzi (a gift from his stepfamily) with a mean streak and a reckless bladder.

Romero, by contrast, was immersed in *all* moments: past, future, and present. He was an equal opportunity enthusiast, as passionate about the present as about the time gone and the time yet to come. He didn't just dream, he pursued: hoarding everything from the past, immersing himself in the dynamism of the moment, and charting out the plans for what was to come. He remembered every date, every name, every game. To preserve the past, he kept letters, magazines, disks, Burger King pay stubs, pictures, games, receipts. To inflate the present, he pumped up any opportunity for fun, telling a better joke, a funnier story, making a crazier face. Yet he wasn't manic, he knew how to focus. When he was on, he was on—loving everything, everybody. But when he was off, he was off—cold, distant, short. Tom Hall came up with a nickname for the behavior. In computers, information is represented in bits. A bit can be either on or off. Tom called Romero's mood swings the bit flip.

That fateful morning of September 20, 1990, Romero's bit flipped right on. It was a date he seared into his memory and Carmack would soon forget, but it was equally important to both. Carmack had used his laser focus to solve an immediate challenge: how to get a PC game to scroll. Romero used Carmack's solution, Dangerous Dave in Copyright Infringement, to envision what would come. Carmack had created a palette that Romero used to paint the future. And the future, it became clear, had nothing to do with Softdisk.

After seeing Carmack, Romero couldn't contain his excitement. He darted around the office, pulling others to come in and check out the game. "Oh my God, look at this," he said, as a couple of employees watched the demo play. "Is that the fucking coolest thing on the planet or what?"

"Oh," one of the guys replied lethargically, "that's pretty neat."

"That's pretty neat?" Romero responded. "Wait a minute: this is like the fucking coolest thing ever! Don't you understand?"

The guys shrugged and said, "Whatever," then returned to their offices.

"Fucking idiots!" Romero declared. By the time everyone else arrived, he was on the verge of exploding. Tom, Jay, Lane, and Adrian were all in the Gamer's Edge office, watching amusedly as Romero held court, playing the demo. "Oh my God," Romero said, "this is the fucking coolest thing ever! We are fucking gone! We have to do this! We have got to start our own company and get out of here with this, because Softdisk ain't doing anything with it! No one's going to see this! We need to do this on our own! This is too big to waste on this company!"

Jay was hanging on the doorway, his fingertips gripping the frame. "Eh, come on," he said, chortling. He'd seen Romero's giddiness before. It was an enthusiasm that bordered on hyperbole. Romero got this excited when he won a round of Pac-Man. He was a human exclamation point.

Romero froze, hands in the air. "Dude," he said gravely, "I'm totally serious."

Jay stepped in and shut the door behind him. Romero explained his rationale. First off, this was a robust, sixteen-color game; Softdisk was interested only in doing four-color games that appealed to the lowest common denominator of users. Second, this was essentially the Nintendo-style game made for a PC, something on par with the bestselling console title in the world: Mario. That meant the game was sure to sell, because everyone was getting a PC and, naturally, everyone would want a fun video game to play. It was perfect.

They already had the ideal team: Carmack, the graphics guru and resident Whiz Kid; Romero, the multitalented programmer and company cheerleader; Adrian, the artist and dark visionary; and Tom, game designer and comic book surrealist. Although Romero was still displeased with Lane, he was willing to give him one more chance to pull through. Regardless, the core chemistry was potent. Carmack's steadfastness balanced Romero's effusive passion, Adrian's grisly tastes countered Tom's cartoon comedy. All they needed was someone to do the business side — handle the finances, balance the books, manage the team. Everyone looked to Jay. "Dude," Romero told him, "you've got to be a part of this too."

Jay gave them his biggest bartender smile and agreed. "Here's what I think we should do," he said. "This needs to be taken right to the top of Nintendo. Now!" If they could get a deal to do a PC port of Super Mario Brothers 3, they could be in business, *serious* business. They decided to take the weekend to make a complete demo of the game, with a few added levels as well as the inclusion of the Mario character, and Jay would send it off.

There was only one problem, but it was sizable. If they were going to moonlight this game, they didn't want Softdisk to know. This meant they couldn't do it in the office. They would have to work on it at home. Thing was, they didn't have the computers they needed to get the job done. The five of them sat quietly in the Gamer's Edge office, pondering the problem as Dangerous Dave looped across the screen.

Carmack and Romero had both been without the computers they wanted earlier in life. So this wouldn't be the first time they came up with a way to get them.

The cars backed up to the Softdisk office, trunks open, waiting in the night. It was late Friday night, long after all the other employees had returned home to their families and television sets. No one would use the PCs from the office on Saturday and Sunday, so they might as well make use of them, the gamers figured. They weren't *stealing* the computers, they were *borrowing* them.

After loading Softdisk's computers in their cars, Romero, Jay, Carmack, Tom, and Lane caravanned out of downtown. They drove away from the run-down buildings, down the highway, until the scenery began to change to low-hanging trees and swamps. Late-night fishermen lined a bridge with their lines in the purple-black murk. A bridge led them to South Lakeshore Drive, the border of Shreveport's main recreational front and main water supply, Cross Lake.

Carmack, Lane, Jay, and an Apple II programmer at Softdisk named Jason Blochowiak had scored a enviable coup not long before when they found a four-bedroom house for rent right along these shores. Jay had bought a cheap boat, which they docked there and used for frequent outings of kneeboarding and skiing. In the large backyard was a swimming pool and a barbecue, with which Jay, a cooking enthusiast, grilled up Flintstonean slabs of ribs. The house itself had plenty of windows looking out on the scene, a large living room, even a big tiled bathroom with a deep earth-tone-tiled Jacuzzi tub. Jay had installed a beer keg in the fridge. It was a perfect place to make games.

Over the weekend while making the Super Mario demo, the gamers put the house to the ultimate test. They hooked two of the Softdisk computers up on a large table that Carmack had been using to hold all-night Dungeons and Dragons sessions with the guys. Romero and Carmack sat there programming together. Tom did all the graphics and Lane animated the familiar little turtle. Earlier they had videotaped the entire game play of Super Mario Brothers 3. To capture all the elements, Tom kept running back and forth, pressing pause on the VCR so he could copy the scenes.

Over those seventy-two hours, they fell into crunch mode. No one slept. They consumed huge quantities of caffeinated soda. Pizza deliveries came repeatedly. Jay worked the grill, churning out a stream of burgers and hot dogs, which often went uneaten. They got the game down to a T: Mario's squat little walk, the way he bopped the animated tiles, sending out the coins, the way he leapt on the turtles and kicked their shells, the clouds, the Venus's-flytraps, the pipes, the smooth scrolling. By the time they finished, the game was virtually identical to the bestselling hit in the world. The only noticeable difference was the title screen, which, under the Nintendo copyright, credited the makers, a company name the guys borrowed from Romero and Lane, Ideas from the Deep.

With the game done, Jay put together a letter explaining who they were and how they wanted Nintendo to take the unprecedented step of licensing Super Mario for the PC. Hopes high, the boys taped up the box and sent it on its way to Nintendo. When the response came back a few weeks later, it was short and sweet. Nice work, the company said, but Nintendo had no interest in pursuing the PC market. It was happy where it was as the world leader in consoles. It was a disappointment for the group, especially following the elation of the lake house programming marathon. But it was not the end by any means. There had to be someone out there who would appreciate their accomplishment. Romero knew just the guy.

Not long before, Romero had received his very first fan letter while working at Softdisk. It was typewritten and cordial. "Dear John," it read, "Loved your game. Just wanted to let you know it was a great game and I think you are very talented. Have you played The Greatest

Pyramid? It is almost the same as your game. I was wondering if you made that game too? Or if you were inspired by it? I can send you a copy if you want. Also what's your high score for your game? Have you been programming long and what language did you use? I am thinking about writing a game and any tips you have would be helpful. Thanks from a big fan! Sincerely, Byron Muller."

Romero, the pack rat, had immediately taped the letter up on his wall and showed it off to Carmack, Tom, Lane, and Adrian. A couple weeks later, he got another fan letter, handwritten and a bit more urgent. "Dear John," it read, "I loved your game (Pyramids of Egypt), it is better than another pyramid type game that was in Big Blue Disk a few issues ago. I finished the game after staying up until 2:00 A.M. last night! Great fun! What's your best score on the game? Is there a secret key that advances to the next level automatically? Do you know of any similar games? Please call me collect if you want . . . or please write. Thanks a million, Scott Mulliere. P.S. I think I found a minor bug (undocumented feature?) in the game!"

Wow — Romero beamed — *another fan!* He taped this letter up on the wall next to the other one and, again, bragged to Carmack and Adrian, who rolled their eyes. Soon after, Romero was flipping through *PC Games Magazine* when he came to a brief article about Scott Miller, a twenty-nine-year-old programmer who was having great success distributing his own games. Intrigued, Romero read to the bottom of the article, where it listed Scott's address: 4206 Mayflower Drive, Garland, Texas 75043.

He paused. Garland, Texas. Garland, Garland, Texas? Who did he know in Garland, Texas, on Mayflower Drive? He set down the magazine and looked up on his wall. The fan letters! By now he had accumulated several of them and, to his amazement, though they all were signed by different names, each and every one had the same return address: Mayflower Drive, Garland.

Romero was pissed. Here he was showing off to the other guys about all his supposed fans, when in fact it was just some loser fucking with his mind. *Who the fuck does Scott Miller think he is?* Romero whipped around to his keyboard and banged out a letter in fury: "Scott: You, sir, have serious psychological problems. . . . What's the deal with the 15 million odd names you've been writing under to reach me? Huh, Byron Muilliere, Brian Allen, Byron Muller? How old are you, really? 15?" Romero fumed for a couple pages, then left the letter on his desk. The next day, he came back cooled off and wrote another note.

"Dear Mr. Miller," he typed, "I have taken a considerable amount of time to reply to your last letter. The reason is because I was infuriated when I found out that you had written to me previously about 3–4 other times, all under different names and I didn't know what was going on. My previous reply is a real scorcher; that's why I didn't send it earlier. I am sending it anyway just so you can see how pissed I was at the time. I am writing this cover letter to soften the previous reply and to tell you that I am somewhat intrigued by your numerous approaches." He sealed up both letters together and sent them to Garland once and for all.

A few days later, Romero's home phone rang. It was Scott Miller. Romero laid into him about sending those fake fan letters, but Scott had other things on his mind. "Fuck those letters!" Scott said breathlessly. "The only reason I did that was because I knew my only chance to get ahold of you was to go through the back door."

Game companies at the time were extremely competitive and secretive, especially when it came to their programming talent. When Romero had been a young gamer, programmers like Richard Garriott or Ken and Roberta Williams always got top billing, their names advertised in big letters on the box. But by the early nineties, times had changed. Companies were not above poaching. As a precaution, many game publishers would loom over their staffs, monitoring calls to make sure that no one was trying to make a steal. Scott, well aware of the sensitivity of his call, had chosen instead to try to lure Romero into contacting him. It worked, though ironically not as originally intended. He hadn't meant to piss Romero off. But now that he had his attention, he wasn't about to let it go.

"We gotta talk," Scott continued eagerly. "I saw your game Pyramids of Egypt. It was so awesome! Can you do a few more levels of it? We can make a ton of money."

"What are you talking about?"

"I want to publish your game," Scott said, "as shareware."

Shareware. Romero was familiar with the concept. It dated back to a guy named Andrew Fluegelman, founding editor of *PC World* magazine. In 1980, Fluegelman wrote a program called PC-Talk and released it online with a note saying that anyone who liked the wares should feel free to send him some "appreciation" money. Soon enough he had to hire a staff to count all the checks. Fluegelman called the practice "shareware," "an experiment in economics." Over the eighties other hackers picked up the ball, making their programs for Apples, PCs, and other computers available in the same honor code: Try it, if you like it, pay me. The payment would entitle the customer to receive technical support and updates.

The Association of Shareware Professionals put the business, largely domestic, between $10 and $20 million annually—even with only an estimated 10 percent of customers paying to register a shareware title. *Forbes* magazine marveled at the trend, writing in 1988 that "if this doesn't sound like a very sound way to build a business, think again." Shareware, it argued, relied not on expensive advertising but on word of mouth or, as one practitioner put it, "word of disk." Robert Wallace, a top programmer at Microsoft, turned a shareware program of his called PC-Write into a multimillion-dollar empire. Most authors, however, were happy to break six figures and often made little more than $25,000 per year. Selling a thousand copies of a title in one year was a great success. Shareware was still a radical conceit, one that, furthermore, had been used only for utility programs, like check-balancing programs and word-processing wares. It had never been exploited for games. What was Scott thinking?

As they talked, it became clear to Romero that Scott knew exactly what he was doing. Scott, like Romero, was a lifelong gamer. The son of a NASA executive, he was a conservative-looking guy with short, dark hair. He had spent his high school days in Garland hanging out in the computer lab during the day and at the arcade after school. He even wrote a strategy guide called *Shootout: Zap the Video Games*, detailing all the ways to beat the hot games of 1982, from Pac-Man to Missile Command. Scott soon took the inevitable path and started making games of his own.

When it came time to distribute the games, Scott took a long, hard look at the shareware market. He liked what he saw: the fact that he could run everything himself without having to deal with retailers or publishers. So he followed suit, putting out two text-based games in their entirety and waiting for the cash to roll in. But the cash didn't roll; it didn't even trickle. Gamers, he realized, might be a different breed from those consumers who actually paid for utility shareware. They were more apt simply to take what they could get for free. Scott did some research and realized he wasn't alone; other programmers who had released games in their entirety as shareware were broke too. People may be honest, he thought, but they're also generally lazy. They need an incentive.

Then he got an idea. *Instead of giving away the entire game, why not give out only the first portion, then make the player buy the rest of the game directly from him?* No one had tried it before, but there was no reason it couldn't work. The games Scott was making were perfectly suited to such a plan because they were broken up into short episodes or "levels" of play. He could simply put out, say, fifteen levels of a game, then tell players that if they sent him a check he would send them the remaining thirty.

In 1986, while working for a computer consulting company, Scott self-published his first game, Kingdom of Kroz—an Indiana Jones–style adventure—as shareware, making the initial levels available through BBSs and shareware catalogs. There was no advertising, no marketing, and virtually no overhead—except for the low cost of floppy disks and Ziploc bags. Because there were no other people to pay off, Scott could price his games much lower than most retail titles: $15 to $20 as opposed to $30 to $40. For every dollar he brought in, Scott was pocketing ninety cents. By the time he contacted Romero, he had earned $150,000 by word of mouth alone.

Business was so good, Scott explained, that he'd quit his day job to start his own shareware game publishing company, called Apogee. And he was looking for other games to publish. Romero was making perfect shareware games and he didn't even know it, Scott said. An ideal shareware game had to have a few ingredients: short action titles that were broken up in levels. Because the shareware games were being distributed over BBSs, they had to be small enough for people to download them over modems. Large, graphically intensive games, like those being published by Sierra On-Line, were simply too big for BBS-based distribution. Games had to be small but fun and fast, something adrenal and arcade-style enough to hook a player into buying more. If Romero would give him Pyramids of Egypt, Scott would handle all the marketing and order processing; the guys would receive some kind of advance plus a 35 percent royalty rate, higher than they'd get from any major publisher.

Romero was intrigued, but there was a problem. "We can't do Pyramids of Egypt," he explained, "because Softdisk owns it." He could hear the disappointment in Scott's sigh. "Hey," he added. "Screw that game! It's crap compared to what we're doing right now."

A few days later, Scott received a package with the Super Mario Brothers 3 demo from Ideas from the Deep. When he fired up the game, he was knocked out. It looked just like the console version—smooth scrolling and everything. He grabbed the phone and talked to Carmack for hours. This guy is a genius, Scott thought. He's outthinking everybody. By the time they were through talking, Scott was more than ready to make a deal. The gamers said they would use this new technology to create a title specifically for Apogee to release as shareware. "Great," Scott said. "Let's do it."

Now they just had to come up with a game.

After their initial conversation, Romero asked Scott to show them his seriousness by sending them an advance. Scott responded with a check for two thousand dollars, half his savings. There was only one thing he wanted in return: A game by Christmas, two months away.

Romero, Carmack, Adrian, Lane, Tom, and Jay convened in the Gamer's Edge office to come up with the game. Tom was quick to point out that, because they were using this console-style technology, they should make a console-style game, something like Mario but different. Fueled by the energy, he was quick to volunteer himself with a fair amount of the bravado that was becoming a requisite part of their clan.

"Come on, what theme do you want?" Tom said. "Tell me. I can do anything. How about science fiction?"

They liked the idea. "Why don't we do something," Carmack said, "where a little kid genius saves the world or something like that? Mmm."

"Okay, yeah!" Tom said. "I have a great idea for something like that." And in a blur he sped from the room and locked himself in his office in the Apple II department. He could feel his head opening up, the ideas pouring out in what sounded like the voice of Walter Winchell. Tom had long been a huge fan of Warner Bros. cartoons; Chuck Jones, the Looney Tunes animator, was a god to him. He'd also watched Dan Aykroyd's impression of *The Untouchables'* Eliot Ness as a kid. He thought about all these things, plus Mario, plus, for flavor, a routine by the comedian George Carlin about people who use bay leaves as underarm deodorant and go around smelling like bean with bacon soup.

Tom typed until he had three paragraphs on his paper. Pulling it out of the printer, he dashed back into the Gamer's Edge office and read these words in his best Winchell impression:

Billy Blaze, eight-year-old genius, working diligently in his backyard clubhouse, has created an interstellar spaceship from old soup cans, rubber cement, and plastic tubing. While his folks are out on the town and the baby sitter is asleep, Billy sneaks out to his backyard workshop, dons his brother's football helmet, and transforms into. . . . Commander Keen— defender of justice! In his ship, the Bean with Bacon MegaRocket, Keen dispenses justice with an iron hand!

In this episode, aliens from the planet Vorticon VI find out about the eight-year-old genius and plan his destruction. While Keen is out exploring the mountains of Mars, the Vorticons steal his ship and leave pieces of it around the galaxy! Can Keen recover all the pieces of his ship and repel the Vorticon invasion? Will he make it back before his parents get home? Stay tuned!

He looked around. Silence. Then, in a burst, everyone was laughing, even the generally stoic John Carmack, who not only laughed but applauded. Commander Keen was on board. Where he would take them, they hardly knew.

The gamers weren't just Softdisk guys anymore, they were, as they called themselves, the IFD guys, co-owners of Ideas from the Deep. Softdisk, as a result, took on an even greater pallor. But it was a day job, a job they all needed since there was no real money coming in yet and no guarantee that it would come in at all. They decided, then, to continue working on titles for Gamer's Edge during the day while they churned out Commander Keen from the lake house at night.

They became all the more efficient at "borrowing" the Softdisk computers. Every night after work they'd back their cars up to the office and load the machines. The next morning they'd come in early enough to bring the computers back. They even got a little cocky about it. Though the machines were top of the line, they wanted some minor adjustments made. Jay began moseying on down to the Softdisk administration office to request new parts. Al Vekovius took notice of the requests but didn't think too much of them. He was still gung ho about Gamer's Edge and the potential to break into the PC marketplace. So whatever the gamers wanted, the gamers would have.

From October to December 1990, they worked virtually nonstop to get Keen done for Scott by Christmas. And it wasn't just one Keen; it was a trilogy called Invasion of the Vorticons. Trilogies were common in the games industry for the same reason they were common in books and films; they were the best way to build and expand a brand identity. Tom, who assumed the role of creative director, mapped out the game plan.

Mario, this was not. As a hero, an eight-year-old misfit who steals his dad's Everclear for rocket fuel was more identifiable than a middle-aged Italian plumber. It was as if the gamers had followed that golden rule of writing about what they knew. Tom, as a kid, used to walk around in a Green Bay Packers helmet and red Converse sneakers, just like Billy Blaze. And, in a sense, they were all Billy Blazes, oddball kids who modified technology to create elaborate means of escape. Keen was a punk, a hacker. And he was saving the galaxy, just as countless hackers like Carmack and Romero used technology to save themselves.

The roles were set: Carmack and Romero were the programmers, and Tom the lead designer—the person in charge of coming up with the game play elements, from the story and setting to the characters and weapons. Carmack and Romero were happy to leave Tom to the creative work; they were too busy programming. Carmack was refining his engine, getting the smooth scrolling down to the point where Keen could move as fluidly left or right as he could up or down. Romero, meanwhile, was working the editor, the program that allows the developers to put together the graphics of the game—characters, rooms, monsters. It was essentially a game designer's construction kit. Carmack and Romero were in sync.

Not everyone else gelled quite as well. Lane was now officially kicked out of the Keen development. Despite Romero's fondness for him as a friend, he felt that Lane's energy was lacking. Adrian was having problems of his own. Though he was recruited later to help them work on Keen, Adrian hated the project. It was too . . . cutesy. Tom had a target audience in mind: "kids," he said, "or those who have kidlike mentalities like we do." Adrian hated kiddie stuff. Even more, he hated cutesy. Worst of all was cutesy kiddie. And now here he was having to sit all night drawing pizza slices, soda pop, and candy. Tom came up with a little character called a Yorp with a big fat green body and one periscopelike eye over his head. Even the monsters were cute. In most games, when a character died, it would simply disappear, vanish. But Tom had other notions. He was eager to incorporate some "larger philosophical ideas," as he said. He loosely based characters on ideas he'd read in Freud's *Civilization and Its Discontents;* a guard was made to represent an id. He wanted to teach kids that when people or even aliens die, they *really* die, they leave corpses. So he wanted the dead creatures in the game to just . . . remain: not graphic or bloody corpses, just dead Yorps. *Cute* dead Yorps.

The cuteness of the characters wasn't the only thing bugging Adrian, it was the cuteness of their creator. Tom was getting on his nerves. He would run around the house, craning his neck and making sounds to show Adrian exactly what the alien creatures in the games were supposed to look like. Romero would usually crack up at these displays. Adrian took a liking to Romero, who shared his taste in heavy metal and his appreciation of sick humor; but Tom, in Adrian's mind, was just plain annoying. To make matters worse, they had to share a desk, and Tom was so full of energy that he kept bobbing his knee up and down, inadvertently hitting the table when Adrian was trying to draw. But it was better than working at the last open space in the house, next to the litter box used for John Carmack's cat, Mitzi. Tom had no idea how Adrian felt. He thought he was just quiet.

For the majority of the time, however, those late nights at the lake house were a perpetual programming party. With Iggy Pop or Dokken playing on the stereo, the guys all worked into the wee hours. Occasionally, they'd take a break to play Super Mario on the Nintendo or maybe a round of Dungeons and Dragons. Carmack had been building a large D&D campaign for the guys, and on Saturday nights they'd gather around a table and play into the early morning hours. With Carmack as Dungeon Master, the game took on depth and complexity. It was quickly becoming the longest and deepest D&D game he'd ever created. And there were no signs of it letting up.

Other times, they'd cruise the lake on the boat. Jay quickly became the designated driver; his impeccable focus gave him the ability to drive not only fast but steady. A couple times they let Romero drive, but he was having too much fun, steering the boat precipitously off course. Jay also fell comfortably into the role of manager or, in a sense, frat house president. While the guys worked, he would grill up ribs on the barbecue or restock the sodas. They were under the gun and needed all the help they could get.

They didn't need any help getting motivated, however. Carmack, in particular, seemed almost inhumanly immune to distraction. One time, Jay tested Carmack's resolve by popping a porno video into the VCR and cranking it to full volume. Romero and the others immediately heard the "oohs" and "aahs," and turned around cracking up. Carmack, though, stayed glued to his monitor. Only after a minute or so did he acknowledge the increasingly active groans. His sole response was "Mmm." Then he returned to the work at hand.

Back at Softdisk, Al Vekovius was beginning to grow suspicious of his star gamers. Jay was continually requesting parts for the computers.

And the other guys were behaving more curtly and elusively. His first suspicion came shortly after they were working on their new game for Softdisk, a ninja warrior title called Shadow Knights. Al had never seen a side scrolling like this for the PC. "Wow," he told Carmack, "you should patent this technology."

Carmack turned red. "If you ever ask me to patent anything," he snapped, "I'll quit." Al assumed Carmack was trying to protect his own financial interests, but in reality he had struck what was growing into an increasingly raw nerve for the young, idealistic programmer. It was one of the few things that could truly make him angry. It was ingrained in his bones since his first reading of the Hacker Ethic.

All of science and technology and culture and learning and academics is built upon using the work that others have done before, Carmack thought. But to take a patenting approach and say it's like, well, this idea is my idea, you cannot extend this idea in any way, because I own this idea—it just seems so fundamentally wrong. Patents were jeopardizing the very thing that was central to his life: writing code to solve problems. If the world became a place in which he couldn't solve a problem without infringing on someone's patents, he would be very unhappy living there.

Carmack was becoming more blunt and insulting about other topics as well, most notably the rest of the Softdisk staff. "You've got a lot of terrible programmers here," he said. "They just stink." It was as if Carmack simply didn't care how he alienated himself from the rest of the employees.

Al began dropping by the Gamer's Edge office more often, only to discover more strange behavior. He once walked in to find Carmack, Romero, and Tom huddled around Romero's computers with their backs to the door. When Al made his presence known, they quickly dispersed. He stepped over and asked them what was going on. "Nothing but dirty jokes, Al," Romero replied, gingerly. When Al looked at the screen, it was suspiciously blank. Later he commented to Carmack that Romero was acting strangely, which struck Al as odd since Romero was always so nice. Carmack considered this momentarily, then, as always, blurted out his unedited perception of the truth: "Romero was just being friendly," Carmack said. "When you turn your back, he hates your guts."

By Thanksgiving, the guys were immersed in the death schedule back at the lake house. Sleep was not an issue. Neither was showering. Eating was something they essentially had to remind themselves to do. To help keep them fed while they crunched on Keen, Scott had begun sending the team weekly hundred-dollar checks labeled "pizza bonus," playing off the pepperoni slice icon that appeared in Keen. Pizza was id's fuel. It was, as Carmack enjoyed noting, the perfect invention: hot, quick, and containing a variety of food groups. When Jay opened an envelope from Scott and waved the check in the air, everyone would declare "pizza money!"

Scott was confident he'd see a return on his investment. He had initiated a full-on blitz. Because of his own success, he had built strong ties with the heads of various BBSs and shareware magazines across the country. He called every one of them, preparing each for a game that would revolutionize the industry. Before long, whenever people logged on to a BBS, they would see a title screen reading: "Coming soon from Apogee: Commander Keen." Scott was putting his reputation on the line. But there was never a doubt in the gamers' minds that Keen would deliver.

Tom was in overdrive on the design, bouncing ideas like Ping-Pong balls off Romero. If Romero doubled over laughing, he knew he was on the right track. Scott offered his own advice for the game. "One of the reasons for Mario Brothers popularity," he wrote them in a letter, "is that you can continue playing the game in search of secret or hidden bonuses, et cetera. I would really like to see something like this implemented in Keen—it would really add to the game I think."

"Like . . . duh!" The guys responded. They loved finding secrets in games. Already secrets were like a subculture among programmers. Sometimes there were secret levels, or inside jokes, or tricks that had no real bearing on the outcome of the game. These were called Easter eggs. The mother of all eggs occurred in 1980, when intrepid Atari 2600 geeks stumbled on a secret room in the geometric role-playing game Adventure, only to find the flashing words "Warren Robinett."

Some players haplessly shot at the name. Others just scratched their heads. Robinett was a disgruntled Adventure programmer who wanted recognition following a corporate takeover.

Tom came up with some tricks for Keen. In episode one, players could find a secret hidden city if they pulled a combination of moves, like throwing themselves in the line of fire of an ice cannon. Around the game he inserted cryptic signs written in what was supposed to be the Vorticon alphabet. If players stumbled into a secret area, they could get the translations.

The guys were so enthusiastic that they decided to put in a preview of their upcoming games, which, at the time, didn't exist. They described more installments of Keen as well as a new game based on characters and elements of Carmack's evolving Dungeons and Dragons world. "*The Fight for Justice*," they wrote. "A completely new approach to fantasy gaming. You start not as a weakling with no food—you start as Quake, the strongest, most dangerous person on the continent. You start off with the hammer of thunderbolts, the ring of regeneration, and a trans-dimensional artifact . . . all the people you meet will have their own personalities, lives, and objectives. . . . *The Fight for Justice* will be the finest PC game yet."

The lake house was filled with the sense of unlimited possibilities. And the bond between Carmack and Romero was becoming stronger by the day. It was like two tennis players who, after years of destroying their competition, finally had a chance to play equals. Romero pushed Carmack to be a better programmer. Carmack pushed Romero to be a better designer. What they shared equally was their passion.

This was most clear to Carmack one late weekend night. He was sitting in the house working at his PC as lightning flashed outside. Mitzi curled lazily on top of his monitor, her legs draping over the screen. The heat of her body was causing Carmack's heat-sensitive display to ooze its colors. He pushed Mitzi gently from the monitor, and she scurried away with a hiss.

A rainstorm had picked up, and it was mighty. Cross Lake spilled into the backyard like the prelude to a horror movie. The lake was so high that it pushed the ski boat to the top of the boathouse. Long black water moccasins slithered toward the deck. The bridge leading to Lakeshore Drive was completely washed out. When Jay arrived after having been out for the day, there was no way to get in. It was, as he described it, "a turd floater" of a storm, bringing everything from the bottom of the lake to the surface. He turned away to wait it out.

Romero arrived with a friend later to find the bridge even worse than when Jay got there. There was simply no way he was going to get his car over the flooded expanse. And there were probably alligators and moccasins now making it their home.

Back in the house, Carmack resigned himself to working on his own that night. After all these hours, he had come to appreciate Romero's diverse range of talents, gleaned from years of making his own Apple II games. Romero had been not only a coder but an artist, a designer, and a businessman. On top of all that, he was fun. Romero didn't just love games; in a sense, he *was* a game, a walking, talking, beeping, twitching human video game who never seemed to let anything get him down. Like a game character, he could always find an extra life.

Just then the door behind Carmack swung open. Mitzi dashed under his feet. Carmack turned to see Romero standing there with his big thick glasses, soaking wet up to his chest, lightning flashing behind him, a big smile on his face. It was a real moment, a moment so impressive that Carmack actually saved it in his thin file of sentimental memories. This one he wanted for future access: the night Romero waded through a stormy river to work.

On the afternoon of December 14, 1990, Scott Miller pressed a button on his PC and uploaded the Commander Keen shareware episode Marooned on Mars to the first BBS. For $30, players could purchase the other two episodes, which Scott would ship on floppy disks in Ziploc bags. Before Keen, Scott's total shareware sales were about $7,000 per month. By Christmas, Keen was approaching $30,000.

The game was, as Scott told the numerous editors and BBS controllers who were deluging him with calls, "a little atom bomb." No one had seen anything like it for the PC—the humor, the graphics, the side-scrolling Mario-type action. "Superlative alert!" heralded one reviewer. "Be prepared to hear praise like we have rarely heaped on any program." Keen "sets a new standard for shareware games," declared another. "For stimulating, velvet-smooth and cutting edge PC arcade action," wrote a third, "there is nothing better than Commander Keen from Apogee Software. *Nothing*." The game wasn't just on par with Nintendo, it concluded, it was better.

Fans couldn't agree more. They were deluging Apogee with letters of praise and letters inquiring about the next games in the Keen series. All the main BBSs were ablaze with conversation about Keen—tricks, secrets, strategies. Gamers were pleading for information to decode the Vorticon alphabet. Scott was so swamped that he recruited his mother and his first employee, a teenage programmer named Shawn Green, to help with the demand. When Shawn showed up for work the first morning, he was greeted by Scott's mother, standing in her bathrobe holding two cordless phones. The second she handed him one, it started to ring.

Romero, Carmack, and the rest of the group celebrated with a huge party at the lake house on New Year's Eve. The stereo cranked Prince. The grill smoked. Revelers boated around the lake. Romero, who rarely drank, made this night a special occasion. It had been a great year but a tough year—one that had cost him his wife and kids. Faced with the choice, he'd chosen the game life over the family life. Though he spoke frequently with his boys and saw them as often as he could, he was living with a new family now: the gamers. And he wanted this night together to last.

He, Tom, and Jay were drunk on white wine and champagne in the kitchen. Romero saw Carmack standing in the corner by himself, sober. "Come on, Carmack," he slurred, "you gotta drink, don't be a baby! It's going to be 1991!"

Normally in these situations Carmack wanted nothing less than to disappear into the wallpaper. This kind of scene—socializing, cavorting—was never his domain. He would rather be reading or programming. But contrary to what the other guys might have thought, he wasn't inhuman. He was fun loving too, just in his own way. He was thrilled to be working for himself, making games, collaborating with people he admired and respected. It took only a little coaxing from Romero to get Carmack to join them in downing several glasses of champagne. The strongest thing they'd seen him drink before was Diet Coke.

Some time later Romero found Carmack leaning quietly against the kitchen wall. "Hey, man," Romero said, "you feeling buzzed yet? You getting drunk, Carmack?"

"I am losing control of my faculties," Carmack replied. "Mmm." Then he stumbled away. Romero got a lot of mileage out of that response, repeating it robotically to everyone throughout the night. It was good to see Carmack loosen up.

Two weeks later, Jay walked out to the mailbox and came back brandishing an envelope. It was the first residual check from Apogee. "Pizza money!" they all said, as he opened it up. The check was for $10,500. With barely any overhead expenses, it was gravy. At this rate they'd be making more than $100,000 in their first year, more than enough for them to quit their day jobs at Softdisk.

Al Vekovius still had no idea that they were moonlighting on the Keen games, let alone doing it on the company computers. Gamer's Edge was doing quite well, and their latest games, Catacomb II and Shadow Knights, were drawing raves. Softdisk had about three thousand subscribers who had paid $69.95 per year to receive Gamer's Edge every month. They knew he was counting on them and weren't sure how he'd react to their mass departure.

Carmack and Romero made it clear they didn't care. This was their break, after all. Tom, by contrast, was nervous about the move. He was worried about getting sued by Softdisk, ruining their chances not only for making it on their own but for enjoying the fruits of Keen's success. Romero scoffed at his worries. "Dude, what's Al going to do if he sues you? You don't have anything for him to get. All you have is a piece-of-shit couch," he said, pointing to the broken sofa in the living room. "I mean, what the fuck? What are you worried about losing?"

Jay also expressed concern, urging the guys to handle this delicately with their boss. "Don't drop a bomb on him," he implored.

"Don't worry," Romero said with his characteristic optimism. "Everything's going to be fine."

However, Al's suspicions began to mount when an employee mentioned something about the Gamer's Edge guys moonlighting on their own games. Al confronted Carmack, who he knew had a tough, if not impossible, time telling lies. It was like feeding questions into a computer or adding numbers on a calculator—the answer always came out right. "I admit it," Carmack said. "We've been using your computers. We've been writing our own games on your time." Later he and Romero broke the news: They were going to leave, and they were taking Adrian Carmack, their art intern, with them.

Al felt like he'd walked into his house to find that someone had broken his windows and stolen his television. But he didn't let himself get too far down. Immediately he tried to turn the situation around. "Look," he said, "let's try to salvage something out of this. Let's go into business together! Let's form a new company! I'll support you. And you guys write whatever games you want and I'll handle selling them. We'll split everything fifty-fifty. And I won't take any legal action against you."

The offer caught them by surprise. They had assumed Big Al was going to sue them, not finance their business. Now there was a new golden opportunity. All they wanted to do was have their own business, and they had no interest in dealing with the hassles of taxes and distribution. If Al was going to handle that stuff, what the hell? They agreed.

But when Al returned to the Softdisk office, he walked into a mutiny. The entire company had gathered to demand an explanation. "Carmack and Romero came back from lunch and bragged about some big special deal they were getting," one of the employees said. "What's the deal? Here these jokers had cheated the company, used the company computers, and now you're giving them half of a new company? Why are you rewarding them?"

"Because it's good business!" Al said, "because these guys are good! They're going to make money for the company. We'll all be successful."

No one was buying it. Either the gamers go, they said, or all thirty of them were going to quit. Al sighed deeply and walked back to the

Gamer's Edge office. "You guys went and told everyone about this and created a nightmare," he said. "Do you realize what you have done?"

"Well," Carmack replied, "we wanted to be truthful."

"Yeah, but I could have positioned it a lot better," he said. "I can't afford to lose my staff. The deal's off."

After several weeks of negotiations and threatened lawsuits, it was agreed that they would contract with Softdisk to write one new game for Gamer's Edge every two months. It was demoralizing, not only for the Softdisk staff but for Al. He saw that, despite their talent, the Gamer's Edge guys really were just boys living by their own rules, and cheating when necessary. Worst of all, they had no sense of guilt. For them it was something to laugh about. They never considered the people who worked at Softdisk. Before Carmack left, Al pulled him aside and asked, "Did you ever think about the people who have worked so hard and supported you?"

Carmack listened, but Al's words didn't compute. He was looking into the face of the past, of opportunities unrealized, of all the old authority figures who had ever stood in his way. As always, he was blunt to a fault. "I don't care about them," Al would recall Carmack replying. "I'll go back to making pizzas before I stay at this crummy place."

On February 1, 1991, id Software was born.

FIVE

More Fun
Than Real Life

Romero wanted to summon the demons. Or at least, he said, figure out how. It was four in the morning at the lake house. Empty soda cans littered the floor. Mitzi dozed on top of Carmack's computer monitor. The smell of pepperoni lingered in the air. The guys sat around the large makeshift table in the living room, several hours into yet another round of Dungeons and Dragons. Since leaving Softdisk, they had more time to devote to their recreational D&D campaign. It was truly evolving into an alternate world, which, like all fiction, deeply reflected their own. It wasn't just a game, it was an extension of their imaginations, hopes, dreams. It mattered.

The deepness of their Dungeons and Dragons adventure was due in no small part to Carmack. Whereas most Dungeon Masters would create small episodes that lasted for a few hours of play, Carmack's world was persistent; players returned to it every time they regrouped. The game they played now was the same one he had been writing since he was a kid in Kansas City. It was as if a musician had been composing an opera for several years. The guys would pass Carmack's room on the way to the bathroom in the middle of the night and see him hunched over pages of notes, sketching out the details of their game.

Carmack's D&D world was a personal masterwork of forests and magic, time tunnels and monsters. He had a fifty-page glossary of characters and items such as "Quake," a fighter with a magical "Hellgate Cube" floating above its head, the "Chalice of Insanity . . . a chalice from which you get Jellybeans of Insanity which, if ingested, will cause you to go nuts and fight everyone around you" and the Mighty Daikatana sword. He relished the feeling of creating a place others could explore. The way D&D was played, he, as Dungeon Master, would invent and describe the set and setting. Then it was up to the players to dictate how they wanted to proceed.

In their game, the guys created an imaginary group of adventurers called Popular Demand: Romero named his character Armand Hammer, a fighter who liked to dabble with magic; Tom was a fighter named Buddy; Jay, a thief-acrobat named Rif; Adrian, a massive fighter named Stonebreaker. With each adventure, Popular Demand gained power and prestige. They were a living metaphor of id. As Carmack had said, the game had the power to bring out someone's true personality. And on this fateful night, Romero wanted to make a deal with the devil.

In Carmack's game, he had designated two different dimensions of existence: a material plane (which Popular Demand inhabited) and a plane of demons. After months traversing the material plane, however, Romero was getting bored. To spice things up, he wanted to retrieve the dangerous and powerful Demonicron, a magic tome that gave a knowledgeable user the power to summon the demons to the material plane. Carmack consulted his D&D rule book. If used thoughtfully, he told them, the Demonicron meant enormous strength to the group, guaranteeing them all the riches of the world. With it, Romero thought, he might get his hands on an ultimate weapon like the Daikatana. But there were risks. If the Demonicron fell into the hands of a demon, it would cause the world to be overrun with evil. Even though Carmack had made up the game, he respected its limitations, its rules, its *science.* If a player did something that would destroy the world, then the world would die.

Romero and the rest discussed the options. Though Adrian and Tom were hesitant, Romero's excitement and enthusiasm won them over once again. "Come on," he said. "We can't lose!" They decided to seize the Demonicron from its palace of supernatural beasts. Carmack rolled the die to determine the outcome of their battles: Popular Demand was victorious. The Demonicron was theirs. What they would do with it, they didn't know. For the time being, there were others matters at hand. In the earthly dimension, it was getting late and there were other games to attend to: the ones by id Software.

When the guys christened their company, they shortened the Ideas from the Deep initialism and simply called themselves id, for "in demand." They also didn't mind that, as Tom pointed out, id had another meaning: "the part of the brain that behaves by the pleasure principle." In early 1991 their pleasurable games were indeed in demand. Keen was number one on the shareware charts, emerging as the first and only game to break the coveted top ten. The first Keen trilogy was now bringing in fifteen to twenty thousand dollars per month. It wasn't just pizza money anymore, it was computer money. They used it to outfit the lake house with a fleet of high-end 386 PCs. Carmack was only twenty years old, Romero, twenty-three, and they were in business.

Despite the success and the fact that Romero, Carmack, and Adrian had decided to leave Softdisk immediately that February, Tom and Jay chose to stay behind. In Tom's case, it was a temporary solution. Always conscientious, he felt bad about leaving the company high and dry and was more comfortable waiting until they found a replacement for him. Jay felt an obligation to fulfill his duty at Softdisk, which included the completion of an important Apple II product. But he would stay at least a friendly part of the id group, D&D campaign included, for some time.

Heading into the spring of 1991, id rode on the high of its newfound freedom. Though under contractual obligation to Softdisk, they now could work on the games completely in the comfort of their lake house. Carmack immersed himself in programming what he wanted to be the next generation of his graphics engine. The first engine had enabled the primary breakthrough of side-scrolling action; now he wanted to create more elaborate and immersive effects. He methodically researched while the rest utilized the existing technology to create their first free-lance games for Softdisk.

The freedom from Softdisk and the success of Keen were inspiring new kinds of games. Rescue Rover was about a young boy who had to rescue his dog, Rover, after the dog had been kidnapped by aliens. A clever maze game, it challenged the player to maneuver a series of mirrors to reflect deadly rays being cast by alien robots so the boy could find and save his dog. It combined what was emerging as something of an id formula: humor plus violence, the more over the top, the better. The title screen for Rescue Rover showed the slaphappy pooch with a wagging tail surrounded by sinister alien weapons aimed at his skull.

While Rover took one step in the dark humor direction, their next game, which they began working on in March, Dangerous Dave in the Haunted Mansion, broke more sinister ground. For this one Romero wanted to recast his most beloved character in a more gothic situation. Using the Keen graphics engine, they set about putting together a more realistic looking Dave. This time they wanted him to pull up to a wretched Shreveport-style house in a pickup truck, decked out in a hunting cap, jeans, and brandishing a shotgun, which he would use to rid the house of zombies and ghouls.

Of all the id guys, Adrian was particularly juiced over the grisly theme. It was a chance for him to exorcise all the gore he had seen when he worked at the hospital. Though he didn't tell the group, he still hated Commander Keen. If they were going to make a kids' game, he thought, they should be doing something gross and funny in the spirit of a popular TV series at the time, *Ren and Stimpy*. With Dangerous Dave in the Haunted Mansion, Adrian finally found an outlet. While Tom and Romero worked at their machines, Adrian, unbeknownst to them, began creating what he called "death animations": three or four tiles that would play in rapid sequence after Dave died. In most games, characters would simply vanish or, as Tom had instructed, Keen floated up the screen to heaven, presumably. Adrian had other ideas.

Late one night Romero hit a button and watched Adrian's animation play: Dave took a zombie fist to the face, which smashed out his eyes in a bloody pulp. Romero almost hyperventilated with laughter. "Blood!" He cackled. "In a game! How fucking awesome is that?"

Violent fantasy, of course, had an ancient history. Readers had been fascinated by the gore of *Beowulf* for over a thousand years ("The demon clutched a sleeping thane in his swift assault, tore him in pieces, bit through the bones, gulped the blood, and gobbled the flesh"). Kids played cops and robbers, brandishing their guns and flying backward in imagined bursts of blood. As the id guys came of age, in the 1980s, the action movie genre—with films like *Rambo, The Terminator,* and *Lethal Weapon*—conquered the box office, just as horror movies like *The Texas Chain Saw Massacre* and *Friday the 13th* had done in the recent past.

Violence in games was nothing new either—even the very first computer game, Spacewar, was about destruction—but *graphic* violence certainly was. In the past graphical violence was always limited, partly because of the inability of technology to render detail and, mainly, because game developers avoided it. Back in 1976, an arcade game called Death Race had caused a ruckus. The object was to drive a car over a bunch of crudely drawn stick figure blips. When the player hit the screaming figures, they were replaced by crucifixes. The cabinet was painted with skulls and grim reapers. It was a far cry from the big hit of the day, Pong. It was also the first video game to be banned.

Adrian's macabre work was too good to pass up. Fueled by Romero's enthusiasm, he added more and more gruesome details, including chunks of bloody flesh that would fly off a zombie's body when it was shot. When the guys at Softdisk saw the gore, however, they didn't get the joke and insisted that id redraw the death animations—sans blood. "Maybe one day," Adrian said, "we'll be able to put in as much blood as we want."

While the other guys were pushing their envelopes, Carmack was pushing his own, specifically, into 3-D. Because he was a craftsman engineer, 3-D was the obvious next step for him. Three-dimensional graphics were the holy grail for many programmers as well. To split hairs, the games weren't really three-dimensional in the 3-D movie sense of the term; the term meant that graphics had a real sense of solid dimensions. Often these games were created from the first-person point of view. The whole idea was to make the player feel as if he were *inside* the game.

Though Carmack was not aware of it, he was joining a pursuit that had begun thousands of years before. The dream of a realistic, immersive, interactive experience had consumed humankind for millennia. Some believed it to be a primal desire. Dating from 15,000 B.C.E., cave paintings in Lascaux, in the south of France, were considered to be among the first "immersive environments," with images that would give the inhabitant the feeling of entering another world.

In 1932, Aldous Huxley described a futuristic kind of movie experience called feelies in his novel *Brave New World*. Combining three-dimensional imagery as well as olfactory and tactile effects, the feelies, he wrote, were "dazzling and incomparably more solid looking than they would have seemed in actual flesh and blood, far more real than reality." Ray Bradbury imagined a similar experience in his 1950 short story "The Veldt," which presented, essentially, a view of the first virtual reality room. A family has a special room that can project any scene they imagine on the surrounding walls. Problems arise when an African vision becomes entirely too real.

Soon technologists began efforts to realize these immersive environments. In 1955, the Hollywood cinematographer Morton Heilig described his work on "the Cinema of the future," which, he wrote, "will far surpass the Feelies of Aldous Huxley's *Brave New World*." With a novelty machine called the Sensorama, which combined sights, sounds, and smells of urban landscapes, Heilig's aim was to create an illusion considerably more immersive than those of the tacky 3-D movies of the time. The goal, he said, was a situation "so life-like that it gives the spectator the sensation of being *physically* in the scene."

Convincing immersion was not just a matter of multimedia preening, it was a matter of interactivity—an essential ingredient and allure of computer games. Interactive immersive environments were the pet project of a University of Wisconsin computer artist named Myron Krueger. Throughout the 1970s, Krueger created Veldt-like experiences, sometimes achieved by projecting the images of audience members—even those in remote locations—on giant landscape screens. "The environments," he wrote, "suggest a new art medium based on a commitment to real-time interaction between men and machines. . . . This context is an artificial reality within which the artist has complete control of the laws of cause and effect. . . . Response is the medium!" One such project, called MAZE, let audience members try to navigate through an image of a maze that was projected in a room.

By the 1980s interactive immersions had taken on a new name: virtual reality. The author William Gibson coined the term *cyberspace* in his influential 1984 novel, *Neuromancer*, to describe an interactive online world that existed between computer networks. In the late 1980s, Scott Fisher, an engineer at the NASA–Ames Research Center, combined a head-mounted display and data-transmitting hand gloves in what became the archetype of the virtual reality interface. Through these tools, users could enter a virtual world in which they could manipulate objects and proceed in a first-person three-dimensional point of view.

The end effect, Fisher wrote in 1989, is a "kind of electronic persona. For interactive theater or interactive fantasy applications, these styles might range from fantasy figures to inanimate objects, or different figures to different people. Eventually, telecommunication networks may develop that will be configured with virtual environment servers for users to dial into remotely in order to interact with each other's virtual proxies. . . . The possibilities of virtual realities, it appears, are as limitless as the possibilities of reality. They can provide a human interface that disappears—as a doorway to other worlds."

Carmack's research into 3-D computer games was on a more intuitive level. Though he was a fan of science fiction, enamored of *Star Trek*'s Holodeck, his focus was not on chipping away at some grand design of such a virtual world but, rather, on solving the immediate problem of the next technological advance.

He had been experimenting with 3-D graphics since making his wire-frame MTV logos on his Apple II. Since then several games had experimented with first-person 3-D points of view. In 1980, Richard Garriott employed this perspective in his very first role-playing game, Akalabeth. Two years later an Apple II game from Sirius Software called Wayout wowed gamers and critics with a first-person maze game. But it was flight simulations, putting the player in the cockpits of a variety of airplanes, that exploited this kind of immersion. In 1990,

Richard Garriott's company, Origin, released a space-themed combat flight simulator called Wing Commander, which became a favorite around the id lake house.

Carmack figured he could do better. Flight sims, he thought, were painfully slow, bogged down by their heavy graphics and leaving the player to snail through the game play. What he and the others preferred was the fast action of arcade games like Defender, Asteroids, and Gauntlet. While the other guys worked on Rescue Rover and Dangerous Dave in the Haunted Mansion, Carmack tried to see how he might do something that hadn't been done before: create a fast-action game in 3-D.

The problem, he found, was that the PC was not powerful enough to handle such a game. Carmack read up on the topic but found nothing adequate for his solution. He approached the dilemma as he had in Keen: try the obvious approach first; if that fails, think outside the box. One of the reasons for a 3-D game's slow speed was that the computer had to draw too many surfaces at once. Carmack had an idea. What if he commanded the computer to draw only a few surfaces at a time, the way one would put blinders on a horse? Rather than draw, in this case, arbitrary polygons, he designed a program that would draw only sideways trapezoids—in other words, walls but no ceilings or floors.

To get the computer to draw at the fastest possible speed, Carmack tried another nontraditional approach, known as raycasting. Instead of drawing out a large slab of graphics, which required a lot of memory and power, raycasting instructed the computer to paint a thin vertical strip of graphics at a time, based on the player's point of view. The bottom line: raycasting meant speed.

Carmack's final challenge was to add characters in the 3-D world. The solution was to incorporate simple though convincing graphical icons or sprites. Wing Commander had used a calculation that told the computer to reduce or scale the size of the sprite depending on the player's location. By combining these so-called scaled sprites with his limited polygons and raycasting, Carmack was able to brew up a fast 3-D world.

Carmack emerged from his research after six weeks, two weeks longer than he had spent on any other game. When Romero saw the technology, he was once again impressed by the Whiz Kid. They discussed what kind of game could best exploit the new engine. They settled on a futuristic world in which the player, driving a tank, had to rescue people from nuclear Armageddon. Released in April 1991, Hovertank was the first fast-action, first-person shooter for the computer. Id had invented a genre.

Despite Hovertank's innovations, it was no Commander Keen. The game looked rather ugly with its big, solid-colored walls. But it included id's increasingly ghoulish touches. Adrian relished the chance to draw a cast of nuclear-mutated beasts reduced to puddles of blood. Like the Yorps in Keen, the puddles would linger through the game, so if a player returned to a spot he would see the remnants of his carnage.

As May began, id Software continued to innovate its games and expand its business, returning specifically to its first emerging brand, Commander Keen. To fulfill a game for Softdisk, id decided to make a new episode called Keen Dreams. Though they had experimented with first-person 3-D gaming in Hovertank, they wanted to preserve Keen's side-scrolling integrity while adding something new. An obvious choice was to create a more compelling sense of moving through a landscape, for example, allowing the foreground and background to move at different speeds. This effect was known as parallax scrolling. In the past, a character might run past a static forest. In a parallax-scrolling game, the trees would move very slowly while the character ran past. It seemed more real.

Again Carmack was faced with the limits of PC technology. After a few attempts, he realized that there was no way to create parallax scrolling in a convincing manner. Since the computers were too slow to draw a moving foreground *and* background, Carmack decided to fudge it. He wrote a program that could temporarily save or cache an image on the screen so that it didn't have to be redrawn every time a character passed by. To create the illusion of depth, he realized that he could temporarily save two images together, say, a little section of a sidewalk and a little chunk of a tree in the background, for quick recall. Once again he had pushed the graphics of the PC into a place no one had gone this quickly before. Keen Dreams was completed by the end of the month.

In June 1991, id began work on the next trilogy of games for Scott Miller and Apogee. Keen 4, 5, and 6 would be released in the same manner as the first set: one initial chunk uploaded as shareware to tease players into purchasing the whole group. At this point Apogee was comfortably ruling not just the shareware gaming world but the *entire* shareware world. The Keen games were at the top of the charts, bringing in close to sixty thousand dollars per month. If they followed the same plan, Scott assured them, they would earn at least as much.

Tom wrote the story line of this trilogy, Goodbye Galaxy. This time around, Commander Keen discovers a plot to blow up the galaxy and must head off in his Bean-with-Bacon MegaRocket to save the world. First, he has to tend to his parents, whom he temporarily immobilized with a stun gun. The stun gun was a new and necessary addition to the game, Tom thought. After the first Keen trilogy, Tom began opening letters of complaint from concerned parents who didn't like the dead Yorps corpses hanging around on screen. *Why couldn't the characters just disappear when they die, like in most games?* Tom still wanted kids to see the effects of their violence, but he didn't want to stir up unnecessary controversy. He decided that, beginning with this game, the creatures would simply be stunned when hit. They wouldn't die; they would just remain frozen, circles of stars surrounding their heads.

By August, id had a working prototype, or beta, of Commander Keen 4: Secret of the Oracle. At the time Romero had met a smooth-talking gamer in Canada named Mark Rein. Mark had been a big fan of the first Keens and asked Romero if they needed anyone to play-test their next games. Romero said they did and sent Mark a beta of Keen 4. At the end was a teaser description of the next episode, "The Armageddon Machine," which promised the game would be, among other things, "more fun than real life!"

Mark replied with a detailed list of bugs, impressing Romero. Mark wasn't just a gamer, he was an aspiring businessman who was so sure he could get id some deals that he offered to fly himself down to Shreveport to meet with the guys. Romero, from the moment he saw the Dangerous Dave in Copyright Infringement demo, had been looking for ways to expand the business. Maybe Mark could fill that void.

Carmack was making this great technology, after all, so why not have someone in the company who would exploit it for all it was worth?

Carmack didn't jump at the suggestion. As he was fond of pointing out, he wasn't interested in running a big company, he just wanted to program games. But he recognized that without Romero id wouldn't have been in the business in the first place. He agreed to bring Mark Rein on as id's probationary president for six months.

Within weeks Mark had scored a deal to release a retail version of Commander Keen with a company called FormGen. He raved about the opportunity for id to cash in on the commercial marketplace. They were going to make three games anyway; all they had to do was take one of them and release it with FormGen as retail. For id, it seemed like a great idea, a second way to cash in. They could release one Keen in the shareware market and another in retail.

Id had no contract with Apogee, but they called Scott Miller to tell him of the opportunity. Their relationship was going well. Earlier in the summer, Scott had brought a coterie of game developers to visit at the boys' invitation. Romero had decided to host a seminar to encourage other game developers to license id's technology. Licensing made sense, Romero thought, because Carmack's technology was clearly so impressive. Why not let others *pay* to use it themselves? Over a weekend the id guys showed how the Keen engine could be used by creating an impromptu PC version of Pac-Man that they dubbed Wac-Man. They completed it in a night and sold their first license to Apogee.

When the id guys told Scott later about the FormGen opportunity, he was dismayed. "This is a big problem," he said to them. "You're breaking the magic formula of the trilogy. If you release a shareware game and don't let people buy the full trilogy, it's not going to sell as well." It's too late, they told him. They had already signed the deal.

By August 1991, id Software's growing ambitions were leading them not only into new business, new games, and new technologies but to a new home. Tom and Romero wanted out of Shreveport. Despite the fun days at the lake house, they were getting tired of the depressing environment. Romero hated driving past all the poor people fishing for food off the Cross Lake bridge. He had another motivation too: a girlfriend, Beth McCall.

Beth worked at Softdisk in the shipping department. A former debutante from New Orleans, she was bright and cheerful, and laughed at all Romero's silly jokes. The relationship was light and fun, just the tonic Romero felt he needed after his divorce. Though his relationship with his ex-wife was strained, he still felt close to his sons. With Beth, he was able to fill a void. Best of all, she wanted out of Shreveport too.

Tom had an idea where to go. He missed the change of the seasons and culture of his college town and begged them to relocate to Wisconsin. Romero agreed to accompany Tom to check out Madison, a college town. They returned convinced that this was the place to go. Their other lake house roommate, Jason Blochowiak, had gone to school in Madison and quickly offered to leave Softdisk and come along. The other guys didn't think Jason was quite motivated enough; he had once commented how he made more money from his investments than from his computer programming. He drove a van with a vanity license plate that read AUTOCRAT. But Carmack thought he was a smart, talented programmer and was happy to have him.

Carmack was fine with going to Madison; as he often told the others, he didn't care where he was as long as he could code. Adrian was much more reluctant. Shreveport, after all, was his lifelong home. Though he explored dark worlds in his art, in real life he craved stability. Romero begged and pleaded, promising Adrian that their apartments would be only the best. After much convincing from his friends and family, Adrian agreed to go. Jay, however, to everyone's disappointment, was not on board for this ride. Feeling obliged to complete his projects at Softdisk, and leery of risking a start-up venture, he chose to stay behind.

On a warm morning in September, the id guys loaded up their cars and drove away from the lake house one last time. The computers in their trunks were their own.

SIX

Green and Pissed

or once, reality didn't live up to Romero's hype. The id guys arrived at the apartment in Madison on a gray day in September 1991 to find it considerably less fun than he and Tom had described. They were in a sprawling complex in which every building looked the same. Compared with their Shreveport house, it was a dump: no lake, no yard, no boat. When they walked down the hall they didn't pass trees, they passed two scary-looking guys dealing drugs.

At least they had some semblance of an id office: a three-bedroom apartment in the complex. Because Carmack didn't care, he agreed to live in the upstairs bedroom while all the other guys got their own apartments elsewhere in the complex. Adrian, who was instantly miserable being out of his element, had even more problems because his apartment was on the far side of the development. While the other guys walked across a parking lot to get to the id office, Adrian had to drive.

But Romero was delighted. He was starting fresh: he had a new girlfriend and new games. Tom shared in the enthusiasm, happy to be back home, refreshed by the collegiate environment. The only real sore point for the two of them was Jason, who had become Carmack's friend. He seemed to be on a completely different wavelength. Still, Carmack wasn't ready to let him go.

Despite their mixed feelings about their new situation, the id team buckled down to finish the second Commander Keen trilogy. After their long months working together, the team had formed into a collective personality. Romero and Carmack were now in a perfect groove, with Carmack improving the new Keen engine—the code that made the graphics—while Romero worked on the editor and tools—the software used to create the game elements. Nothing could distract them. One night Beth and a few other women showed up at the apartment. The guys were hard at work. Beth did her best to attract Romero's attention. When nothing elicited a response, she threw up her hands and said, "Why can't we just have our men come home and have sex with us?"

"Because we're working," Romero said. Carmack laughed.

Tom was just as dedicated, feeling particularly giddy about the success of the project, which inspired him to new heights of creative design. He populated Keen's world with gun-toting potato men, tongue-wagging poisonous mushrooms and, his favorite, the Dopefish—a green fish with big dopey eyes and giant front teeth.

Adrian, as usual, didn't share Tom's glee. But he put all his efforts into bringing the silly characters to life. His artwork was taking on more color and precision, rivaling that of the best games on the market. He was also finding a way to vent his mounting frustrations with Tom, Keen, and Madison. One time he played around with the Commander Keen image, creating a graphic of Keen with his eyes gouged out and his throat ripped open. Adrian had a good laugh switching between the images of Keen all happy and chipper and Keen sliced and diced.

With the work on the new Keens progressing and checks continuing to pour in, Carmack was able to go back to his pet project: 3-D first-person shooters. The latest step was inspired by something he had heard from Romero. Carmack and Romero had developed another aspect of their collaboration. Though Carmack was gifted at creating game graphics, he had little interest in keeping up with the gaming world. He was never a player, really, he only made the games, just as he was the Dungeon Master but not a player of D&D. Romero, by contrast, kept up with *everything,* all the new games and developers. It was through one of these developers that he first learned about an important new development called "texture mapping."

Texture mapping meant applying a detailed pattern or texture to a tile of graphics on the computer screen. Instead of drawing a solid color on the back wall of a game, the computer would draw a pattern of bricks. Romero heard about texture mapping from Paul Neurath, whose company, Blue Sky Productions, was working on a game called Ultima Underworld, which would be published by Richard Garriott's Origin company. Neurath told Romero that they were applying texture mapping to shapes or polygons in a three-dimensional world. Cool, Romero thought. When he hung up the phone, he spun his chair to Carmack and said, "Paul said he's doing a game using texture mapping."

"Texture mapping?" Carmack replied, then took a few seconds to spin the concept around in his head. "I can do that."

The result was Catacomb 3-D, which incorporated texture-mapped walls of gray bricks covered in green slime. To play, the gamer ran through the maze, shooting fireballs out of a hand that was drawn in the lower center of the screen, as if one was looking down on one's own arm, reaching into the computer. By including the hand, id Software was making a subtle but strong point to its audience: You are not just playing the game, you're inhabiting it.

The game ended up being published six months before Neurath's Ultima Underworld. Though Ultima Underworld, a role-playing adventure, received more attention because of the Garriott connection, together the games took the 3-D gaming experience to a new, more immersive place. When Scott Miller saw Catacomb 3-D, he had one thing to say: "We need to do something like this as shareware."

As Thanksgiving 1991 neared, life in Madison was turning increasingly ugly. The drug-dealing neighbors had been arrested after the cops pounded down their door. Someone siphoned gasoline from their cars. Adrian was particularly miserable because he lost the cap to his water bed and couldn't find a replacement. He spent months in a sleeping bag on the floor. Carmack had been sleeping on the floor for months too, though by choice. He simply didn't feel he needed a mattress. Finally Romero got fed up with the situation and bought his partner a mattress, leaving it for him on his floor. "Dude," he said, "it's time you got a good night's sleep."

Madison was growing cold—really, really cold. Snow dumped from the sky. The entire parking lot of the complex was glazed over in ice. Every afternoon when he'd wake up, Adrian would have to sit in his car for twenty minutes warming the engine so he could drive to the other side of the development. One time they all went out to buy a pizza but ran back to their cars without the pie. They were so cold they decided to leave the pizza and drive home. No one was willing to run back inside.

The result was that they barely left their apartment. Though they were used to spending endless hours together in a small room, in Shreveport at least they had the *opportunity* to go outside and kneeboard around the lake. Here they killed even more time playing Dungeons and Dragons. In an effort to expand the game, they even drew up flyers that they posted around town.

At the top of the page, Adrian had drawn each of the id guys as his character in the game—Tom with a beard and a large ax, Romero with a huge sword, Adrian standing high with a belt that had the word *die* on a cloth, and Carmack, dressed as a wizard, holding the rule book. Next to them was a blank stick figure with a question mark for a head. The flyer read: "WANTED: CLERIC and/or THIEF! Party playing in an awesome, character and event-driven campaign. . . . Just moved our business here, need one or two new players. . . . Things you will enjoy in this campaign: character interaction, good balance, cool stuff happening, pizza. Things you won't be doing in this campaign: Dominating the world."

Tensions began to rise, however, about who was trying to dominate the apartment. Adrian was fed up with Tom and Romero bopping around making alien noises and imitating the characters from Keen. Even Carmack was growing tired of their antics. Worse was the trouble with Jason, who was becoming something of a fifth wheel. Carmack was still defending him, though; so instead of firing him they assigned him to bang out a fast, easy game by himself that could fulfill an obligation on the Softdisk contract.

With the Softdisk game being handled by Jason and the second Keen trilogy wrapping up, id could focus on its next project for Apogee. At this point, a hierarchy had been established. Carmack was the technology leader, coming up with the latest engines with which they could construct a game. Tom, as creative director, was in charge of spearheading the game stuff that would go around Carmack's technology. Romero fit nicely between the two, able to help Carmack with tools and at the same time goof around with Tom on creative ideas. Adrian would fulfill their orders for artwork, injecting, when he could, his own menacing visions.

When the four sat down late one night to discuss a new game, those roles unexpectedly began to shift. The trouble started with Tom. Buoyed by the blockbuster success of the first trilogy months before, he had long imagined doing three trilogies, similar to the plan his hero George Lucas had mapped out for the *Star Wars* films. But Carmack's technology was clearly headed toward another idea: a fast-action, first-person game. Keen was neither fast-action nor first-person; it was a side-scrolling adventure like Mario. It was implicit that the next game, at least, would call for something else.

Tom was disappointed, but he shifted into high gear, brainstorming for a new first-person game. He had an immediate idea. "Hey," he said, "remember in the movie *The Thing* when the guy comes out of the cage where the dogs are going insane from that alien, and everyone asks him what's in there? And he says, 'I don't know, but it's weird and pissed off'? Well, that's just like a video game, because in video games you have no idea why you're shooting the monsters other than that they're green and pissed off. Why not do a game like that? Something about these mutant lab experiments you have to hunt down?" He started jotting down potential titles at his PC as he read them aloud to the group: "Mutants from Hell!" "Die, Mutants, Die!" "3-Demons!" "Texture-Mapped Terence and the Green Shits!" Or, he concluded, they could just cut to the chase and call the game "It's Green and Pissed."

Everyone laughed. "Yeah," Romero said, "imagine some game dude wandering into a computer store and saying to the clerk, 'Um, excuse me, but do you have It's Green and Pissed?'" Despite their approval, Tom quickly retreated from his idea. He didn't want to be controversial for controversy's sake.

"Yeah, I don't know," Romero said. "That's so hackneyed. That's something you always hear of. It's like 'yet again the mutated lab full of bullshit, blah blah blah.' We need to do something cool. You know, it'd be really fucking cool if we made a remake of Castle Wolfenstein and did it in 3-D."

Wolfenstein! It was a word that struck an immediate chord with both Carmack and Tom, who, like Romero and every other hard-core Apple II gamer, had grown up playing the classic action title created by the legendary Silas Warner in the early 1980s. They immediately *got* Romero's vision. Wolfenstein was perfect for Carmack's technology because it was, at its core, a maze-based shooter. The player had to run through all these labyrinths fighting Nazis and collecting treasure, then doing away with Hitler. Despite the game's blocky, low-resolution graphics, it was unique in its implication of a larger virtual world. When Castle Wolfenstein was released, most games for computers or arcades, like Pong, existed on one static screen. But in Wolfenstein the conceit was that each screen the player saw represented one room of a large castle. Each room was a maze of walls. When the player ran through the maze, the screen would change, showing a new room. Though there was no scrolling, the *feeling* was one of true exploration. Part of the appeal was that the player never knew what awaited in the next room: often it was a Nazi screaming in German.

Encouraged by everyone's sympathetic reaction, Romero exploded with ideas. In the original Wolfenstein, the characters could search the bodies of dead soldiers. "How cool would that be to have in first-person 3-D?" he said. "You could go through and, like, drag the bodies around a corner and rifle through their pockets! *Prɔʃhh prɔʃhh prɔʃhh!*" he said, imitating the sounds. "We have this opportunity to do something totally new here, something fast and texture-mapped. If we can make the graphics look great and fast, and make the sound cool and loud, and make the game explosively fun, then we're going to have a winner, especially with the theme."

The computer game industry was still meek, after all. SimCity, a hit game, challenged players to build and micromanage a virtual town. Civilization, another success, was a heady Risk-like strategy game based on famous historical battles—blood not included. Wolfenstein could be like nothing the industry had ever seen. "It will be just shocking," Romero concluded, "a totally shocking game."

Carmack gave his blessing. Once behind an idea, Romero was always charismatically convincing. And Carmack was growing to appreciate Romero's talent for taking his technology into a new world, a place he himself would never have conceived. Adrian, who wasn't familiar with the original Wolfenstein, was eager to do anything other than Keen, and the idea of 3-D art intrigued him. Tom, though stung by the rejection of Keen, assumed that they would return to his games after this one. He was still the company's game designer, after all. So, true to his conciliatory nature, he was willing to go along for the ride. It was a ride all the more immersive because of Carmack's technology and all the more wild because, for the first time in id's brief history, it was being steered by Romero.

On a cold winter day, Carmack laced up his shoes, slipped on his jacket, and headed out into the Madison snow. The town was blanketed in the stuff, cars caked in frost, trees dangling ice. Carmack endured the chill because he had no car; he'd sold the MGB long before. It was easy enough for him to shut out the weather, just like he could, when necessary, shut Tom and Romero's antics out of his mind. He was on a mission.

Carmack stepped into the local bank and requested a cashier's check for $11,000. The money was for a NeXT computer, the latest machine from Steve Jobs, cocreator of Apple. The NeXT, a stealth black cube, surpassed the promise of Jobs's earlier machines by incorporating NeXTSTEP, a powerful system tailor-made for custom software development. The market for PCs and games was exploding, and this was the perfect tool to create more dynamic titles for the increasingly viable gaming platform. It was the ultimate Christmas present for the ultimate in young graphics programmers, Carmack.

The NeXT computer wasn't the only new spirit ushering in the new year. Times were changing in the world of id. They had finally fired Jason, narrowing the group to Carmack, Romero, Adrian, and Tom. But something else was in the air. The Reagan-Bush era was finally coming to a close and a new spirit rising. It began in Seattle, where a sloppily dressed grunge rock trio called Nirvana ousted Michael Jackson from the top of the pop charts with their album *Nevermind*. Soon grunge and hip-hop were dominating the world with more brutal and honest views. Id was braced to do for games what those artists had done for music: overthrow the status quo. Games until this point had been ruled by their own equivalent of pop, in the form of Mario and Pac-Man. Unlike music, the software industry had never experienced anything as rebellious as Wolfenstein 3-D.

The title came after much brainstorming. At first they assumed they had to use something other than the Wolfenstein name, which had been created by Silas Warner at Muse Software. Tom banged out a list of options from the strained — The Fourth Reich or Deep in Germany — to the absurd — Castle Hasselhoff or Luger Me Now. He even played around with some German titles — Dolchteufel (Devil Dagger), Geruchschlecht (Bad Smell). To their surprise and relief, they discovered that Muse had gone bankrupt in the mid-1980s and let the trademark on the Wolfenstein name lapse. It would be Wolfenstein 3-D.

When they ran the idea by Scott, he loved it. He had been pleading with them to do a 3-D shareware game for months. He too knew Castle Wolfenstein and cracked up at Romero's plans for their version: loud guns, fast action, mowing down Nazis. Money was still rolling in from the Keen games. The second trilogy was out in the shareware market too. Its numbers were disappointing, about a third of the original, but Scott knew this was not so much a sign of the game's appeal as verification of his original concern: that the retail release of a Keen game for FormGen would cut into his sales because it left him with only two episodes, not three. Nevertheless, the guys at id were his stars, and he believed wholeheartedly in their technology and vision. He guaranteed them $100,000 for Wolfenstein.

Id had no intentions to stop there. Mark Rein, still id's probationary president, had scored with FormGen to release two more retail id products. Id was excited but concerned; FormGen's first game with them, Commander Keen: Aliens Ate My Babysitter, didn't sell well. Id blamed in part what they thought was a terrible box cover, designed by a company that had done packages for Lipton tea. But the prospect for another shot was enticing. Again, it would allow them to earn revenues from two lucrative markets: shareware and retail. No one, not even Origin and Sierra, was doing this. Though Mark and FormGen were reluctant to, as they said, "stir up the World War II stuff," they agreed to take Wolfenstein retail. The id guys were growing accustomed to getting their way.

Mitzi enjoyed her new perch atop Carmack's spacious black NeXT computer. She stretched out lazily on the monitor, letting her legs dangle over the screen. Surrounded by empty pizza boxes and Diet Coke cans, Romero, Carmack, Tom, and Adrian sat at their computers, working on Wolfenstein 3-D. The calmness of the outer world was in stark contrast to the world unfolding on the screens. Wolfenstein had taken on two imperatives: it would be brutal, as originally imagined by Romero, and it would be fast, as engineered by Carmack.

Carmack knew he could up the speed and, thus, the immersion — thanks to the leaps he had made by combining raycasting with texture mapping on Catacomb 3-D. For Wolfenstein, he didn't so much take another leap as improve his existing code: cleaning up the bugs, optimizing the speed, making it more elegant. A key decision was to let the graphics engine focus on drawing only what the player needed to see. That meant, once again, drawing the walls but not the ceilings and floors. Also to speed things up, characters and objects in the game would not be in true 3-D, they would be sprites, flat images that, if encountered in real life, would look like cardboard cutouts.

Romero, in pure Melvin mode, imagined all the crazy stuff they could do in a game where the object was, as he said, "to mow down Nazis." He wanted to have the suspense of an Apple II game pumped up with the shock and horror of storming a Nazi bunker. There would be SS soldiers and Hitler. Adrian hit the history books, scanning images of the German leader to include throughout the game.

But that wasn't enough. "How about," Romero suggested, "we throw in guard dogs? Dogs that you can shoot! Fucking German shepherds!" Adrian cracked up, sketching out a dog that, in a death animation, could yelp back. "And there should be blood," Romero said, "lots of blood, blood like you never see in games. And the weapons should be lethal but simple: a knife, a pistol, maybe a Gatling gun too." Adrian sketched as Romero spoke.

Tom came up with ideas for objects the player could collect through the game. In a paradigm dating back to the early text-based adventures, the gamer had two essential missions: to collect and to kill. Tom came up with treasures and crosses for players to find. There was also the issue of health items. A player would begin with his health at 100 percent. With every shot, the health would decrease until, when it hit 0 percent, the player would die. To survive, a player could pick up so-called health items. Tom wanted these items to be funny; he said, "Why not turkey dinners?"

"Yeah," Romero agreed, "or even better, how about dog food?" They were having German shepherds in the game, so what the hell? Tom began cackling at the thought of a player slurping up dog food. "Or how about this?" Tom added. "When the player gets really low on health, at like 10 percent, he could run over the bloody guts of a dead Nazi soldier and suck those up for extra energy." *"Flllippp slrrrrrp,"* Romero said, making the sounds and wiping his chin while cracking up. "It's like human giblets, you can eat up their gibs!"

The work would go late into the night. Carmack and Romero perfectly embodied the two extremes. While Carmack tweaked his code, Romero experimented with the graphics and new ways to exploit the tools. Carmack was building the guitar that Romero would bring to life. But their friendship was not traditional. They didn't discuss their lives, their hopes, their dreams. Sometimes, late at night, they would sit side by side, playing a hovercraft racing game called F-Zero. For the most part, though, their friendship was in their work, their unbridled pursuit of the game.

Carmack and Romero shared a vision the others didn't possess. Tom, deep down, was still closer to Keen, concerned about violence, about being too controversial, too bloody. Adrian liked the gore; he sketched out dead Nazis lying in pools of blood. But he still harbored a desire to get back to something more gothic and horrific, like Dangerous Dave in the Haunted Mansion.

Carmack and Romero, however, were in sync. Carmack didn't so much care about the accoutrements of the game as he enjoyed Romero's passion for showing off what his engine could do. Romero *got* what he was doing—trying to make a sleek, simple, fast game engine. And he was the one who dreamed up the sleek, simple, fast game to go around it. Romero even began excising parts of the game just to adhere to that dictum. At first they had programmed the game so that players could drag and search dead Nazis, as in the original Castle Wolfenstein. But they didn't like the outcome.

"Ugh." Romero groaned as he watched Tom drag a body across the screen. "That's not going to help the game be bad ass, it's slowing the game down. It's a neat idea, but when you're running down hallways and blowing down everything you see, who cares if you drag shit? We gotta rip that code right out of there. Anything that's going to stop us from mowing shit down—get rid of it!"

The brutality was not just a graphic and game play concern, it had to be a matter of sound too. Id had developed a relationship with an out of town computer game musician named Bobby Prince. Bobby had worked with Apogee and come highly recommended by Scott Miller. He had done some work on the Keen games. For Wolfenstein, they needed him even more badly. The weapons had to sound suitably *killer*. To accomplish this, they would, for the first time, use digital sound. Bobby came up with a few suggestions, including a staccato rip for the machine gun.

Late one afternoon Romero got ready to play the sound effects for the first time. The game had really taken shape. On the suggestion of Scott Miller, Carmack had gone from the 16-color palette of EGA graphics to the new Video Graphics Adapter or VGA, which allowed 256 colors. Adrian took full advantage of the expanded color range. He had drawn out soldiers with little helmets and boots. He created a special animation sequence that would show the soldiers twitching back in pain, blood spurting from their chests, when they were shot.

Romero loaded up the test portion of the game. He looked down the barrel of his chain gun as the Nazi approached him. He hit the fire button, and the roaring fire of the machine blast Bobby had programmed tore through the speakers as the Nazi went flying back. Romero flew back himself, hands off the keyboard, and fell to the floor laughing, holding his stomach. It was another moment, a variation on when he saw Dangerous Dave in Copyright Infringement for the first time.

"You know," he said, as his laughter finally subsided, "there's never been another game like this."

On screen, the little Nazi bled.

One afternoon in February 1992, Roberta Williams opened a package. She and her husband, Ken, were sitting in a gorgeous office in Northern California atop one of the largest empires in the business, Sierra On-Line. They were among the leaders in the computer game industry, which had grown from $100 million per year in 1980 to nearly $1 billion. Their early graphical role-playing games had given way to a slew of titles, all created around Sierra's inherent philosophy: building brands by making game designers into celebrities.

Sierra, as a result, received submissions for games all the time. This day the contents of the package would catch Roberta's eye. There was a cover letter from a young programmer named John Romero. He had heard that she was becoming interested in children's games and was including one he and his friends had made. It was doing rather well in the shareware market, he wrote. It was called Commander Keen in Goodbye, Galaxy!

Roberta and Ken were impressed and requested a meeting. The id guys were awestruck. They had grown up playing Sierra games; now they were being asked to visit the king and queen in their lair. And the timing couldn't have been more perfect. Wolfenstein was coming into shape. If Sierra made them an offer they couldn't refuse, they might strike a deal. They decided to put together a short demo of the game to show the Williamses.

When the id guys showed up at Sierra's offices, it was clear that they hadn't left their apartments for a month. Romero had been growing out his hair. Tom had an unkempt beard. Carmack had holes in his shirt. They were all in ratty, torn jeans. Before they met with Ken and Roberta, they were given a tour of the offices. For the guys, particularly Romero and Tom, it was a tour of the gamers' hall of fame. Back in a CD duplication room, they were introduced to Warren Schwader. Romero and Tom looked at each other and immediately fell to their knees, bowing. "We're not worthy, we're not worthy," they said. Schwader, they knew, had designed one of their favorite old Apple II games, Threshold. "Dude!" Romero beamed. "*Threshold!* You are the Daddy!"

But the allure soon wore off. Around the corner Carmack fell into a conversation with a programmer. As Romero, Tom, and Adrian watched, Carmack chipped away at the programmer's work, challenging what to him was an obvious waste of time. When he was through, the Sierra programmer just sat there, completely belittled by Carmack's superior skills. Romero patted Carmack on the back as they walked away. "God," he said, "you just wiped them down." Carmack shrugged modestly. Romero was proud.

The Williamses were not as impressed. The boys struck them as nothing more than highly talented and highly naïve kids. When Ken Williams showed up at a fancy restaurant called Edna's Elderberry House with this ragtag group of guys in shabby clothes, he was pulled aside by the maître d'. Williams had to explain that these were important guests before they were led to a private room with a long oak table and a burning fire.

The food came, and conversation flowed. Williams prided himself on discovering and nurturing young talent. But the inexperience of this group, he thought, was palpable. They didn't seem to have a business bone in their bodies. When they told Williams how much they were making on Commander Keen, he blanched. "You're telling me," he said, "you're making fifty thousand dollars a month just from shareware?"

They showed him the numbers. Scott had upped their royalty to 45 percent. There was virtually no overhead, they explained. The shareware model let Apogee keep ninety-five cents for every dollar that came in. "We make the best stuff in shareware," Romero proclaimed, "that's why we're making so much money. If you think that's awesome," he said, "check this out."

Tom took out a laptop, set it on the table, and urged Williams to hit the key. Wolfenstein came on the screen. Williams played the game with a poker face. The guys were dying with anticipation. Finally Williams said, "Ah, that's neat." He closed the program. A final screen came up, with the face of Commander Keen and a green monster from Aliens Ate My Babysitter. In big words in the middle it said: "id Software: Part of the Sierra Family?"

"Do you mind removing the question mark?" Williams said. Then he offered them $2.5 million.

The id guys returned to their snowed-in apartment to discuss the deal. Two and a half million dollars was a lot of money for four or five guys to split. But they didn't jump the gun. They didn't want just to do a stock deal, they wanted some up-front cash. So they returned to the approach they'd originally taken with Scott Miller. "Why don't we do this?" Romero suggested. "Let's ask for a hundred thousand down. If they're interested, then we'll sell. If they don't, then we don't do it."

When presented with the request, Williams balked. Though he was impressed by their work, he wasn't ready to fork over such a large chunk of cash. The deal was over. Clearly, id thought, he just didn't *get* what they were doing. He didn't understand the potential of Wolfenstein 3-D. If he had, he would have immediately handed over the cash. It was a disappointment, not so much because they missed out on the money but because their hero and his company had let them down. This game was going to change things, they knew; there was nothing on a computer like it. Fuck Sierra and their loser programmers, Romero told them, id would remain independent. And, independently, they would rule.

Fueled by the trip to Sierra, id's burgeoning egos exploded into their Dungeons and Dragons fantasies. Games, once again, had become expressions of their own inner worlds. In recent rounds Romero had been toying with the Demonicron, the darkly powerful book he had encouraged them to seize from the demons. It was a dangerous move, one that would either help them rule or destroy the world. Carmack grew increasingly distressed at Romero's recklessness. He didn't want to see the game he had spent so long creating get ruined. In a desperate move, he called Jay Wilbur back in Shreveport, asking him if he could fly up to Madison to reprise his D&D character and help stop Romero. But Jay couldn't make the trip. Ultimately, Carmack decided to test Romero's resolve, to see just how far his partner was willing to go.

Late one night Carmack the Dungeon Master brought the devil in to play. He told Romero that a demonic creature in the game had a bargain to make: *Give him the Demonicron and he will grant you your greatest wishes.* Romero said, "If I'm going to give you this book, then I want some really kick-ass shit." Carmack assured him the demon would oblige with the Daikatana.

Romero's eyes widened. The Daikatana was a mighty sword, one of the most powerful weapons in the game. Despite the pleas of the others, he told Carmack he wanted to give the demon the book. It didn't take long to find out the consequences. As the rules of the game dictated, Carmack rolled the die to randomly determine the strength of the demon's response. The demon was using the book to conjure more demons, he told the group. A battle of epic proportions ensued until Carmack declared the outcome. "The material plane is overrun with demons," he said, flatly. "Everyone is dead. That's it. We're done. Mmm."

No one spoke. They guys couldn't believe it. After all those games, all the late nights around the table in Shreveport, the adventures here that cured all the cold nights of Madison, it was over. A sadness filled the room. Romero finally said to Carmack, "Shit, that's fun playing that game. Now it's ruined? Is there any way to get that back?" But he knew the answer. Carmack was always true to himself and to his game. "No," he said, "it's over." There was a lesson to be learned: Romero had gone too far.

With the D&D world destroyed, the Sierra deal blown, and Madison growing even colder, the id guys turned up the heat literally and figuratively. They needed help to get Wolfenstein done, they decided, and they knew just the person to call: Kevin Cloud.

Kevin was the editorial director at Softdisk and had been acting as an informal liaison between id and their former home. Artistic, diligent, and well organized, he seemed like the perfect complement to their team. Born in 1965 to a teacher and an electrician, Kevin grew up in Shreveport reading comics and playing in arcades. While pursuing a degree in political science, he took a job as a computer artist at Softdisk. It ended up changing his life.

Kevin immediately struck up a friendship with the Gamer's Edge guys, emerging as one of their few allies during the rising mutiny. He spoke in a slow southern drawl and was partial to cowboy boots and blue jeans. He was polite and laid-back, but he could also be darkly funny, enjoying scatological humor and riffing just as sickly as Romero and Tom. Unlike them, though, Kevin could tether it all in on a dime, returning to a steady focus that their creative giddiness didn't seem to allow. After they left the company, Kevin distinguished himself for his diplomatic skills—able to keep Softdisk at bay, letting id maintain maximum freedom.

The id guys called him from Wisconsin and said they'd like him to join their team. There was only one condition. He had to move to Madison. Kevin didn't hesitate. He was growing tired of Softdisk. He had also just gotten married and was ready to begin a new life. So he packed up all his belongings and hit the road with his wife for a nineteen-hour drive. He arrived early the next morning and knocked on id's apartment door. After a minute or so, Carmack appeared in his underwear, bleary-eyed, his hair matted. "Come back later," he said, and shut the door, leaving them standing with their bags in the cold.

Kevin turned to his wife. "Um, let's go get some coffee." Later he came back and met with the guys. The deal was made, Kevin would join the team. Elated, he told them that he had already found an apartment and would sign the lease the following morning. Inspired, id decided it was time for them to move too. So Romero and Tom went out in search of spacious new digs. That night they reported back to Carmack and Adrian. They had found a stylish new apartment complex, but Romero's bit, it seemed, had flipped. "Yeah, we can move across town," he said, "but I'm telling you, this fucking snow and ice, this shit sucks. I hate it here."

"Yeah!" Adrian said.

"I really don't want to stay here anymore," Romero said. "I didn't know it'd be this bad in Wisconsin. Wouldn't it be cool to go to California, mountains and trees? You know, that's what I like—a place where a human can be outside around the year and live, not die if he has nothing. I'm into that. It's like, okay, heat versus freezing winter? I choose heat! I'd rather not have to bundle up, slide around, crack my skull open, and not be able to move my fingers. I'd rather be sweating my ass off in a fucking tank top out by the lake! We're a developer, we don't have to be in any one location. We can be anywhere." Wherever he went, he knew, his girlfriend, Beth, would be happy to come along.

As the midnight hour passed, they stretched a map across a table and discussed all the places they could move: "Jamaica!" Tom suggested. Adrian spoke: "How about Dallas?" *How about Dallas!* It had a lot going for it. It was warm, in the South. And Apogee was there. Scott Miller, in fact, had long raved about the city, telling the guys how there was a huge lake, just like the one in Shreveport, where they could go skiing and maybe even get a house. Still better, Tom added, Texas had no state income tax, which meant they could make even more money. Dallas it would be.

There was only one problem: Kevin Cloud. He was about to sign a lease for an apartment, which would commit id to staying in Madison for at least another six months. He had to be stopped. It was 3:00 A.M. In a panic the id guys left a flurry of messages at Kevin's hotel. He woke up a few hours later and got the messages: "Don't sign the lease! Call immediately! We are the wind! We are the wind!"

"Oh my goodness," he said to his wife, "they must have looked at their budget and realized they can't hire me." He was relieved to hear the real news. Despite the long drive, he agreed to head with the guys down to Dallas, closer to home. "We are the wind," they repeated, as if it summed up everything about them: their spontaneity, their speed, their elusiveness.

A few weeks later, a moving truck backed up to their apartment. The guys waited as the driver went to open the back of the truck. The gate slid up. Their jaws dropped in disbelief. Sitting alone in the back of the truck, like a vision, like an omen, was a Pac-Man machine. Here it was: the game they had all grown up with, the one Romero had plastered with his high scores all around Sacramento, the one they had copied in Shreveport in their Wac-Man demo. Romero gulped and asked the driver, "Is that your machine?"

"It's mine now, I guess," the driver said. "Someone left it on my truck. They didn't want it in their house."

The id guys looked at each other, nodding. "Hey, dude," Romero said, "can we buy it from you?"

The driver looked at these kids with long hair and torn jeans. They didn't look like they could afford a haircut, let alone a fancy arcade machine. "Sure," he said brashly, "for a hundred and fifty bucks!"

Carmack reached into his pocket. "No problem," he said, peeling off the cash from a fat wad of bills. "Leave it on the truck." The game was coming to Texas.

SEVEN

Spear of Destiny

In Texas video games made the long list of evils. Games were bad, corrupting the kids, causing them to blow their milk money on nonsense. So the upright citizens of Mesquite, a small town just southeast of Dallas, took their cause to the courts. They wanted the games banned. The case went all the way to the Supreme Court, which, ultimately, shot the Texans down. This was in 1982. The games at the center of the debate were arcade hits like Pac-Man, the very machine that arrived on the truck when id Software, Mesquite's first gaming company, pulled into town on April Fool's Day 1992.

Carmack and Romero couldn't have been happier to be in the heat again. Everything in Dallas was big. The highways were big. The trucks were big. The car dealerships were big. Even the people were big, from the towering cowboys to the statuesque blondes. Id settled on Mesquite to be near Scott Miller, who ran Apogee from his hometown of Garland, just a few minutes up the road. Mesquite, as it so happened, had what the guys considered a suitably killer place to live. La Prada Apartments, off Interstate 635, boasted sprawling lofts with ten-foot black windows overlooking crystal blue swimming pools and gardens. When id arrived, women in bikinis lounged by the pools, the sweet, tangy smell of barbecue floated up from the grills, water polo balls flew over the nets. They were home.

Scott was thrilled to have his star gamers as neighbors. He and his partner, George Broussard, took them out for a big Tex-Mex dinner of burritos and nachos, then off to SpeedZone, a *big* arcade, for go-cart racing and games. The id guys chased each other around the tracks in their Formula One model cars. Afterward they admired the authentic sports cars being driven by Scott and George. Apogee was clearly reaping the rewards of Keen's continued success. "Oh man," Romero told Carmack, "they're driving bad-ass cars while we drive ass cars. It's time for us to kick ass."

There was plenty of reason for them to succeed. In addition to the guarantee of a hundred thousand dollars, Scott upped their royalty to 50 percent—unheard of in the industry. He was eager to keep the boys happy. He had made other concessions too. He knew they hated their obligation to Softdisk. In order to let id focus on Wolfenstein, he told them that Apogee would create a game to fulfill the Softdisk contract. Unbeknownst to Softdisk, the next game they received, ScubaVenture, came not from id Software but from Apogee.

Scott had increasingly big plans for Wolfenstein. At the moment, the idea was to follow their existing shareware formula: release one episode, containing ten levels, for free, then charge gamers to receive the remaining two episodes. After talking with Romero and Tom, Scott learned that it was taking the group only about one day to make a level of the game. *Ka-ching! Dollar signs!* Instead of just three episodes, why not have six? Scott said, "If you can do thirty more levels, it would only take you fifteen days. And we could have it where people could buy the first trilogy for thirty-five dollars or get all six for fifty dollars, or if people buy the first episode and later want the second episodes it will be twenty dollars. So there's a reason to get them all!" After some consideration, id agreed.

Not everything about the future was looking up. The guys abruptly decided to part ways with their president, Mark Rein, after a difference of opinion. "That's fucking it," Romero declared. "Boom! He's gone."

But gone too was id's one and only biz guy. Official biz guy, at least. Unofficially, of course, Carmack and Romero had been running businesses for years. Though coders by trade, they'd been working for themselves since they were teenagers. Carmack had put a team of his friends together to make Wraith, then he managed his own freelance programming career. Romero had grown up as a one-boy band, churning out dozens of titles and pawning them off to small publishers. Like most artists or programmers, however, they enjoyed doing their craft more than cutting a deal.

And the more immersed they became at id, the less interested they were in handling the mounting production tasks: paying bills, ordering supplies, fielding calls. They needed someone who could be a front man for the company, someone as brash and iconoclastic in business as they were in game development. There certainly were plenty of candidates, as budding executives across the country began sniffing out id. But id didn't want just anyone. They wanted their old friend Jay Wilbur.

Here's the deal, they told Jay on the phone: as id's new chief executive officer, he'd get 5 percent of the company and free rein to run the business side of things. All he had to do was say yes and drive the few hours from Shreveport to Dallas. Tired of Softdisk and feeling that he had fulfilled his obligation to Al Vekovius, Jay agreed. Fire up the barbecue, he told them, he was coming to Mesquite.

"Dance, motherfuckers!" Romero screamed. "Lay down! *Brrrrrschh! Brrrrrschh! Brrrrrschh!*" The SS guards were everywhere—down the hall, under the Hitler portrait, careening by the shit buckets. And Romero was there—*dude, fucking right there*—storming down the hall with the chain gun, mowing down Nazis and running over their bloody, bony chunks of gibs.

It was well past midnight at the id pad in the La Prada Apartments. Romero was at his perch on the second floor of the loft, Adrian to his right, Tom behind him. To his left was a snarl of cables and controllers; at the moment, the office's favorite new obsession, a one-on-one brawl game called Street Fighter II, was jammed in the Nintendo. Downstairs by the kitchen, Carmack sat at his stealth black NeXT machine. Kevin sat to his right, Jay behind them. The floor was piled with pizza boxes. Carmack sat above a pile of empty Diet Cokes. It had been only days, and id had settled in.

Romero had been growing more and more enthused over Wolfenstein's progress. This was easy to tell; all one had to do was listen to the volume of his screams. Game playing, everyone was beginning to notice, was more than just a part of work for Romero, it was a part of life. He was spending much of his time testing out Wolfenstein. When he wasn't testing it himself, he was contacting gamers across the BBS world who were play-testing it for him.

"Hey, you know what we should have in here?" Romero called out, as he paused the game. "Pissing! We should have it so you can fucking stop and piss on the Nazi after you mow him down! Heh heh! That would be fucking awesome!"

Adrian and Tom chuckled heartily beside him. Tom reached below his desk, then hurled one of his many wads of paper at Romero. Romero, who had his own stash, responded with three or four more. One or two sailed over the loft and hit Kevin, who, as usual, responded with his own litany of paper bombs. Carmack tried to focus. Paper fights. Nazi yells. Romero's violent fantasies. They were becoming the norm since the guys had arrived in Mesquite. Carmack never participated in the revelry; no one expected him to. So far his powers of concentration were good enough to shut out the distractions so he could deal with his immediate problems: optimizing the Wolfenstein engine for maximum speed and stability.

Though he could tolerate the paper fights, the bigger annoyance was the push walls. Push walls were essentially secret doors in a game. The idea was that the player could run down against a wall and, if he pushed in the right spot, a portion of the wall would slide back, revealing a secret room full of goodies. Tom had been needling Carmack incessantly about adding this special feature. Secrets, he lobbied, were an essential part of every good game. There had been secrets in their early games—like the Vorticon alphabet in Keen or the spot where Keen would moon the player if the player paused too long without doing anything. Wolfenstein was in dire need of something like that. And creating a way for players to find secret rooms through push walls seemed like a natural.

But Carmack wasn't biting. It was, he said, "an ugly hack." This meant that it was an inelegant solution to an unnecessary problem. Making a game, writing code, for Carmack, was increasingly becoming an exercise in elegance: how to write something that achieved the desired effect in the cleanest way possible. The Wolfenstein engine simply wasn't designed to have walls sliding back into secret rooms. It was designed to have doors slide open and shut, open and shut. It was a matter of streamlining. The simpler Carmack kept his game, the faster the world would move, therefore, the deeper the immersion. Nope, he'd say, push walls were out.

Tom didn't relent. He'd bring it up whenever he sensed an opening. Soon Romero joined Tom's crusade. "We understand that you're overloaded on programming stuff because of this new engine," Romero told Carmack. "How about just this one thing? Put push walls there and we'll be happy. We'll put 'em fucking everywhere." Carmack still said no. It was, notably, the first time since they had begun that the team experienced creative conflict.

During the day they took occasional breaks, playing football in the pool. One time, with Carmack out there, Romero pleaded Tom's case again. "Dude," he said, "we need push walls! You can't just run down these hallways and not find secret stuff! Everything you're doing is awesome. Just doing this one thing will make me and Tom really happy with the design. This is really simple design-wise."

"Forget about it," Carmack snapped.

More new tensions began to surface. With the extra levels ordered by Scott, the id guys were putting in sixteen-hour days, seven days a week. Kevin and Jay did ease the burden somewhat. Kevin was able to assist Adrian with the character work, as well as help out with some packaging and marketing designs. As CEO, Jay's main asset wasn't so much strategizing the company as being the office "biz guy." He made sure there was enough computer paper, enough disks, enough toilet paper, enough pizza. He made sure bills got paid. One of the reasons he got the job was he was the only one who balanced his checkbook.

Despite the help of Kevin and Jay, though, nothing could dissipate the reaction everyone was having to the shenanigans of Romero and Tom. They were over the top with energy. They used to jump around, bleeping and blurting, imitating sounds and characters from Keen. But now they had a microphone. Literally. Bobby Prince, their freelance sound designer, had temporarily set up camp in the id apartment, turning the loft into a mini–sound studio. With an artillery of effects and mikes, Tom and Romero went overboard. They'd stay up well into the morning recording demented screeds.

One night they got the idea to record answering machine messages for the id phone. The first started with jazzy piano and Romero speaking over the music. "Id Software is brought to you today by the letter *I* and the number five," he said, like at the end of *Sesame Street*. Tom followed by singing in a strange high voice, "Five strawberry pies!" Screams and thunderclaps followed into the beep. For another, they cranked up the distortion to make them sound like gravel-voiced demons. "Id Software is not available right now," the demon belched, "because I'm eating them!" In a third, Tom began by saying that he was standing in the rubble of id Software. Suddenly, the demon appeared and said, "Are you in any way related to id Software?" Tom told the demon that he was just there doing the answering machine message. "Goodbye, ass!" the demon bellowed, followed by a blaze of thunder, fire and, at the end, Tom's screams.

Adrian got so fed up with their noise that, on the night of the answering machine revelry, he simply left. Carmack, for the time being, would stay behind.

Tensions were building outside the office too. One day Scott received a call from FormGen, with whom he had been in contact since the company decided to do a retail version of Wolfenstein. FormGen would often appeal to Scott when they were having difficulty negotiating with id. Scott had had some concerns of his own: most notably that Wolfenstein was nothing more than a maze game, Pac-Man with guns. He wondered if people would see it for what it was. FormGen's latest concern, however, was even bigger.

"Look, Scott," an executive said, "we don't think they should be showing blood and stirring up the World War II stuff. We're really worried about this. It's too realistic. We're going to make a lot of people upset. There's never been a game like this."

"Let me see what I can do," Scott replied. He dialed id. "Hey," he said, "FormGen thinks the game needs to be toned down." He could hear the guys huffing on the other end of the line. It was time for id to do something about the violence, he conceded. "Beef it up!" he said. They wholeheartedly agreed.

Adrian filled the game with all kinds of gruesome details: skeletons hanging by their wrists from chains, corpses in jail cells slumped against the bars, blood and flesh chunks randomly spotting the laby-rinthine walls. It was a welcome change from the art Tom was having him create for the game, novelistic elements like pots and pans hanging in the kitchen and still-life plates of turkey dinners. Adrian, who was growing to despise the game's realism, was longing for more splatter-punk, demonic gore. He pumped in as much blood as he could.

Tom and Romero upped the shock value in other ways, most no-tably the screams. They stayed up late into the night, recording hellish German commands and orders: "Achtung!" and "Schutzstaffel!" They recorded last words for dying Nazis: "Mutti!" (Mommy), and, for Hitler himself, a final good-bye to his wife: "Eva, auf Wiedersehen!" To cap it off, they used a digital version of the Nazi party anthem, "Horst Wessel Lied," to open the game.

They also threw in something they called a Death Cam. After the final enemy, known as "the boss" of an episode, got killed, a message would appear on the screen saying, "Let's see that again!" Then a de-tailed animation would slowly play, showing the big, bad boss meeting his grisly demise. This Death Cam was id's version of a snuff film. They decided to include a screen at the beginning of the game that would say, "This game is voluntarily rated PC-13: Profound Carnage." Though tongue-in-cheek, it was the first voluntary rating of a video game.

With the game nearing completion, there was one major issue left unresolved: the push walls. Romero and Tom figured it was worth one last try and asked Carmack to put them in. To their surprise, he spun around in his chair and said it was already done. Carmack, in the end, agreed that it was, as he was fond of saying, the Right Thing to Do. Secrets *were* fun. Tom and Romero were right. It was striking, they thought, and worth remembering. Carmack was stubborn but, if some-one argued a point strongly and convincingly, he was willing to give in.

Tom and Romero went to town putting in all the secrets. A player would run up to a section of a wall, say, a banner of Hitler, and push, by hitting the space bar on the keyboard. Then—*blam!*—the wall would creak back. They filled rooms with treasures and health items, turkey dinners and ammo. They even made a completely secret level, based on a first-person 3-D version of Pac-Man, ghosts and all.

There was a psychology and a philosophy to video game secrets. Secrets rewarded the player for thinking outside the box, pushing a wall that should be solid to see if it would open. This principle also applied to cheating. Many games included what were known as cheat codes, little commands the player could type in that would give him added health items or weapons. But there was a price to pay. If a player cheated, he was disabled from posting a high score. Behavior in games, as in life, had consequences and rewards.

At 4:00 A.M. on May 5, 1992, the shareware episode of Wolfenstein 3-D was complete. Id had wrapped up all the little finishing touches. Tom typed the back story: "You're William J. 'B.J.' Blazkowicz, the Allies' bad boy of espionage and terminal action seeker. . . . Your mission . . . to infiltrate the Nazi fortress." In most games, players could choose from difficulty levels, such as easy, medium, and hard. In Wolfenstein, a player would boot up the game and see the question "How Tough Are You?" Below were four responses; each had an accompanying image of the player's imagined face, ranging from the hardest ("I Am Death Incarnate"), with the face of a snarling, red-eyed B.J., to the easiest ("Can I Play Daddy?"), which showed B.J. with a baby's bonnet and pacifier. In that spirit, they added taunts that would appear on the screen when the player tried to quit. "Press N for more carnage; Press Y to be a weenie" or "For guns and glory, press N; For work and worry, press Y."

Details done, errors or bugs checked, the game was ready to be uploaded to Software Creations, id's adopted home BBS online community in Massachusetts. Gamers, already hooked on Keen, waited anxiously for the newest title to arrive. "Who knows?" Tom said. "If gamers like this, Wolfenstein might do twice as well as Keen." Keen was currently number one on the shareware market.

Carmack, Adrian, Romero, Jay, Kevin, and Scott gathered around the computer that was connected, by modem, to the Software Creations BBS. Crickets chirped outside. The Pac-Man machine blinked in the corner. With the hit of a button, the data file labeled Wolf 3-D split into abstract bits and streamed through the telephone line out of Mesquite, out of Dallas, up through Texas, heading for New England.

Okay, the guys all agreed, it was time to go to bed. They'd see what happened tomorrow.

"**Pizza money!**" Jay hollered, opening up the first royalty check for Wolfenstein 3-D. They really had no idea what they would make. Keen was bringing in about $30,000 per month; they expected, at best, to double that. Wolf, after all, was still being distributed through the relative underworld of shareware catalogs and BBSs, without advertising. The closest thing to marketing were the BBS techies who wrote little teasers of text about the game on their computers. But the guys certainly expected, at least, to break even rather soon. The game had cost, if one considered id's only overhead—the rent of the apartments and their $750 per month salaries—roughly $25,000 to make.

The check was for $100,000. And this reflected only the first month. Together with the continued sales of the Keen games, id was heading for annual sales in the millions. By releasing the first episode as shareware, they'd instantly hooked the gamers, leaving them craving more. It defied logic—the thought of giving something away for free. But Scott's plan had worked.

Wolfenstein evolved into an underground sensation. Before the press picked up on it, the gamers online were abuzz about the game's immersive blend of high technology and gruesome game play—the synthesis of Carmack's and Romero's personal passions. Forums on the various BBSs and on the emerging commercial online services— Prodigy, CompuServe, and America Online—brimmed with discussion about the game. The Internet's discussion forum, Usenet, was on fire. E-mails poured in to the office.

"There's no surprise that this game is the hottest download on many BBS systems and the talk of Usenet," wrote one fan. "I *love* this game. The feeling as you round a corner at full speed and blow away three guards and an SS who are firing at you, then quickly pivot to take out the guy coming up from behind is indescribable. The anticipation as you open each door and wonder what's waiting behind it is intense."

One employee at Microsoft raved about "how popular Wolf 3-D is here at Microsoft. It seems like I can't walk down a hall without hearing 'Mein Leben' from someone's office." He also mentioned how he hoped id would port a version of the game for Microsoft's new operating system, Windows.

By summer, the press was echoing the praise. One shareware magazine gushed that the game was "more like an interactive movie than an arcade game." Another said it was "single-handedly justifying the existence of shareware." Even *Computer Gaming World*, the industry's veteran publication, picked up on the craze, saying that this was "the first game technologically capable of . . . immersing the player in a threatening environment . . . a peek at part of interactive entertainment's potential for a sensory immersed virtual future." *Virtual reality*, now a buzzword in the mainstream press, was a term being applied to Wolfenstein. Shareware magazines were dubbing it a virtual reality game. A Kentucky entrepreneur hooked up a version of Wolfenstein to virtual reality goggles and brought in five hundred dollars a day at the Kentucky State Fair.

But players didn't need virtual reality goggles to feel immersed. In fact, the sense of immersion was so real that many began complaining of motion sickness. Calls were coming in even at the Apogee office saying that people were throwing up while playing the game. Wolfenstein vomit stories became items of fascination online. Theories abounded. Some players thought the game's animation was so smooth that it tricked the brain into thinking it was moving in a real space. Other gamers thought it had something to do with the "jerkiness" of the graphics, which induced the feeling of seasickness. Some felt it was simply disorienting because there was no acceleration involved; it was like going from zero to sixty at light speed. Gamers even exchanged tips for how to play without losing one's Doritos.

The motion sickness wasn't the only source of controversy. The violence was another. "This game certainly goes heavy on the ketchup," wrote one reviewer. "Enemies spurt great gobs of blood as you mow them down. If you're sensitive to violence in video games, this is a game to avoid at all costs." Most people weren't protesting much about shooting human beings; they were upset that players could shoot dogs.

Nevertheless, it was gore they delighted in. "Wolfenstein 3-D may have no socially redeeming value," one magazine wrote, "but we couldn't stop playing it."

If the violence could be stomached, for some, the enemies couldn't. Jay received a letter from the Anti-Defamation League protesting the game's inclusion of swastikas and Nazis. An even bigger problem was Germany itself. Wolfenstein had made its way there online, as it had to other countries, through CompuServe, which had an international presence. It didn't take long for the game to come to the attention of the German government. Germany, after World War II, had forbidden the inclusion of Nazis in popular entertainment. So Wolfenstein was banned. Apogee began receiving unopened packages containing the game. Soon Scott started fulfilling orders by sending the games in nondescript packages.

When CompuServe learned of the German ban, it pulled Wolfenstein from its service until it heard from German counsel. The move gained attention from pundits and lawyers because it was one of the first examples of the emerging legalities of cyberspace: what happens when a game, or any item—image, book, film—is uploaded in one country but breaks the law of another? The Wolfenstein case prompted one lawyer to publish an article, "Nazis in Cyberspace!" He found it "intuitively wrong" for the game to be taken down. Cyberspace, he argued, should be treated as its own "independent nation." The article was illustrated by a flag with a coiled, snakelike mouse cord and the dictum: "Don't Tread on Our BBS."

Wolfenstein began empowering gamers in creative ways as well: they started making modifications, or mods. People, including Carmack and Romero, had been hacking into games for years. There had even been some computer games, such as the 1983 game Lode Runner, which had special programs, level editors, to allow users to create their own versions of the game. That same year three fans of Silas Warner's original Castle Wolfenstein programmed a parody called Castle Smurfenstein—with Smurfs substituted for the Nazis.

A game as sophisticated as id's Wolfenstein 3-D was considerably more difficult to hack—requiring someone to effectively *write over* the original content. But not long after Wolfenstein came out, the guys at id booted up a modified version. It seemed the same except for one notable difference. The music had been replaced by the "I Love You, You Love Me" theme song from the children's show *Barney*. And instead of killing the SS boss at the end of the episode, players had to destroy the smiling purple dinosaur.

Carmack and Romero couldn't have been more pleased. Others didn't feel that way. Kevin, always business minded, was concerned over copyright issues, over the thought of people messing with their content. Scott agreed. What if people started making their own versions of the game and tried to sell them? It would cut into everyone's profits. But, with Carmack and Romero wholeheartedly behind the idea of open, free, fun hacking, the issue was temporarily pushed aside.

Despite their success, id didn't rest on their laurels. The work ethic, if anything, got more intense. Immediately after the Wolfenstein shareware was uploaded, the guys buckled down to complete the remaining five episodes. The pressure was palpable. Thousands of gamers were sending in their checks; id had to deliver the goods. When they did take a break, it was several weeks later and the occasion was significant. Kansas City was hosting a big Apple II festival. For the id guys, weaned on Apple II, it seemed like the perfect respite. An Applefest, after all, was kind of where Romero had met Jay. Now they could return to show off how far they'd come. So they piled into Tom's Toyota and drove thirteen hours, a brand-new seven-thousand-dollar laptop with Wolfenstein in the trunk.

The festival was being held at a community college. All the out-of-town guests were staying in a school dormitory. Upon checking in, the id guys noticed a sign telling of a special guest speaker: Silas Warner. They looked at each and gasped. "No way!" Silas was the creator of the original Castle Wolfenstein. As far as they knew, he had no idea that they had remade his game. Nervously, they filed into the lecture hall, computer in tow, and waited for him to arrive.

Silas sauntered onstage like King Kong. He was a massive man: 320 pounds of gamer meat with fingers that could crush a computer mouse with a pinch. But he was funny and articulate, telling the story of his own start-up, Muse Software, the rollicking ride of its rise and fall. Silas was flocked by fans when it was over. The id guys stood in the back, holding their laptop, and waited their turn. "Hey, Silas," Romero finally said breathlessly, "we're id Software, and we just did a remake of Castle Wolfenstein and put it on the market and we brought it here so you can check it out and look at it and sign our manual!"

Silas looked at this motley group of programmers with the fancy PC laptop and raised his brow. "Oh yes," he said slowly. "I remember that someone called me about it." Eagerly, they fired up the laptop and showed him the game. To their relief, he complimented them on their work and signed autographs. Later that night they returned to the dorm. It was a memorable night. Everyone hung out in the hallways, talking about games, checking out Wolfenstein. There were even celebrities in the Apple II community, like Burger Bill, a programmer who was known to keep a hamburger in his desk and nibble on it occasionally for days on end. But with the crowd gathering around id's laptop, it was clear that Burger Bill wasn't the only game in town.

Id's first taste of fame came the next month, during their first real company vacation. They had just completed all the remaining episodes of Wolfenstein and decided to celebrate by spending $5,000 each on a weeklong stay at Disney World. They spent the days riding Space Mountain over and over again, checking out the action. One night they regrouped in a hot tub at the Grand Floridian Hotel, right off the theme park. Life was good. So good, they decided, that they were going to give themselves raises when they got back: up to what, at the time, felt like a substantial amount of money, $45,000 per year. Wolfenstein, they cheered, had done them well.

"Did someone say Wolfenstein?" asked a guy in the pool nearby. He nudged his friend. "We love that game!"

The id guys looked at them dubiously. But the gamers were for real. They rushed over to the hot tub and began raving about the game. It was a striking moment, especially for Romero, who had spent so many years being a fan himself. Now here he was, sitting in a hot tub under giant palm trees, surrounded by a theme park, money flowing, being treated like a legend. He could deal.

As their success grew, Carmack's and Romero's personalities came into even sharper contrast. Carmack sank deeper into his technology; Romero, deeper into game play. Tom documented their differences in a hint manual he wrote for Wolfenstein 3-D. He characterized Romero as the ultimate player and Carmack the ultimate technician—or, as he put it, the Surgeon and Engine John.

"John Romero," he wrote, "at this point in time, is the world's best Wolfenstein player. His current record for getting through all of episode one in Bring 'Em On mode—five minutes, twenty seconds! That's not going for anything but the shortest, fastest path to each elevator. We call him The Surgeon, after the way he surgically takes out guys and keeps going. He welcomes all challengers to his record. John's advice: 'Play with the mouse and keyboard and use the up arrow and right shift to run most of the time. Don't sit and wait for the enemy to come—charge and lay waste to them before they know what hit 'em. There's no room for wimps in World Class Wolfenstein play.'"

Further down he described the work of Carmack. "*Engine John,*" he wrote. "We call the part of a program that actually gets the graphics onto the screen 'the engine.' The cool, texture-mapped engine for Wolfenstein 3-D was written by our resident technical 'soopah genius,' John Carmack. However, he's already disgusted with the technology. He's excited about his new ideas on rendering holographic worlds."

It was true, Carmack was over his previous accomplishment, just as he was over his past. Right now the next obvious step was for him to further enrich his virtual worlds. The spirit was in the air. In May 1992, when Wolfenstein was released, an author named Neal Stephenson published a book called *Snow Crash,* which described an inhabitable cyberspace world called the Metaverse. Science fiction, however, wasn't inspiring Carmack's progress; it was just his science. Technology was improving. So were his skills.

The opportunity to experiment came during the development of Spear of Destiny, the commercial spin-off of Wolfenstein that id was now making for FormGen. The game was named for the mythical spear used to kill Christ, an object later sought by Hitler for its supposed supernatural powers. In the game, Hitler steals the spear and B.J. must fight to win it back. FormGen's original concerns over violence had faded with Wolfenstein's success, so id was free to continue on its gory path.

Because Spear of Destiny was built using the original Wolfenstein engine, Carmack could work on new technology while the rest of the guys completed the game. At first, he fiddled with countless little experiments, using art resources from the existing games. He played around with making a racing game like F-Zero, the hovercraft title he played now and then with Romero. Carmack covered the floor of his computer screen with an angular blue matrix of lines. Then he started laying down images that together would make up roads. The only digital images around were big banners of Hitler from Wolfenstein, so he put those down back to back, making a highway of Hitlers surrounded by a sprawling web. Carmack could lose himself in the abstract mathematical imagery of this world, working on the acceleration of movement, the sense of speed, velocity, decline.

Soon his experiments became part of a deal for a game called Shadowcaster, an upcoming title from a small game development company named Raven. The id guys had met the owners of Raven while living in Wisconsin because they were the only other game company in town. Run by two brothers, Brian and Steven Raffel, Raven had started making games for the Amiga game console. Romero was so impressed by their work that he wanted to cofinance their development of a PC game for Apogee. Raven turned him down, saying that they weren't interested in the PC at the time. But they stayed in touch. Now they had a contract with Electronic Arts to make a PC game after all. Id suggested a deal: let Carmack make the engine for a cut of the profits. Everyone agreed. Carmack got busy.

Others in the office weren't quite as immersed. Everyone but Romero, it seemed, was burned out on Wolfenstein. Adrian was tired of churning out realistic Nazi images. He began hanging out more with Kevin, who was now collaborating with him. Tom, meanwhile, was getting increasingly frustrated with the design direction of the games. On occasion he would pull Romero aside and ask him when they were going to start working on the next Keen trilogy. Romero would tell him that it was still on the table, but privately he was getting tired of the badgering. Tom was clearly not motivated to work on Spear. Romero tried to motivate him as best he could, telling Tom to think about that nice new Acura he was going to buy when all the money rolled in. Other times they'd just take the easy way out: leaving their work altogether to kick-punch each other in Street Fighter II.

The more bored Tom got, the more they played. And since Tom was bored much of the time, the games were lasting longer into the night. Downstairs, Carmack was trying to focus on Shadowcaster. He was really on to something here, he could see it, the Right Thing, something different unfolding on his screen, but the distractions were getting worse. After months of shutting out the paper fights and answering machine messages and assorted screams, he finally gave way. Carmack stood up and began to unplug his machine. Everyone else stopped what he was doing and watched. "I think I'm going to get more done doing this by myself in my apartment," Carmack said. He picked up his stealth black NeXT machine and walked out the door. He wouldn't return for weeks.

When Spear of Destiny came out, on September 18, 1992, it further cemented id's fame and fortune. Once again they won the shareware awards for best entertainment software. They were also winning continued accolades from the press as well as their peers. At the annual Computer Game Developers Conference, an executive from Electronic Arts spoke at a marketing workshop about how Wolfenstein had become such a sensation with no marketing at all. Scott Miller was the first to agree. But the orders were rolling in. The conventional wisdom, at the time, was that at best 1 to 2 percent of the people who downloaded the shareware version would actually pay for the game. To make matters worse, there was nothing stopping someone from buying the game and simply copying it for friends. Despite all these forces, the sales continued to soar. Id was getting checks totaling $150,000 per month.

And the opportunities were coming in from really unlikely places. The most unlikely of all: Nintendo. Despite having turned id away when they tried to sell Nintendo on a PC version of Mario, the company had changed its tune. Id was paid $100,000 to port Wolfenstein for the Super Nintendo machine. But Nintendo had one condition: tone the game down. Nintendo was a family system, and they wanted a family version of the game. This meant, first of all, getting rid of the blood. Second, they didn't like the fact that players could shoot dogs. Why not substitute something else, Nintendo suggested, like rats? This being Nintendo, id agreed.

Even more ironic was an offer from a company called Wisdom Tree, makers of religious-themed games. One day a representative called Jay to inquire about licensing the Wolfenstein engine to make a game based on the story of Noah's Ark. They wanted a first-person 3-D version in which the player was running around the ark and hurling apples and vegetables to keep the animals in order. Jay had a good laugh. Nintendo, he knew, didn't allow any kind of religious imagery in a game, whether Satan or Noah. But Wisdom Tree had plans of its own: putting the game out independently as a rogue title for the Super Nintendo. Jay agreed to license them the technology.

For the time being, though, there was something more important to attend to: Carmack's technology. He returned to the id apartment with the results of his labors on the Shadowcaster engine. It was, everyone immediately saw, quite a leap. There were two noticeable firsts: diminished lighting and texture-mapped floors and ceilings. Diminished lighting meant that, as in real life, distant vistas would recede into shadows. In Wolfenstein, every room was brightly lit, with no variation in hue. But, as any painter knows, light is what brings a picture to life. Carmack was making the world alive.

For greater immersion, he had also learned how to apply textures to the floors and ceilings, as well as add variable heights to the walls. The speed was about half that of Wolfenstein, but since this was an adventure game, built on exploration, it seemed appropriate to have a steadier pace. The leaps didn't come easily to Carmack. It took a hefty amount of time for him to figure out how to get just the right perspective down for the floors. But his diligence and self-imposed isolation had paid off in a big way. He even had slopes on the floors, so the player could feel like he was running up or downhill. Kevin spent about twenty minutes just running up and over a little hill in the game. It was incredible. And, it was clear, it was time for id to turn this technology into their next game.

With Wolfenstein and Spear of Destiny done, everyone, particularly Tom, was ready to move on to different subject matter. The last two games had drained him. Blocky maze games and shooters were nothing like Keen, and he was anxious to return to his pet project, to finish his long-awaited third trilogy. Carmack, to his delight, seemed to go along with the idea. He even described how great it'd be to see the Yorps dancing around in three dimensions.

There was another idea on the table too: *Aliens*. Everyone at id was a huge fan of this sci-fi movie. They thought it would make a great game. After some research, Jay found that the rights were available. He thought they could get a deal. But then they decided against it. They didn't want some big movie company telling them what they could and couldn't put in their game. The technology Carmack had come up with was way too impressive to compromise, they thought. So it was back to the brainstorming.

To Tom's dismay, the Keen 3-D argument didn't go far. Carmack's technology was too fast and brutal for another kids' game, they all said. Tom looked to Romero, his friend and sidekick, but even he clearly didn't want to do the game. The computer bit in Romero's head flipped off for Keen. It wasn't surprising. Wolfenstein, after all, had originated with Romero, and clearly he preferred its gore to the cuteness of Keen. Tom knew how Adrian felt. Even Carmack, who had once shown interest in Keen 3-D, had moved on to another idea, something about as far removed from Keen as possible: demons.

Carmack, of course, had a long history with demons. There were the demons of Catholic school, the demons Romero had summoned in their Dungeons and Dragons game, the demons who'd destroyed the D&D world. Now it was time for them to make another appearance. Here was this amazing new technology, so why not have a game about demons versus technology, Carmack said, where the player is using high-tech weapons to defeat beasts from hell? Romero loved the idea.

It was something no one had done before. Kevin and Adrian agreed, snickering at the potential for sick, twisted art, something in the spirit of their favorite B movie, *Evil Dead II*. In fact, they all agreed, that was what the game could be like: a cross between *Evil Dead II* and *Aliens*, horror and hell, blood and science.

All they needed was a title. Carmack had the idea. It was taken from *The Color of Money*, the 1986 Martin Scorsese film in which Tom Cruise played a brash young pool hustler. In one scene Cruise saunters into a billiards hall carrying his favorite pool cue in a stealth black case. "What you got in there?" another player asks.

Cruise smiles devilishly, because he knows what fate he is about to spring upon this player, just as, Carmack thought, id had once sprung upon Softdisk and as, with this next game, they might spring upon the world.

"In here?" Cruise replies, flipping open the case. "Doom."

EIGHT

Summon the Demons

"**G**ggggggggggrrrrrrrrrrrrrrrrrrggggaaaaaaaaawwwwwwww||||||!!"
It was a scream from hell—a throaty cry, desperate, almost underwater, like somebody gargling blood. Worse, it was coming from right next door to the new office the id guys had christened Suite 666.

Once id had decided to spring upon the world with Doom, they'd relocated to this suitably dark workplace: a seven-story, black-windowed, cube-shaped building called the Town East Tower. The Tower was, like the gamers themselves, an anomaly in the suburban cowboy domain of Mesquite. On either side of the bordering Lyndon B. Johnson Highway were the consumer biospheres indigenous to the area: Big Billy Barrett's Used Cars, Sheplers Western Store, and the city's biggest attraction, the Mesquite Rodeo. Though the Tower housed ordinary offices of lawyers and truck driving schools, compared with the rest of town, the stealth cube looked like it had dropped from outer space.

And now it sounded like someone was birthing an alien in the dentist's suite next door. In actuality, it was a patient who needed an emergency tracheotomy—which the dentist had performed himself. The screams of patients and drills would become a regular backdrop of life at id. For a group of guys making a game about demons, they sounded just right.

In fact, *everything* felt right for id that fall of 1992. Wolfenstein and Spear of Destiny were the talk of the computer and shareware magazines. Such accolades positioned id, and its publisher, Apogee, as nothing less than the heroes of the shareware movement. The two companies dominated the shareware charts with two Commander Keen titles, Wolfenstein 3-D, and Apogee's own original game—a side-scrolling shooter starring a brash, Schwarzenegger-style hero called Duke Nukem—occupying the top four positions. The press declared Apogee one of "the most remarkable, if unheralded success stories in the entertainment software industry. . . . [Apogee] is ready to confront the Big Boys."

One of the only companies, it seemed, not caught up in the fanfare over Apogee was id. The guys believed that Scott Miller, despite their friendship, had not been fulfilling his responsibilities. This information came from Shawn Green, an Apogee employee whom Romero had befriended since Keen's release. Shawn was a hard-core gamer and aspiring programmer from Garland, Texas. With long hair and a lust for loud rock music, he'd grown up as an outcast in his conservative town—required to attend night school because he refused to cut his hair. At Apogee, Shawn toyed with people who would call in to complain about killing dogs in Wolfenstein by explaining that "you can kill people too."

He told Romero that there were more serious complaints—calls from people who could not get through to order id's games. Apparently, many of the Apogee lackeys spent their days engaged in rubber band fights. Many were simply young students Scott had hired by putting up flyers in computer stores that said, "Do you like to play games? Can you handle talking on the phone and playing games all day for six bucks an hour?" To make matters worse, there was no computer network. Orders were scrawled on scraps of paper and then jammed on metal spikes.

Kevin Cloud, who was emerging as one of the more business-minded members of id, tried calling Apogee himself and found that he couldn't get through. Something had to be done. Sure Scott was their friend, and he'd given them their start, but now he was unnecessary. Why give up 50 percent of their sales when they could do the self-publish completely on their own? Doom would surely be as big as, if not bigger than, Wolfenstein. Jay, Tom, Adrian, and especially Romero—who, from the moment he suggested they leave Softdisk, had always been looking for ways to grow the business—agreed. The only dissonant voice was Carmack's.

In an increasingly stark opposition to Romero, Carmack expressed a minimalist point of view with regard to running their business. As he often told the guys, all he cared about was being able to work on his programs and afford enough pizza and Diet Coke to keep him alive. He had no interest in running a big company. The more business responsibilities they had—things like order fulfillment and marketing—the more they would lose their focus: making great games.

Jay assured him that life would only get better. "We will truly become independent," he said. "We'll rely on nobody. We need to create our own opportunities. We don't wait for them to knock. We open the door. We grab opportunity by the scruff of the neck and pull it through." Carmack could be left alone to work on his technology. Ultimately, he agreed. Scott had to go.

Scott took the news in stride. In fact, he had suspected for some time that id would jump ship. He felt grateful that the relationship had lasted as long as it did. The id games had helped put Apogee on top and buy Scott and his partner, George Broussard, nice sports cars. By this time id was also far from the only company making successful games for Apogee. Scott was continuing to publish many other authors, such as Tim Sweeney, a gifted programmer from Maryland who churned out popular titles under his company, Epic MegaGames. Apogee's own title, Duke Nukem, was number one on the shareware charts, right above Wolfenstein, with a sequel on the way. Though Scott didn't want to lose id, he was confident he'd survive.

Scott Miller wasn't the only one to go before id began working on Doom. Mitzi would suffer a similar fate. Carmack's cat had been a thorn in the side of the id employees, beginning with the days of her overflowing litter box back at the lake house. Since then she had grown more irascible, lashing out at passersby and relieving herself freely around his apartment. The final straw came when she peed all over a brand-new leather couch that Carmack had bought with the Wolfenstein cash. Carmack broke the news to the guys.

"Mitzi was having a net negative impact on my life," he said. "I took her to the animal shelter. Mmm."

"What?" Romero asked. The cat had become such a sidekick of Carmack's that the guys had even listed her on the company directory as his significant other—and now she was just *gone*? "You know what this means?" Romero said. "They're going to put her to sleep! No one's going to want to claim her. She's going down! Down to Chinatown!"

Carmack shrugged it off and returned to work. The same rule applied to a cat, a computer program or, for that matter, a person. When something becomes a problem, let it go or, if necessary, have it surgically removed.

Tom didn't like what he saw the moment he set foot inside the black cube. Compared with the creative boiler room atmosphere of the lake house and apartments, the new id domain felt isolated and detached. Everyone would have his own office. Everyone, it turned out, except Tom.

On the first day, each guy chose his space. Carmack and Romero took side-by-side offices, while Adrian and Kevin, who were growing increasingly close, decided to share a space. Tom liked an open corner spot in a large room with a window. "This would be a great office area," he said, "we just need to put some walls up." The rest agreed. But the walls were slow to come. Whenever Tom asked Jay about it, Jay would say they were on their way. Out of humor and frustration, Tom put down two long strips of masking tape where the walls of what he called his creative corner would go.

Those weren't the only invisible barriers around. Romero seemed to be pulling away or, as Tom had often joked, flipping his bit from the moment they moved. Tom would sit at his desk behind his tape and watch Romero laughing down the hall with Adrian and Kevin. It felt sad to him, the inability to connect. Some of this, he thought, surely had to do with their emerging creative differences. There seemed to be a widening chasm between the factions of design and technology. It started the moment Romero chose Wolfenstein—a fast, brutal game that would emulate Carmack's graphics engine—over a more robust, character-driven world like Keen. Tom was still id's game designer, but he didn't feel like he was designing what he wanted at all. Yet he held out hope that things might prove different for Doom.

The early meetings suggested that they might. The discussions took place in a conference room overlooking the LBJ Highway through black Venetian blinds. Everyone sat around a large black table. Over pizza they brainstormed about Carmack's demons from hell idea. They all agreed on making a fast-action game that had the sci-fi suspense of *Aliens* combined with the demonic B-movie horror of *Evil Dead II*.

But Tom, who maintained the role of creative director, was determined not just to make another plotless first-person shooter. In Wolfenstein there was no emotion, no feeling for the people getting blown away. Tom, who had left dead Yorps in Keen to impart a truer representation of death, wanted to bolster Doom with a more gripping kind of depth, something cinematic.

"How about we tell this story of scientists on this moon at the butt-end of space," he said, "and they're studying this anomaly and it rips open and they think aliens are coming out? But as you get further along you realize it's mythological demons from hell and that's, like, the shock. It gets creepier and creepier as you go on. And you have an episode where that's discovered and there's, like, magnetic poles on the moon where there's two anomalies. So you go in and walk through a slice of hell and you come out and hell's come out in our dimension and perverted everything you're used to in the first episodes."

Though Romero was somewhat supportive at first, Carmack had other ideas. "Story in a game," he said, "is like a story in a porn movie; it's expected to be there, but it's not that important." Tom gnashed his teeth. Furthermore, Carmack added, the technology was going to be different this time around. He didn't want to do another game consisting of levels and episodes. Instead, he said, "We've got to make this one contiguous world, a seamless world." Rather than running through a door, say, and having an entire new level load up, the player would have a sense of invisibly progressing through one massive space.

Tom hated this concept. It went against their winning formula. Players liked the sense of having completed one section or level of a game, then moving on to the next. He looked to Romero. But once again Romero sided with Carmack. Tom returned to his desk to wait for his walls.

Romero wasn't the only one realizing the importance of Carmack's vision. One afternoon Jay and Kevin went outside for a smoke and talked about the company purchasing what was known as key-man insurance in case anything happened to Carmack. When Kevin suggested that the company buy the insurance for everyone else as well, Jay replied, "Everyone else is expendable." Because of his technological innovations, Carmack remained the resident Dungeon Master, the guy in charge, the one holding the rule book.

It was clear that Doom would look like no other game. All the features Carmack had experimented with in the Shadowcaster engine were coming to life. Most notable were the diminished lighting effects—the concept that would allow a virtual space to fade gracefully to black. Carmack's first innovation was just to think up the idea of diminished lighting. But, equally important, he was willing to make the difficult choices that would make this technology possible. That meant letting something go.

Programming is a science based on limited resources; one can program only within the range of power available in a computer's hardware and software. In the fall of 1992, Carmack was still programming in VGA, which allowed only 256 colors. His challenge was achieving the effect of fading to black with these limited resources.

The solution was to choose the colors on the palette so that there might be, for example, sixteen shades of red, ranging from very bright to black. Carmack then programmed the computer to apply a different shade based on where a player was within a room. If the player walked into a big, open space, the computer would make a quick calculation and then apply the darkest shades to the farthest section. As the player moved forward, the computer would brighten the colors; the colors nearer would always be brighter than the ones farther away. Cumulatively, the world would seem not only more real but more evil.

But this was not all. Both Carmack and Romero were eager to break away from the tile-based architecture of their earlier games; Keen and Wolfenstein were constructed like building blocks, piecing little square tiles of graphics together to make one giant wall. What the Two Johns, particularly Romero, wanted now was to create a more fluid, free-form design, a world, like the real world, that could have walls of varying heights, rooms that felt huge, twisted, and strange. In Wolfenstein walls had to be at ninety-degree angles; in Doom they would be at all kinds of angles.

Carmack felt ready for the challenge; computers were getting more powerful, and so were his skills. He began experimenting with ways to draw larger, more arbitrarily shaped polygons, as well as add textures to the ceilings and floors. When Romero looked over Carmack's shoulder, he was impressed—just as he had been on so many occasions before. Carmack explained his progress with diminished lighting and arbitrary polygons. He also talked about some other things he might do: make some special concessions so that hackers could more easily modify the game, as well as add some kind of networking component that could let players compete head-to-head.

Romero immediately saw the potential in Carmack's technology, potential that Carmack was, by his own admission, not capable of envisioning himself. And because Romero was a programmer, he could speak to Carmack in a language he understood, translating his own artistic vision into the code Carmack would employ to help bring it to life. The moment Romero saw the diminished lighting effects, his mind went to work imagining what effects he could design. "If you can change the light value," he said, "can we do it dynamically, like on the fly while the game's playing, or does it have to be precomputed?"

"Well," Carmack said, "I can make it dynamic."

"Cool, then let's have strobes! You know, you're fucking running through a room and—*bzzzz! bzzzz! bzzzz!*—the lights flash off!"

Romero raced back to his office. He booted up the map editor—the programming template he and Tom would use to create the Doom worlds. Using it, again, was very much like designing architecture for a house. On screen Romero would look at something resembling a flat overhead blueprint. By clicking his mouse and dragging down a line, he could draw a series of walls. With another click he could switch the point of view to look at his creation from *within* the space. Adrian and Kevin, meanwhile, would provide the texture images, essentially the wallpaper, which a level designer could use to decorate a room's walls.

With those map-editing tools available, Romero was eager to use Carmack's innovations to bring Doom to realization. Carmack was doing amazing work; Romero knew this on two counts—as a programmer who appreciated Carmack's ingenuity and, just as important, as a gamer who had never played through such worlds on a PC, or any other platform for that matter. He played around with rooms that flashed strobe light, with walls that soared and receded at different heights. Every decision he made was based on how he could best show off Carmack's technology. Carmack couldn't have been happier; what more could someone want, after all, than to be both appreciated *and* celebrated? Romero was just as energized; with Carmack's innovations, he too could reach new heights.

Tom, by contrast, felt himself sinking. Since their initial meeting about the game, he had been on his own writing up a treatment, known in the game industry as a design document, for Doom, fleshing out the characters, motivations, story. The game would begin, he wrote, with the player assigned to a military base conducting experiments on a distant moon. The experiments go awry, however, when the scientists accidentally open a portal to hell, releasing an onslaught of beasts—much like what happened with Romero in their Dungeons and Dragons game. The action would start with the player engaged in a game of cards with some other soldiers. Suddenly a burst of light would flash and the demons would come, ripping the player's best friend to shreds. Tom wanted to create an immediate sense of terror as the player watched his pal die a terrible, instant death. He named the doomed character in the game Buddy—the same name as that of the Dungeons and Dragons character he'd played.

But his work fell flat among his own friends. The first blow came when Carmack casually announced that he was no longer interested in pursuing a seamless world for Doom. The game could return to a more traditional level design. "But I've spent the last two months writing a design document based *entirely* on that seamless world *you* wanted!" Tom exclaimed. Carmack's remark meant that Tom had to revise everything he'd done.

"This Doom Bible is not helping us get the game done," Carmack said. Id had never written down anything in the past, why start now? Doom didn't need a back story. It was a game about fight or flight. The player just needed to be scared all the time; he didn't need to know why. Carmack told Tom to drop the Bible and start playing around with the technology, like Romero was doing. "I'm still working on this technology," he explained, "but please *experiment.* Figure out what can be done with this." He suggested Tom go to the library and check out some books about military bases to get some ideas.

Romero agreed. Though he liked much of what Tom had put into the Doom Bible, a character-driven story was clearly not going in the same direction as Carmack's technology. There was no time for guys to sit around and play cards in Doom. Not only was the game going to be brutal and fast, like Wolfenstein, but it was going to be even *more* brutal and fast.

Tom gave up the story once and for all. But another story was falling into place for id. In the company's brief history, a pattern was emerging that emulated Carmack's programming ideology: innovate, optimize, then jettison anything that gets in the way. It happened in their games: how Keen was killed for Wolfenstein, how floors and ceilings were sacrificed for speed. And it happened in their lives: Al Vekovius, Scott Miller, and even Mitzi the cat had all been abruptly deleted from the program. It was impossible to know who or what could be next.

Romero marched into the kitchen at id, waving a crudely drawn caricature of Burger Bill, the renowned gamer rumored to keep hamburgers for days in his desk. Tom, Kevin, and Adrian followed, cackling. Romero stapled Bill's picture to the chair, then grabbed a steak knife from the drawer. It was time for revenge.

Bill had been contracted by id to convert or port Wolfenstein for the Super Nintendo. But with the deadline approaching, he still hadn't delivered an iota. He finally admitted that there was a problem: he had made the mistake of signing id's contract while employed by the game publisher Interplay. His contract with Interplay stipulated that any work an employee did was property of the company; the Super Nintendo port, therefore, was now owned by Interplay.

The id guys flipped. "See," Romero said, "this is just the kind of bullshit you get when you rely on other people." Tom took out a pencil and sketched a hideous caricature of Bill with burger meat dripping from his greasy mouth. Romero swiped it from his hands and said it was time for Bill to pay the price. In the kitchen, they took turns stabbing the picture, yelling and laughing and egging each other on. They began attacking the chair, knifing it, stomping it, trashing it. Days later, when Bill came to visit, the ruins were still on the floor. He took one look at the knife with his name scrawled on the blade and asked meekly, "Um, what's this?" Then they fired him. Carmack would do the port himself.

Such shenanigans were becoming par for the course. The guys had long engaged in a kind of competitive, creative hazing ritual known as the Rip-A-Thon. They would take turns humiliating each other in some artistic way. Adrian programmed a screen opening so that when Romero turned on his computer he'd see a doctored picture of himself engaged in compromising sexual acts. After Tom had some glossy headshots made of himself following Wolfenstein's success, Romero and Adrian went to town defacing them; the most elaborate example involved a bratwurst, clay testicles, and a can of whipped cream.

Id's frat house even had its own house mother in the form of their office manager, Donna Jackson. Donna had a syrupy southern accent and big teased hair, and was partial to bright pink business suits and matching rouge. She quickly took to the role of company matriarch. She made sure everyone was fed and happy and healthy, offering to get more junk food or soda whenever someone was down. When she arrived, her hobby was gambling in Shreveport casinos; she soon became an expert sharpshooter in id's games. She called the id guys, still in their early twenties, "my boys." The boys called her Miss Donna or, sometimes, the id mom.

But since Miss Donna was a mom for hire, no one was in fear of being reprimanded for their outbursts. Office destruction became sport. The office was strewn with broken keyboards, smashed monitors, broken disks. Romero might just walk up to Kevin and joke, "Hey, Kevin, that garbage can is calling you a sad motherfucker." Kevin would reply dryly, "It is?" before pummeling the can into the ground.

More darkness was coming from the art room. Doom was precisely the kind of game Adrian had always wanted to do: something that could allow him to exorcise his most nightmarish visions. Along with the others, he and Kevin dreamed up the most hideous creatures they could imagine: the Imp, a red-eyed Bigfoot-like beast with brown fur covering his muscles and metal spikes protruding from his shoulders and arms; the Demon, a snorting pink bull with bloodstained teeth and horns; and, meanest of all, the Cyber Demon, with a gun for an arm and a ripped-open torso.

This time around, the monsters would look even more lifelike, thanks to a new animation technique. For Wolfenstein, Adrian had had to draw every frame, showing each character in several walking and running positions. Now they decided to try a mixed media approach. They would sculpt the characters in clay, then shoot them in different positions on video. The video frames would then be scanned into the computer, colorized, and programmed as moving digital characters using a program Carmack wrote called the Fuzzy Pumper Palette Shop. "The overall effect is distorted," Kevin said, "but that's Doom."

Adrian and Kevin had so much fun they even began scanning themselves into the game. One day Kevin rolled up his sleeve and stood behind the video camera with his arm extended in front of the lens, taking turns firing toy weapons: a plastic shotgun and pistol from Toys "R" Us; a chain saw—like the one used by the hero of the movie *Evil Dead II*—borrowed from a woman Tom had been dating. The video images would then be placed in the lower center of the game's frame, looking like the player was sighting down the length of his forearm or, in actuality, Kevin's. Inspired, Adrian scanned a pair of his snakeskin boots, which he used to create a serpentlike texture for one level of the game. When Kevin came to work with a bloody wound on his knee, they scanned that in too, to use as a wall texture. In the strange emerging world of Doom, anything could go.

By the new year, there was enough coming together that Tom typed up a press release. "Dallas, Texas, January 1, 1993—Heralding another technical revolution in PC programming," he wrote, "id Software's Doom promises to push back the boundaries of what was thought possible on a computer. . . . In Doom, you play one of four off-duty soldiers suddenly thrown into the middle of an interdimensional war! Stationed at a scientific research facility, your days are filled with tedium and paperwork. Today is a bit different. Wave after wave of demonic creatures are spreading through the base, killing or possessing everyone in sight. As you stand knee-deep in the dead, your duty seems clear—you must eradicate the enemy and find out where they're coming from. When you find out the truth, your sense of reality may be shattered!"

He touted the game's new, improved technologies: texture-mapped worlds, nonorthogonal walls, and diminished lighting. For the hell of it, they threw in a teaser about multiplayer gaming, something they had yet to implement. "Up to four players can play over a local network," Tom wrote, "or two players can play by modem or serial link. . . . We fully expect to be the number one cause of decreased productivity in businesses around the world."

With the bar set, Tom, Romero, Adrian, Carmack, and Kevin had arrived at a genuine look and feel for the game. The player would progress while staring down the barrel of a shotgun jutting out in the lower center part of the screen. The rooms would unfold dark, foreboding, mainly in grays, blacks, and browns, with an occasional royal blue floor. As originally intended, the walls were anything but ninety degrees; they were octagonal, tiered, with steps leading from one room to the next. Carmack had also devised a way to create windows within walls, so a player could look from one room into another, though not know how to get inside. There were actual light sources in the games — strips of fluorescence on the floor or above. But the realism was punctuated by demonic monsters. In one section a player would progress through a locker room, only to find a pink demon floating in the showers.

By the spring, several of these levels were collected into an early demonstration, or alpha, of the game, which was distributed to friends, testers, and select members of the press. *Computer Gaming World* published a glowing preview: "We don't know what nasty sludge is seeping into the Texas water table," it read, "but whatever it is has given these boys some strange visions, and what's worse, the programming sorcery to carry it out. *Doom* is the name of their next creation, and unbelievable graphics technology is their game."

Despite the enthusiasm, the Two Johns were still not happy with Tom's work. Tom had taken Carmack's advice to study military architecture too much to heart. The levels he created had the banality of a real-life military base. He stuck stubbornly close to the scenario of his Doom Bible, creating a room, even, that showed a group of soldiers sitting around a table playing cards. Many of the rooms looked like actual offices: with gray walls, brown-tiled floors, and even office chairs and file cabinets. Tom was trying to appease Carmack at the expense of the game, Romero thought. So he decided to show how the design should be done, even if that meant Carmack would have to make his code faster.

Romero retired to his office, cranked up Dokken, and got to work. Hours into the night, he pointed and clicked, dragged and dropped, creating lines on his map editor, switching back and forth into the first-person point of view. He knew what he was going for: to break out of the concrete box–like military bunkers and into something else, something big, expansive, twisting, weird, and abstract. After a series of late nights, the world emerged just as Romero wanted it. And when he pulled the others into his office, they stepped inside.

It began in a room with a low gray ceiling but angled walls. Walking to the front right, they came to a wall with slats in it, open spaces that revealed an outdoor vista, a sky, but no apparent way to get out. Two large lights stripped the opening of a hallway. It seemed like the way to go. As one walked down the hall, the rooms opened up to a plank leading outdoors. There was a gray sky overhead. Mountains off in the distance. But as one moved, the path only led back inside, now into a room with higher walls than the first. Lights flashed from over-head as a flurry of Former Humans—zombie soldiers possessed by demons—unleashed rounds of fire, emerging from the shadows with bloodstained chests. When Romero was through, everyone agreed. Tom's banal levels were out. Romero's were in. This was the design. *This* was Doom.

From that moment, Tom's attitude went from bad to miserable. It felt like everything he had done, everything he wanted to do, was get-ting thrown out. It was like the end of sixth grade, he thought, when some people are turning into jocks and some people are turning into geeks and you get that realization that you're heading down the wrong path. Romero all but ignored him: no jokes, no destruction, no alien bleeps. The rest made him feel just as alone, striking down anything he would suggest for the game. It soon became too painful for Tom to be there. He found a girlfriend and began spending more time out of the office.

Before long Carmack pulled Romero aside and suggested they fire Tom. But Romero knew what such a change would mean. Though no owner had left or been fired before, the guys had decided how to deal with such a situation if it should ever arise. Just after they formed the company, they sat down and agreed, wholeheartedly, that the fate of id Software had to transcend the fate of the individual owners. They had seen the damage the infighting had caused Softdisk and were deter-mined to insulate their own company from such demise.

They made two agreements. First, there had to be a unanimous vote among the owners to ask someone to go; at the moment, Adrian, Ro-mero, Tom, and Carmack were the main partners, with Jay and Kevin each owning smaller shares. Second, if an owner left, he would lose all his shares and have no future stake in the company; they didn't want anyone's departure to damage the success of id. Tom, in other words, would never see a penny from Doom, let alone Wolfenstein or Keen. He would be on his own.

Romero convinced Carmack to give Tom another chance. Romero

had other things on his mind as well. He was getting married again. His relationship with Beth, the former clerk at Softdisk, had become a deep and meaningful love affair. She could give him the space he needed to build his career as well as be in a relationship. She was fun, loved to cook, loved to have a good time. She didn't have any real interest in games, but at least he could continue doing what he most enjoyed.

Over July 4, 1993, Romero spent his honeymoon in Aruba. When he came back, he was more energized than ever. Though he still maintained close contact with his sons in California, the years without a family in town had been tough. And his relationship with his ex-wife, Kelly, was only getting more strained. But now he had a new wife, a new beginning. Money was rolling in from Wolfenstein to the tune of a hundred thousand dollars per month. Doom had found its voice. All was well. All, he quickly discovered, but Tom. By now, everyone else had had enough. They wanted him out. Finally, Romero gave in.

He wanted to break the news to his old friend himself. So he invited Tom to his house for a meal home-cooked by Beth. Tom was delighted. He hadn't spent quality time with Romero for ages. The dinner was like old times: the two guys joking around, talking movies and games. Romero couldn't bring himself to break the news. The next day a shareholders' meeting was called. Tom walked in to find everyone sitting around the conference room table staring at the floor. "Tom," Carmack finally said, "obviously this isn't working out. We're asking for your resignation."

For Tom, the moment felt unreal. He heard Romero say something about how he'd tried to tell him about this last night but just couldn't bring himself to do it. Tom could not even respond. He found a little sticker on the table, peeled it off, and began rolling it between his fingers. Despite all the warning signs, he hadn't seen this coming at all. He felt depressed, ashamed. Maybe this wasn't just about the games, he thought. He always felt like they resented his upbringing, the fact that he wasn't a delinquent or the product of a broken home. He was just this guy with doting parents and a college education. In a barely audible voice, he began defending himself, talking about all the things he could do for Doom. But there was silence in response. Soon his voice faded too. They asked him to leave the room while they discussed the situation.

As the door shut behind him, something in Tom shifted. A weight rose from his body. He had been so miserable for so long, so dejected, feeling so unwanted, he never had the gumption to recognize the situation for what it was and make a break. It was like those old job interviews when the men in suits kept asking him if the job they were offering was what he really wanted to do. At that time, he realized, it hadn't been what he wanted; what he wanted was to make games. Now, five years later, he accepted that these were not the games he wanted to make. When he stepped back into the conference room, he said, "I think, guys, this is really the thing to do." His games at id were over. The others' were just getting started.

NINE

The Coolest Game

John Carmack stood in the Ferrari dealership admiring a cherry-red 328 sports car and had one thought: *How fast can it go?* As an engineer, he considered speed an efficient way to measure his progress: How much faster could he get the computer to render graphics on screen? A car was much the same. When Carmack looked at the sexy design of the body, he saw straight through to the engine. To the dealer's surprise, the wiry twenty-two-year-old in T-shirt and jeans wrote a check for seventy thousand dollars and took the keys.

It didn't take long for Carmack to feel that the car wasn't quite fast enough. His instinct was to get under the hood and start futzing around, just like he had with his MGB. But this was no ordinary car, this was a Ferrari. *No one* futzed with a Ferrari. The elite manufacturer had very low regard for anyone who dared mess with its pristine design. For Carmack, though, it was another machine to hack.

With Romero's help, Carmack soon found someone who was more than up to the task: Bob Norwood. Norwood had been racing and building cars since he was a thirteen-year-old in Kansas. He held more than a hundred spots in *The Guinness Book of World Records* for speed records in a variety of funny cars and, above all else, Ferraris. When

Romero read in an auto magazine that Norwood now ran an auto shop in Dallas, he suggested Carmack give him a call.

Carmack, as usual, was skeptical. Every other auto guy in town had shrugged off his request. "A Ferrari, eh?" they'd say. "Well, I guess we can put a new exhaust system on it." A new exhaust, Carmack knew, was a wimpy and ineffectual answer to his problem. When he drove into Norwood's, the crusty owner walked out with greasy hands. "I got this 328," Carmack said cautiously, "and I want it to be a little faster." Norwood squinted his eye and replied matter-of-factly, "We'll put a turbo on it." Carmack had found a new friend.

For fifteen thousand dollars, Norwood rigged the Ferrari with a turbo system that would activate when Carmack floored the gas pedal. It was a ballsy bit of hacking, and Carmack immediately felt a kinship with the veteran racing man. The day it was finished, Carmack planned to celebrate by driving to his brother's graduation in Missouri; though his success with Keen and Wolfenstein had helped him mend bridges with his mother, pulling up in a car like this was guaranteed to close the deal.

He showed up at Norwood's with his duffel bag, threw it in the trunk, then hit the road. Just outside Dallas, he saw an open stretch of highway. Slowly, he pushed the pedal down to the floor. As it lowered, he felt a force build until the pedal hit the metal and the car accelerated almost twice as fast, reaching nearly 140 miles per hour. Life was good. He was living his dream: working for himself, programming all night, dressing how he pleased. All those long, hard years without a computer, without a hacker community, were fading behind him. Contrary to what the other guys might have thought, he did have feelings. And at this moment, with the cows and corn blurring beside him, he felt unbelievably happy. He drove the rest of the way with a huge grin on his face.

His car wasn't the only engine Carmack wanted to go faster. Doom, though quick, was still not quite quick enough for his taste. The game had considerable challenges for speed, such as the textured ceilings and floors, as well as the walls of varying heights. While porting Wolfenstein to the Super Nintendo System, Carmack had read about a programming process known as Binary Space Partitioning, or BSP. The process was being used by a programmer at Bell Labs to help render three-dimensional models on screen. In the simplest terms, it broke the model into larger sections or leaves of data, as opposed to sluggishly drawing out many little polygons at a time. When Carmack read this, something clicked. What if you could use a BSP to create not just one 3-D image but an entire virtual world?

No one had tried this. No one, it seemed, had even *thought* about this because, after all, not many people were in the business of creating virtual worlds. With BSPs, the image of a room in Doom would be essentially split up into a giant tree of leaves. Rather than trying to draw the whole tree every time the player moved, the computer would draw only the leaves he was facing. Once this process was implemented, Doom, already fast, soared.

To keep Doom's development going, however, Carmack, Romero, and the rest knew they had to deal with one pressing problem: replacing Tom Hall. As a friend, of course, Tom was irreplaceable, particularly for Romero. There was just no one who possessed that hysterically comic streak. Worse, the split from id was so painful that Romero and Tom had hardly spoken since the firing. But at least Tom had managed to land on his feet. Scott Miller, another casualty on the way to id's success, offered him a job as a game designer for Apogee. It was bittersweet, but Tom accepted; maybe now he would be able to make the games he had always imagined.

Back at id, the guys started sifting through résumés for a new game designer of their own. Kevin had received a résumé from a promising-looking gamer named Sandy Petersen. At thirty-seven years old, Sandy was ancient compared with the id guys and an admirable veteran of the gaming scene. In the early eighties, he had created a pen-and-paper role-playing game, Call of Cthulhu, that featured flesh-eating zombies and tentacle-legged alien parasites. The game became a cult favorite around the world, selling over a hundred thousand copies. Eventually, Sandy went on to create computer games at MicroProse, a company in Baltimore founded by Sid Meier, legendary designer of the historically based strategy series Civilization.

But Romero had a concern about Sandy. At the bottom of Sandy's résumé, he noted that he was Mormon. "Dude," Romero told Kevin, "I don't want anyone who's religious here. We're fucking writing a game about demons and hell and shit, and the last thing we need is someone who's going to be against it."

"Nah," Kevin said. "Let's just meet him, he might be really cool."

Romero sighed. "Okay, dude, but I wouldn't do it."

Several days later, Sandy showed up. He was a heavyset, balding guy with glasses and suspenders. He had a rapid-fire, high-pitched voice that got more excited as he spoke about games. Encouraged, Romero sat him down in front of a computer to see how he could put together a makeshift level of Doom. Within minutes Sandy was drawing what seemed like a mess of lines on screen. "Um," Romero said, "what are you doing here?"

"Well," Sandy chirped speedily, "I'm going to have you come through here and this wall's going to open up behind you and the monster's going to come through it and you're going down this way and I'm going to turn the lights off and all this stuff . . ."

All right, Romero thought, this guy's getting it like—bam! With Sandy on board as id's game designer, Romero would be free to do all the different things he enjoyed—programming, making sounds, creating levels, overseeing business deals.

Sandy was given an offer, but he told Jay he needed more money to support his family. Later that day Carmack approached him and said, "The stuff you've done is really good. I like your work, and I think you'd be good in the company." The next day Carmack stopped him in the hall again. "When I said your work was good," he said, "that was before I knew that you'd asked Jay for more money. So I don't want you to think I told you your work was good in an attempt to get you to ask for less money. Mmm." Then he walked off. It seemed to Sandy like a weird thing to say, as if Carmack thought that he could cajole him out of wanting a higher salary. He doesn't know anything about how humans think or feel, Sandy thought.

It didn't take long for Romero to appreciate Sandy's speed, sense of design, and encyclopedic knowledge of games. Sandy regaled him about the payback a player should receive when blasting the lungs out of a demon with the shotgun. "You really should get rewarded on several levels," he said. "You hear the gun go off, you see the big, manly guy cocking his shotgun, you see the bad guy go flying backwards, or an explosion. It's always you're rewarded for doing the right thing!"

Romero couldn't agree more, adding how, in addition to all that, there would be like tons of blood flying out from the beasts. They had a good laugh. Romero decided to probe the religious issues. "So," he said, "you're Mormon?"

"Yep," Sandy replied.

"Well," Romero said with a chuckle, "at least you're like not a Mormon that keeps pumping out tons of kids and stuff."

Sandy stopped typing. "Actually, I've got five kids."

"Oh, okay," Romero stammered. "But that's not like *ten* or anything. But you know five's a lot but, um, at least you're not a really *hard-core* card-carrying Mormon."

"Oh, I got my Mormon card right here!" Sandy pulled it out.

"Well, at least you don't wear those garments and stuff, right?"

Sandy lifted his shirt. "Got my garments on right here!"

"Okay, okay," Romero said, "I'm going to shut up."

"Look," Sandy said, "don't worry. I have no problems with the demons in the game. They're just cartoons. And, anyway," he added, smiling, "*they're* the bad guys."

While id refined Doom in September 1993, two sons of a preacher from Spokane named Rand and Robyn Scott released Myst, a literary adventure computer game on CD-ROM. The game became an instant phenomenon, topping the computer game charts and eventually selling more than 4 million copies. It also popularized the burgeoning new format of CD-ROM. With the rise of CD-ROM drives on home computers, this spacious format (which could store hundreds of times more data than floppy disks) was becoming the "it" software for game developers. The extra space afforded better sound and even full-motion video—effects exploited in a horror CD-ROM game called 7th Guest, another chart topper.

Shot in a photorealistic manner, Myst set players on a mysterious abandoned island, where they were to explore strange rooms and machines and unlock the secret of their inventor, a man named Atrus. Like Doom, Myst unfolded from a first-person point of view. But in Myst, players didn't run or, for that matter, crawl. They just slowly flowed; clicking a space or item before them would gracefully fade one setting into the next. "Its brilliantly designed and rendered 3-D images," *Wired* magazine raved, "and its funhouse world of mazes, puzzles, and human intrigues will certainly set a new standard for this type of adventure game."

Id hated Myst. It had none of the elements they liked: no real-time interaction, no pace, no fear, no action. If Myst was like Shakespeare, Doom was going to be Stephen King. With Carmack's engine in gear, the rest of the team buckled down on finished elements of the game. Adrian and Kevin churned out dark, demonic art. They drew guys impaled, twitching on stakes (like the impaled farmer Adrian had seen at the hospital long ago), blood-spattered corpses chained to walls. The death animations were more elaborate than ever: monsters stumbling with their skulls ripped open, the Baron of Hell slumping forward with his intestines spilling onto the floor.

The weapons were falling into place: the shotgun, the pistol, the chain saw, a rocket launcher, and the affectionately named BFG, Big Fucking Gun. In Wolfenstein, if the player lost a gun, it would be replaced with the default weapon, a knife. In Doom, the player would be left to duke it out with his bare fists. They digitized Kevin's hand, slugging punches against a blue screen. The killer weapons and monsters needed suitably killer sounds. The guys signed Bobby Prince up again to record the audio. Under Romero's guidance, Bobby gave Doom a techno metal–style soundtrack. A puree of animal groans were used for the game's beasts.

With the guns and monsters and gore, Sandy and Romero went to town on the levels. Romero had found his voice in Doom. He loved everything about the game, the speed, the fear, the suspense, and he tried to play it all up. Romero's levels were deliberately paced. As level designer, he was responsible for not only designing the architecture of the environments but also choosing where to put monsters, weapons, bonus items and objects; it was like being a theater director and haunted-mansion creator all in one.

Romero relished the roles. In a level of his, a player might run into a room and see a window leading outside but wouldn't know how to get there. So the player would run down a room, music pumping, looking for a way. A door would slide open and *Boom!* there'd be a howling Imp. Blast that monster down, run down a brown spotted corridor, open another door, and *Blam!* another herd of beasts. Romero had a knack for staging the battles, letting the player win one small round, then pummeling him with a storm of enemies.

While Romero was raw and brutal, Sandy was cerebral and strategic. One level was littered with green barrels that, when shot, would explode. Sandy made levels in which the only way to kill a monster was to shoot a barrel at the perfect moment. His levels were not nearly as aesthetically pleasing as Romero's; in fact, some of the id guys thought they were downright ugly, but they were undeniably fun and fiendish. They complemented Romero's well.

By the fall of 1993, the pressure was on as gamers began to clamor for Doom. A demonstration for the press leaked out onto the Internet, despite id's best efforts. Small groups of die-hard fans began calling the id office or sending desperate e-mails for information. But the mainstream press didn't seem to know or, for that matter, care. A community television program did a piece on the guys, filming them at work playing games, but that was about it. Calling the big papers and magazines, Jay found, was fruitless.

Instead, Jay—determined to make id's business style as innovative as its games—focused on setting up the company's distribution and marketing. He established a toll-free number to field orders and set up a deal with a fulfillment house. Since they were self-publishing Doom, they would be getting twice the earnings they had on Wolfenstein. Games distributed through the regular retail channels would bleed cash to middlemen. Every time someone bought a game at CompUSA, the retailer would take money, then pay the distributor, the distributor would take money, then pay the publisher, the publisher would take money, then pay the developer. By going shareware, id was cutting them all out, taking eighty-five cents for every dollar sold; the game would be listed at around forty dollars. Jay figured Doom, like Wolfenstein, would rely on word of mouth. While big guns like Nintendo were spending millions on marketing and advertising, id would take out only one small ad in a gaming magazine for Doom. The goal, then, was to get the Doom shareware into as many hands as possible.

At the time, retail stores were selling shareware disks and being forced, by the authors, to cough up a high royalty. Id, which had made some of the most successful shareware games yet, had a different approach: give the Doom shareware to retailers for free, no fee, no royalty, and let them keep all the profits from the sale. The more shareware was distributed, the more potential customers id would be able to collect.

"We don't care if you make money off this shareware demo," Jay told the retailers. "Move it! Move it in mass quantities!" The retailers couldn't believe their ears — no one had ever told them *not* to pay royalties. But Jay was insistent. Take Doom for nothing, keep the profit! My goal is distribution. Doom is going to be Wolfenstein on steroids, and I want it far and wide! I want you to stack Doom deep! In fact, I want you to do advertising for it too, because you're going to make money off it. So take this money that you might have given me in royalties and use it to advertise the fact that you're selling Doom." Jay got plenty of takers.

The buzz around Wolfenstein and Doom brought back old characters. Al Vekovius contacted the boys to see if they wanted to rerelease some of their old Softdisk games. The company, he told them, was having trouble recovering since their departure. They turned him down. More notably, the game turned out Romero's stepfather, John Schuneman. On a trip to Dallas, Schuneman sat across the table from Romero at a dinner at Outback Steakhouse and, for the first time, opened his heart. "You know, I've been a bear sometimes," he said, "but I'm a man, and I remember telling you if you were going to make your mark you had to do business applications. Well, I want you to know that I'm man enough to admit that I was wrong. I think this is great. And I want you to know I was wrong."

Romero accepted the apology. Times were moving on, and there was no reason to hold a grudge. Doom was about to be finished. The best was yet to come.

It was Halloween 1993, and Romero was inside Doom. He stood in a small room with gray walls stained in brown sludge, staring down the barrel of his pistol. An ominous, deep synthesizer chord buzzed, giving way to the eerie plucking of a guitar and, finally, a death-rattle drumbeat. A shotgun lay on the floor. Romero ran forward, grabbing it and storming through a door that slid open to the ceiling. The snarls resounded from everywhere—hideous snorts and belches and groans. Suddenly there were fireballs, big, red, explosive bursts hurling in flames through the air. He had to act fast.

Romero spun once, unleashing his shotgun blast into the chest of a Former Human, who went flying back in a spray of blood. A fireball sailed into Romero's side, bleeding his vision red until he could hear himself wheezing and panting. Another blast, Romero spun. But he couldn't see anything. A blast again, more wheezing. A shadowy beast the color of television static hurled forward. Romero fired once to no avail. Then he saw the barrels, two green heaps of waste. The beast was heading right for them. At the perfect moment, Romero fired into the barrel, leaving the monster in a bloody pile of gibs.

A door opened—the one in Romero's office. Romero snuck a peek over his shoulder and kept playing as Carmack walked in. Carmack liked what he saw on screen. Romero had a real sense of grandeur, he thought, the way his levels were so diverse, so varied in elevation, so *deep*. He made his technology sing.

"What's up?" Romero asked.

Carmack told him that he had enough stuff done to be able to get to the networking part of Doom. Oh yeah, Romero thought, *the networking*. They had mentioned this in their press release in January, the fact that Doom would have a multiplayer component, which would let players compete with and against each other. But after all the other work, the networking had become almost an afterthought.

Carmack told Romero about what he thought were somewhat modest technical challenges. "So what I have to do is write the setup stuff to figure out how to communicate over the IPX properly," he said, "and getting the serial stuff going may be a little bit of work . . ." Romero nodded as Carmack spoke. How incredible networking would be, he mused. There had been other games that let players compete head-to-head: side-by-side fighting games like Street Fighter II and this new game called Mortal Kombat were already the rage. And there were seemingly ancient games like the multiplayer colonization game M.U.L.E., or Multiple Use Labor Element, and the early *Star Trek*–inspired modem-to-modem game, NetTrek. But there had been nothing like a multiplayer Doom—first-person, fast-action, immersive, bloody. Romero's heart raced.

He nailed the key on his keyboard and ran through the level on his screen, E1M7, or, Episode 1, Map 7. He came to an area down one hall that had a long window opening up to an outside platform oozing with green plasma. Romero imagined two players shooting rockets at each other, their missiles sailing across the screen. Oh my God, he thought, no one has ever seen that in a game. Sure, it was fun to shoot monsters, but ultimately these were soulless creatures controlled by a computer. Now gamers could play against spontaneous human beings—opponents who could think and strategize and scream. *We can kill each other!*

"If we can get this done," Romero said, "this is going to be the fucking coolest game that the planet Earth has ever fucking seen in its entire history!"

Carmack couldn't have said it better himself.

Within two weeks, Carmack had two computers networked to each other in his office. One represented his first-person point of view, the other represented the other player's. On cue, he hit the button on his keyboard; his character moved forward on the computer in front of him. He pictured the little packets of data traveling across the network line flowing into the computer across his office, translating instantly into the space marines on screen. The computers were talking to each other. And Carmack knew the result. He glanced over at the computer to the right and saw his character, now represented in third-person, running across that screen. He had made a consensual virtual world, and it was alive.

Romero flipped when he came into the office. "Oh my God," he screamed, "that is sooooo awesome!" He dashed back into his office, and Carmack started the game again, this time with Romero connected from his own machine. Romero watched as the space marine Carmack controlled ran down a hall. Romero chased after him, unleashing a shot from his gun—*boom!*—sending Carmack flying back through the air in a spray of blood and screams. "Suck it down!" Romero cried.

Soon everyone in the company was taking turns in multiplayer mode, chasing each other, hurling off explosions. The office filled with screams, not just digital screams, but real screams, human screams. It was an arena, and they were all in it, competing, running, escaping, killing. They began playing one-on-one matches as well, keeping score manually to see who racked up the most kills. And that was not all, Romero realized. Since they could have four people in a game at one time, why not have them playing cooperatively, moving through a level of monsters as a team? Carmack said it was possible. Romero couldn't contain himself. "Don't tell me you can have a four-people co-op game in here mowing through the monsters?" He gasped. "That is the shit!"

Romero paced. This was big—bigger than the Dangerous Dave moment, bigger than anything he'd seen. He made his way down the hall, the yelps and screams coming from inside the rooms. There was Adrian, twitching and convulsing as he played against Kevin and Carmack and Jay. What *was* this? Romero thought. It was like a match, like a boxing match, but the object wasn't just to knock the other guy out or some wimpy shit like that. This was, like, kill the guy! This was a match to the death. He stopped cold. "This," he said, "is deathmatch."

By the first week of December 1993, the work on Doom was hurtling to a close. People had stopped going home, choosing instead to sleep on the couch, the floor, under desks, in chairs. Dave Taylor, hired to help with supplementary programming, had developed quite a reputation for passing out on the floor. But it wasn't happening just because he was tired, he said. Doom was having some kind of greater effect on him, some *biological* effect. The longer he played, the faster he cruised through the streaming corridors, the more his head would spin. After a few minutes, he would have to lay down on the floor to steady himself. Sometimes, he'd just end up falling asleep. It got to be such a frequent display that, late one night, the rest of the guys took a roll of masking tape and taped a body outline around him.

The pressure mounted as they felt the game approach completion. Random gamers began calling the office and leaving messages like "Is it done yet?" or "Hurry up, motherfuckers!" Others spewed resentment at id for not meeting its originally promised release date of the third quarter of 1993. "You started posting hype about Doom several months ago," one gamer posted on an online newsgroup. "You've been encouraging [us] to go ballistic over how great Doom is going to be. And you've told a *lot* of people that the third quarter of 93 was the date. Now all that anticipation is going to backlash in a massive spurt of flames and ranting against id."

Some posted more forgiving tales of anticipatory dreams based on early screenshots released of Doom. "I was firing the shotgun at a pixelated (yes, my dream was pixelated) demon," wrote one gamer, "when my alarm clock went off (well, it turned the radio on :) . . . Time to schedule an appointment with a local shrink. I can't imagine what shape I'll be in once the game is actually released :)."

Another wrote a poem called "The Night Before Doom": " 'Twas the night before *Doom*, / and all through the house, / I had set up my multi-playing networks, / each with a mouse. / The networks were strung, / with extra special care / in hopes that *Doom*, / soon would be there." The publisher of a computer magazine had a darker vision he printed in an editorial called "A Parent's Nightmare Before Christmas": "By the time your kids are tucked in and dreaming of sugar plums, they may have seen the latest in sensational computer games . . . Doom."

On Friday, December 10, it was finally Doom time. After working for thirty straight hours testing the game for bugs, id was ready to upload the game to the Internet. A sympathetic computer administrator at the University of Wisconsin, Parkside, named David Datta volunteered to let id upload the Doom shareware to a file transfer site he maintained on the school's network. It was a good deal. The university, like most, had high-speed bandwidth for the time, which meant it could accommodate more users. The plan was that id would upload the shareware on cue, then the gamers could download it and transfer it around the world. So much for high-priced distribution. The gamers would do all the work for id themselves. Jay had announced the day before in the chat rooms that Doom would be available at the stroke of midnight on December 10.

As the midnight hour approached, the id guys gathered around Jay's computer. The office was littered with the debris of Doom's creation. Adrian and Kevin's clay models sat on the shelves. Heaps of broken chairs and keyboards were strewn on the floor. A busted garbage can crumpled in the corner. The taped outline of Dave Taylor's body collected dust bunnies on the floor. Jay had the Doom file ready to go.

Online, the Wisconsin file transfer protocol (FTP) site teemed with gamers. Though there was no way for them to communicate through a discussion board or chat room, they had ingeniously found another way to talk. The system had a means that allowed a person to create and name a file that would join another list of files on screen. Someone got the bright idea to talk simply by creating a file and assigning a name like "WHEN IS DOOM" or "WE ARE WAITING." Hundreds more waited in a special channel of Internet Relay Chat (through which people could have real-time discussions in text), where Jay was dropping clues about Doom's coming arrival.

Finally, the clock struck midnight. They would have to wait no more. Jay hit the button to upload it to the world. Everyone in the office cheered. But Jay was silent. He sat wrinkling his forehead and tapping his keyboard. There was a problem. The University of Wisconsin FTP site could accommodate only 125 people at any given moment. Apparently, 125 gamers were waiting online. Id couldn't get on.

Jay phoned David Datta in Wisconsin and hatched a plan. David would extend the number of possible users so Jay could upload Doom to the machine. And he would stay on the phone with Jay to tell him the precise moment, so Jay could be sure to get on. Everyone waited. They could hear the guy typing on the other end of the phone. Then he cleared his throat. Jay's finger hovered over the upload key. "Okay," David said, "now!" But Jay still couldn't get on.

Jay booted up the chat channel, which was filled with gamers. "Look," he typed to them, "I'm sorry, but we have to kick you all off of the Wisconsin site because I can't get this uploaded. And your choices are either I kick you all off and I get this done. Or it doesn't get uploaded at all." They scurried off. Jay hit the button one last time and connected. Doom was finally on its way out.

Elated but exhausted, the team said their good-byes and went home for their first good night's sleep in months. Only Jay stayed behind to watch the game finish uploading. After a half hour, the final bit of Doom data made its way to Wisconsin. The moment it did, ten thousand gamers swamped the site. The weight of their requests was too much. The University of Wisconsin's computer network buckled. David Datta's computer crashed.

"Oh my God," he stammered to Jay over the phone. "I've never seen anything like this."

Neither had the world.

TEN

The Doom
Generation

L ike a lot of parents in 1993, Bill Andersen knew exactly what his nine-year-old son wanted for Christmas: Mortal Kombat. The home version of the violent arcade fighting game was the hottest thing going, eclipsing even Street Fighter II with over 6.5 million sales. Andersen lamented about the game to his boss, an ambitious Democratic senator from Connecticut named Joseph Lieberman. Senator Lieberman listened intently to his chief of staff. He wanted to see the game for himself.

Mortal Kombat defied his imagination. Secret moves let players rip the spines from their opponents in gushes of blood on screen. More distressing to the senator, gamers seemed to *prefer* the brutality; the more graphically gory version of Mortal Kombat for the Sega Genesis home video game system was outselling a blood-free version for the Super Nintendo Entertainment System three to one. The success of the Sega version had dealt a staggering blow to Nintendo, which had demanded that the developer of the game, Acclaim, remove the controversial "death moves" to adhere to the company's family values. By choosing to release the blood-and-guts version, Sega became the new must-have system, racking up nearly 15 million units in sales. Nintendo's squeaky clean perch, for the first time in the industry's history, was gone.

And this wasn't the only such game. Senator Lieberman came across Night Trap, a big-budget title for the new Sega system that included live-action footage of scantily clad sorority girls — including one portrayed by Dana Plato, former child star on the TV show *Diff'rent Strokes* — being attacked by vampires. Violent films like *Reservoir Dogs* and *Terminator 2* had conquered Hollywood; now an edgier, more aggressive video game age seemed to be dawning too. On December 1, 1993, Senator Lieberman called a press conference to blow the whistle.

Beside him sat Democratic senator Herb Kohl of Wisconsin, chairperson of the Subcommittee on Juvenile Justice and chair of the Subcommittee on Government Regulation and Information. Senator Lieberman was also joined by a somber Captain Kangaroo, the children's television host Bob Keeshan. Kohl said, "The days of Lincoln Logs and Matchbox cars" had been replaced by "video games complete with screams of pain [that] are enough to give adults nightmares." Keeshan warned of "the lessons learned by a child as an active participant in violence-oriented video games . . . lessons the thinking parent would shun like a plague. Indeed it could become a plague upon their house." He urged game developers to "understand their role in a nurturing society."

Senator Lieberman took it as a call to arms. "After watching these violent video games," he said, "I personally believe it is irresponsible for some in the video game industry to produce them. I wish we could ban them."

This wasn't the first time that America's political and moral establishment had tried to save youth from their own burgeoning culture. Shortly after the Civil War, religious leaders assailed pulp novels as "Satan's efficient agents to advance his kingdom by destroying the young." In the twenties, motion pictures were viewed as the new corrupter of children, inspiring sensational media-effects research that would be cited for decades. In the fifties, Elvis was shown only from the waist up on television; *MAD* magazine's publisher, William Gaines, was brought before Congress. In the seventies, Dungeons and Dragons, with all its demons and sorcery, became associated with Satanism, particularly after a player enacting the game disappeared under the steam tunnels of a Michigan university. In the eighties, heavy metal artists like Judas Priest and Ozzy Osbourne were sued for allegedly invoking young listeners to commit suicide. In the nineties, video games were the new rock 'n' roll — dangerous and uncontrolled.

This sentiment was a long time coming. The roots were in the thirties, when pinball arcades were thought to be havens for hoodlums and gamblers. New York City mayor Fiorello La Guardia placed a ban on pinball that lasted until the mid-seventies. By then the controversial arcade game Death Race, which featured players driving over pedestrianlike stick figures, had made headlines. As the golden age of arcade and home video games exploded into a $6 billion industry in the early eighties, concerns over the potential ill effects on children exploded.

In 1982 the national Parent Teacher Association issued a statement decrying game arcades. "The PTA is concerned over the increasing number of video game sites which may have an adverse effect on many of the young people who frequent such establishments. . . . Initial studies have shown that game sites are often in close proximity to schools. In many cases there is not adequate control of access by school-age children during school hours, which compounds the problem of school absenteeism and truancy. Where little or no supervision exists, drug-selling, drug use, drinking, gambling, increased gang activities and other such behaviors may be seen."

Cities including Mesquite, Texas; Bradley, Illinois; and Snellville, Georgia, began to restrict or ban access to arcades. "Children are putting their book fees, lunch money, and all the quarters they can get their hands on into these machines," said Bradley's mayor in 1982 after he saw "hundreds of teenagers smoking marijuana in a video arcade in a nearby town." Though the Supreme Court overturned the bans following the Mesquite incident, countries including Malaysia, the Philippines, Singapore, and Indonesia not only banned video games but shut down arcades.

The media began to stoke the flames with headlines like "Video Games — Fun or Serious Threat?" in *U.S. News & World Report* and

"Video Game Fever—Peril or Payoff for the Computer Generation" in *Children's Health*. "The video game craze," said the newscaster Robert MacNeil on PBS, "is it warping young minds or educating them for the future?"

Scientists, academics, and various pundits struggled to come up with the answers. C. Everett Koop, the U.S. surgeon general, fired a sensational salvo when he stated that video games were causing "aberrations in childhood behavior. Children are into the games body and soul—everything is zapping the enemy. Children get to the point where they see another child being molested by a third child, they just sit back."

Newsweek reported on others following suit: "Dr. Nicholas Pott, who treats two such patients at a clinic at North General–Joint Disease Hospital in New York, says disturbed youths may dodge reality and human contacts as well as meteorites. The clinic director, Dr. Hal Fishkin, objects to the repeated kill-or-be-killed theme. 'We don't need more fodder for the violence mill,' he says. Others worry about subliminal messages that the medium may transmit. 'The more you can titillate your emotions, the less tolerant and patient you are going to be for things that don't deliver as fast,' says Fred Williams, professor of communications at the University of Southern California."

Despite the assertions, not all academics found substantiation for the damaging effects of video games. "There is no evidence to indicate that the games encourage social isolation, anger, antisocial behavior, and compulsivity," concluded the *Journal of Psychology*. Sherry Turkle, a sociologist at the Massachusetts Institute of Technology, praised video games' ability to provide encouragement to emotionally disturbed or retarded children. "A lot of kids who are good at this are not good at other things," she said. "This mastery experience is very important." But when the video game industry bloated and crashed in 1983, so did the rhetoric—for the time being.

Ten years later, on the morning of Thursday, December 9, 1993, Senator Lieberman reignited the cause with the first federal hearings on violent video games. The hearings were filled with impassioned statements by expert witnesses who decried the new scourge. Dr. Eugene Provenzo, a professor who authored a book called *Video Kids: Making Sense of Nintendo*, proclaimed that "video games are overwhelmingly violent, sexist, and racist." Robert Chase, president of the National Education Association, suggested that games incite real-life violence. "Because they are active rather than passive, [video games] can do more than desensitize impressionable children to violence," he said. "They actually encourage violence as the resolution of first resort by rewarding participants for killing one's opponents in the most grisly ways imaginable."

Later, Howard Lincoln, the executive vice president of Nintendo of America, and William White, vice president of marketing and communications for Sega of America, took their brawl over Mortal Kombat to the stage. Lincoln portrayed Nintendo as the martyred defender of family values. White argued that the industry was simply growing up, with more and more games being played by people over the age of eighteen. Lincoln bristled at that notion. "I can't sit here and allow you to be told that somehow the video game business has been transformed today from children to adults," he said to the panel. "It hasn't been."

After much debate and media fanfare, the hearings ended at 1:52 P.M. on December 9. Senator Lieberman declared that the video game industry had one year to develop some kind of voluntary ratings system or the government would step in with its own council. He would call a follow-up meeting in February to determine how the publishers and developers were coming along. The gamers had been warned. It was time to change their ways.

The next day, id Software released Doom.

Two hundred feet under Waxahachie, Texas, inside the U.S. Department of Energy's Superconducting Super Collider Laboratory, Bob Mustaine flew back in his chair. The government man was terrified. He wasn't the only one. Across the room, his colleagues also twitched and screamed. This had become a daily occurrence at lunchtime. In all their days studying particle physics at the country's most ambitious research facility, they had never seen anything quite as shocking as the fireballs erupting on their computer screens. Nothing—not even the multibillion-dollar subatomic shower of colliding protons—blew them away like Doom.

Several states away, in Fort Wayne, Indiana, a crowd of students convulsed in the computer lab of Taylor University. Brian Eiserloh, a gifted math student who worked as the lab supervisor, had once again unlocked the doors earlier that night to let the mob of gamers in. The lab, like most around the country, sported the fastest computers available. As a result, he and the other computer enthusiasts had been skipping sleep, class, and food to sit in front of their PCs playing the game. As programmers, they were awed by the graphics, the speed, the three-dimensional views. And as regular dudes, they had never chased each other down with shotguns before. "Oh my God!" Brian exclaimed, checking the clock. "It's seven A.M. again!" That semester, Brian, previously an A student, would get all F's.

A few thousand miles away, Nine Inch Nails' rock star Trent Reznor sauntered off a concert stage as the crowd roared. Security guards rushed to his side. Screaming groupies pushed backstage. Trent nodded and waved, heading back through the crowd. He didn't have time for this. There were more important things waiting. He stepped onto his tour bus, forsaking the drugs, the beer, the women, for the computer awaiting him. It was time again for Doom.

Scenes like these had spread around the world since the game crashed the University of Wisconsin's network on December 10. Without an ad campaign, without marketing or advance hype from the mainstream media, Doom became an overnight phenomenon in an online domain that, as fate would have it, was simultaneously beginning to explode.

Though a global network of computers had been around since the 1970s—when the U.S. government's Defense Advanced Research Projects Agency, or DARPA, linked networks of computers (the DARPAnet and, later, the Internet) together around the world—it was just starting to seep into the mainstream. This evolution began in 1989, when a computer researcher in Europe named Tim Berners-Lee wrote a program that linked information on the Internet into what was called the World Wide Web. Four years later, in 1993, two University of Illinois hackers named Marc Andreessen and Eric Bina created and released Mosaic: a free "browser" program that transformed the Web's unseemly data into more easily digestible, magazinelike pages of graphics and text. With this new user friendliness online, commercial services such as CompuServe and America Online helped court the masses. Among the earliest pioneers, not surprisingly, were gamers — the same ones who had been on online discussion groups and bulletin board systems like Software Creations for years. And all of them, it seemed, wanted to play Doom.

Schools, corporations, and government facilities blessed with fast computers, high-speed modems and, most important, people familiar enough to make them work were overtaken by the game — sometimes literally. Over the first weekend of Doom's release, computer networks slowed to a crawl from all the people playing and downloading the game. Eager gamers flooded America Online. "It was a mob scene the night Doom came out," said Debbie Rogers, forum leader of AOL's game section. "If we weren't on the other side of a phone line, there would have been bodily harm."

Hours after the game was released, Carnegie-Mellon's computer systems administrator posted a notice online saying, "Since today's release of Doom, we have discovered [that the game is] bringing the campus network to a halt. . . . Computing Services asks that all Doom players please do *not* play Doom in network-mode. Use of Doom in network-mode causes serious degradation of performance for the player's network and during this time of finals, network use is already at its peak. We may be forced to disconnect the PCs of those who are playing the game in network-mode. Again, please do *not* play Doom in network-mode."

Intel banned the game after it found its system swamped. Texas A&M erased it from its computer servers. Doom was such a problem that a computer lab supervisor at the University of Louisville created a special software to remedy the problem. "People sprint in here falling all over each other to play the game," he said, "[so] we have a nice little program that goes through the system and deletes Doom."

Early reviews echoed the gamers' glee. *PC Week* called Doom a "3-D tour de force." *Compute* said it signaled a new era in computer gaming: "The once-dull PC now bursts with power. . . . For the first time, arcade games are hot on the PC . . . the floodgates are now open." Others expressed a mix of shock and allure at the game's unprecedented gore and brutality. "The follow-up to Wolfenstein 3-D is even more brilliant, but even more disgusting," wrote a reviewer for *The Guardian* of London. "This is not a game for children or anyone sensitive to violence." As another explained, "This game is so intense, and so genuinely frightening that the deeper you venture into these shadowy chambers the closer your nose gets to the screen—an indication, I believe, of how much you, the player, enter this adventure game's other reality." Despite the pleas of his wife, the reviewer couldn't keep himself away; Doom was, he confessed, a "cyberopiate."

It was also a cash cow. The day after Doom's release, id saw profit. Even though only an estimated 1 percent of people who downloaded shareware bought the remaining game, $100,000 worth of orders were rolling in every day. Id had once joked in a press release that they expected Doom to be "the number one cause of decreased productivity in businesses around the world." The prophecy was true everywhere, it seemed, including their own.

"Good night, monkey!" Romero yelled. "You better fucking hop down! Fuck you, motherfucker! Suck it down!" Shawn Green hunched over his computer at id, his sweaty hand twitching his mouse as this barrage of insults screamed through the wall. Ostensibly Shawn had been hired to handle tech support for Doom, but it wasn't long before a more demanding job—sparring partner—took over. With the bordering office, he was regularly challenged by Romero—the ultimate gamer: the Surgeon, as Tom Hall had christened him back in the Wolfenstein days—to a round of Doom deathmatch. Shawn had quickly subsumed and surpassed Tom's role as Romero's sidekick and gaming pal. And now, to his shock, he was paying the price.

"Come on, monkey fuck!" Romero screamed, pounding his fist on the wall. "Who's your fucking daddy? Let's go!" Shawn checked his watch. It was 8:00 P.M. again. Holy shit! he thought. Another day wasted playing deathmatch. The games with Romero were taking over everything—work time, playtime, mealtime, bedtime. And now Romero was turning this into a deranged sport, hurling insults like a trash-talking jock after school. The most aggressive thing people usually did when they played video games was roll their eyes. But Doom, Shawn realized, called for something more. After winning the next round, he punched the wall back and screamed, "Eat that, motherfucker!" Romero cackled approvingly. This was how games were meant to be played.

The violent revelry was not limited to Romero. Office destruction was even more a part of daily life. Keyboards smashed against tables. Old monitors crashed into the floor. The influx of sample America Online disks and computer sound cards ended up embedded like Chinese throwing stars in the walls. One day even Carmack joined in the action.

This happened after Romero accidentally locked himself in his office. Hearing the pleas, Carmack gave the knob a twist, paused, then deduced the most obvious and immediate solution. "You know," he said, "I do have a battle-ax in my office." Carmack had recently paid five thousand dollars for the custom-made weapon—a razor-edged hatchet like something out of Dungeons and Dragons. As the other guys gathered around chanting, "Battle-ax! Battle-ax! Battle-ax!" Carmack chopped Romero free. The splintered door remained in the hall for months.

Id was on a high. Though Doom had not penetrated the mainstream like Mortal Kombat or Myst, it was the hottest game in the computer underworld since, well, Wolfenstein and Keen. The guys at id were the indisputable rulers of the shareware market, heading toward a year of multimillion-dollar earnings. And that, they soon discovered, was just the beginning. With the help of a New Yorker named Ron Chaimowitz, they were going to conquer retail.

Like the id guys, Ron had hustled his way into the computer industry. Short, balding, and in his forties, he entered the entertainment business by launching the industry's first Hispanic record label in Miami in the eighties. His big coup was to sign an up-and-coming bar mitzvah band called Gloria Estefan and the Miami Sound Machine. He also broke Julio Iglesias in the United States. Naming his company Good Times, he pursued the emerging market for home videos with low-priced, twenty-nine-minute workout tapes starring Jane Fonda. This product landed him a big deal with the Wal-Mart chain, whose executives urged him to explore what they thought was another virgin marketplace: budget computer software. Ron expanded his company into Good Times Interactive, or GTI.

Good Times Interactive first published a Richard Simmons "Deal-A-Meal" CD-ROM and a Fabio screensaver. But that was hardly enough to fill Wal-Mart's shelves, so Ron went looking into the computer game world. At first he cut deals with well-known publishers like Electronic Arts and Broderbund to repackage previously released games that had outlived their shelf life. What would be more lucrative, he realized, would be to publish his own budget games. To do this, he needed budget developers—untapped by the Electronic Arts of the world. He found them in shareware.

Shareware makers were like a farm league, he thought. He just needed to find the right team to release a retail product. Id Software, he discovered, had done gangbusters with Wolfenstein 3-D and now was causing an even greater firestorm underground with Doom. Yet Doom, to his amazement, had no retail representation. Ron had found his next Gloria Estefan.

After flying to Texas to meet with the young millionaires at id, he was surprised to find a group of long-haired kids in shorts. The office was trashed with broken computer parts, rancid pizza boxes, and an artillery of crushed soda cans. But these appearances belied a true business savvy, Ron quickly learned. After he gave the guys the big pitch about his company and his exclusive deal to shelve 2,200 Wal-Mart stores, id played it cool. The guys knew that by selling shareware they were able to eliminate all middlemen and get full dollar value for their product. Furthermore, after the lackluster performance of the Spear of Destiny retail game, they weren't about to throw the shareware model away. Why, they wanted to know, did they need GTI?

Ron didn't relent. "Look," he said, "maybe you'll sell a hundred thousand copies of Doom in shareware, but I believe if you give me a retail version of Doom and, let's call it for lack of a better term, Doom II, I think I could sell five hundred thousand or more units." Id remained unmoved. Ron went back to New York but returned to Texas two more times to plead his case. Finally, they told him their terms. If they were going to do retail, they didn't want to be treated like ordinary developers. They wanted complete creative control. They wanted to own their intellectual property. And they wanted to be featured prominently on all the merchandise so that people would know the game was coming not from GTI but from id. Ron agreed and committed to a marketing budget of $2 million for Doom II. Two million dollars was more than id had spent to develop *all* its games combined. Doom, despite its success, was still relegated to the computer underground. Doom II, which they started working on immediately, would take them mainstream.

For id, Doom II also fit into the now established and unique formula of putting out a retail product based on a shareware release, just as they had done following Commander Keen and Wolfenstein 3-D. It was the best way to milk Carmack's new graphic engines for all they were worth. Doom II would simply be a new set of levels built with the original Doom engine. While the artists and level designers worked on the sequel, Carmack could be free to research his next great graphic engine.

With the influx of cash from Doom and the promise of Doom II, the guys didn't wait long to start spending their money. They were philanthropic. Adrian bought his mother a new house in a safer neighborhood than where she had been living. Romero gave his car, a Cougar, to the manager of a local Mexican restaurant he frequented and paid for a Las Vegas vacation for his grandparents. Carmack bought $3,200 of computer equipment for his former computer teacher at Shawnee Mission East grade school. "I wanted to buy them things that will allow them to explore other areas," he said, "not just what's in books." He also put aside $100,000 to bail an old high school friend out of jail.

Mainly, though, the guys at id spent money on their cars. Kevin bought a Corvette. Adrian bought the Trans Am sports car he'd always wanted. Dave Taylor got an Acura NSX. (The guys even chipped in and bought a new leather couch for the office so, in part, Dave could have something nice to pass out on next time he got what was now widely known as Doom-induced motion sickness.) Carmack and Romero themselves celebrated by going Ferrari shopping.

At a showroom, they admired a gleaming new Testarossa that listed at $90,000. Carmack was treating cars like he treated his games; he had already grown somewhat tired of his current engine. What he really wanted was one of these. "Oh my God," said Romero. "Holy shit! Now *that* is a car. That is fucking daddy car right there! Dude, I can't believe you're getting that car." Carmack paid cash for a red one to match his 328. Romero bought a "fly yellow" Testarossa for himself. They parked them side by side in id's lot—just in the right place so that, during work, they could gaze down at their ultimate machines.

But Carmack's Ferrari didn't stay in the lot for long. Within days he drove it over to Norwood Autocraft and started on the modifications— he wanted to get the car, which ran at four hundred horsepower, at least twice as strong. Bob Norwood, who had become Carmack's automotive mentor, had a master plan: to install a twin turbo system that would not just double but triple the car's horsepower. For added energy, they put in a computer-controlled device that would inject a burst of nitrous oxide. While Romero was enthralled enough by the pure aesthetics of the Ferraris, for Carmack the cars were now less means of a joyride than new engineering materials to be modified to his liking.

As the id guys soon discovered, Carmack wasn't the only gamer who liked getting under the hood.

"**Hey,**" Romero told Carmack one day at the office, "there's something you have to see." He booted up Doom—or at least what was *supposed* to be Doom—on his computer. Instead, the trumpeting theme of the *Star Wars* movie began to play. The screen filled with not Doom's familiar opening chamber but instead a small, steel-colored room. Romero hit the space bar, and a door slid open. "Stop that ship!" a voice commanded from within the game. Carmack watched as Romero jolted down the hall past bleeping droids, white Stormtroopers, laser guns, the deep bellows of Darth Vader. Some hacker had completely altered Doom into a version of *Star Wars*. Wow, Carmack thought. This is gonna be great. We did the Right Thing after all.

The Right Thing was programming Doom in such a way that willful players could more easily create something like this: StarDoom, a modification, or mod, of their original game. It was an idea hatched after seeing the early modifications that players were creating for Wolfenstein 3-D. That small phenomenon had caught Carmack by surprise, even though he had long hacked games like Ultima himself. The Wolfenstein modifications were different, however, because players weren't just finding the code that they could change to increase their characters' health; instead, they were changing their characters altogether, replacing the bosses with Barney.

Though Carmack and Romero were intrigued and inspired by these actions, they were concerned over the destructive quality of the mods. Players had to erase the original Wolfenstein code and replace it with their own images; once a Nazi was changed into Barney, there was no way to bring the Nazi back quickly. For Doom, Carmack organized the data so players could replace sound and graphics in a nondestructive manner. He created a subsystem that separated the media data, called WADs (an acronym suggested by Tom Hall, it stood for Where's All the Data?), from the main program. Every time someone booted up the game, the program would look for the WAD file of sounds and images to load in. This way, someone could simply point the main program to a *different* WAD without damaging the original contents. Carmack would also upload the source code for the Doom level-editing and utilities program so that the hackers could have the proper tools with which to create new stuff for the game.

This was a radical idea not only for games but for any media. It was as if a Nirvana CD came with tools to let listeners dub their own voices for Kurt Cobain's or a Rocky video let viewers excise every cranny of Philadelphia for ancient Rome. Though there had been some level-editing programs released in the past, no programmer — let alone *owner* — of a company had released the guts of what made his proprietary program tick. Gamers would not have access to Carmack's graphical engine, but the stuff he was making available was more than just subtly giving them the keys. It was not only a gracious move but an ideological one—a leftist gesture that empowered the people and, in turn, loosened the grip of corporations. Carmack was no longer a boy dreaming of computers in his Kansas City bedroom; he was the twenty-three-year-old owner of a multimillion-dollar company, and he could do whatever the fuck he wanted. He could live the Hacker Ethic big time.

It wasn't a popular way to rule. With the exception of Romero, the only other hacker-minded programmer at id, Carmack's generosity caused much consternation at the company—especially among the more conservative-minded businessmen, like Jay and Kevin. "This is a *crazy* idea," Kevin said. "No one's ever given away their tools to make new content. And we have to worry about legal questions. What if someone takes our content and combines it with their product and releases it? What if someone takes all the content that's developed on the Internet and sells it on the shelf and suddenly we're competing with our own product?"

Carmack rolled his eyes. They didn't get this at all, he thought, because they weren't programmers so they didn't *get* the hacker joy of it. They weren't really gamers either. They weren't part of the gaming community that was growing up there. To Carmack's appreciation, Romero came loudly to his defense. "Dudes," Romero told the others, "we're not going to lose that much money. We're making a ton of money right now. Big deal. Who cares?"

Even before Doom was officially released, plenty of people certainly did care about the ability to modify it. One group was so eager, they hacked the leaked alpha version of Doom. As the official release approached, Carmack had e-mailed the Wolfenstein mod makers about the new faculties in Doom. He didn't anticipate how far these gamers would go. In only a matter of weeks after Doom's release, hackers began releasing crude level or map-editing programs. These tools let players modify existing rooms of the game, say, adjusting walls, moving around floors, or making other minor adjustments.

On January 26, 1994, the hackers got all the more real. A student at the University of Canterbury in New Zealand named Brendon Wyber uploaded a free program called the Doom Editor Utility, or DEU. Wyber had created the program with the help of an international online coalition of gamers who, through bone-breaking hack work, had found a way to break apart Doom's code. Though Carmack had provided source code, he gave no clue of how actually to tear the goods apart. The DEU broke everything apart and explained how to make a level from the ground up. Soon a Belgian student named Raphael Quinet collaborated with Wyber to release a more readable version of the DEU, which hit the Net on February 16, 1994. "You can do almost anything to any level," they promised in the program, "move, add or remove monsters and powerups, change the wall colours and positions, create new lifts, doors, acid pools, crushing ceilings . . . or even create a new level from scratch!"

The DEU was a watershed. Suddenly, all those with the gumption could make a level of a game. They didn't need to be programmers or artists or anything. If they wanted they could just tweak what was there. Or they could dress it up, using their own sounds, images, ideas. There could be Doom Barneys, Doom Simpsons, Doom shopping malls, Doom subways. A University of Michigan student named Greg Lewis delved further into the netherworld of Doom code and created a program called DeHackEd. This software — also distributed for free — did the unthinkable by allowing a user to modify not the WADs containing the graphics, sounds, and levels but the very *core* of the game itself, known as the executable file. The executable contained all the technical information for how the game was played: how monsters behaved, how weapons fired, how text was displayed.

"DeHackEd is capable of heavily restructuring the way Doom works," Lewis wrote in the file describing his program. "Make fireballs invisible, make missiles do 2000 points of damage, make demons float! Edit the Ammo tables to help your struggling Marine with more ammo. Edit the Frame tables, and create new looking items, or extra-fast shooting weapons. And save your changes in patch files to distribute to your friends. Create new types of deathmatches, with plasma 'mines' and super-fast wimpy rockets. Wad developers can modify monster types to distribute with their levels . . . great new possibilities!"

Hacker tools for Doom became another means of immersion in what was already the most immersive game around. Doom immersed players in a fast-action 3-D world. It immersed competitors in an arena of deathmatching where they could hunt each other down. The Doom mod tools immersed programmers as creators, as ones who could take this incredible world and sculpt it to their own divine desires. The game made them into little gods. Doom hackers began swapping their levels for free in forums on AOL, CompuServe, and across the Internet. Gamers who had been failing out of school because of deathmatching now had an even more addictive compulsion: hacking. They hacked all night. They hacked all day. They even hacked naked; at the Taylor University computer lab, gamers stripped down for regular "skinny-hacking" parties. Doom wasn't just a game, it was a culture.

And it was a culture that made the skeptics within id even more queasy. After much arguing in the company, Jay was granted permission to post legal terms for prospective Doom hackers. "Id Software requires no fees or royalties," he posted online. "You may require user payment for your work; Your utility *must* not work with the shareware version of Doom; You *must* represent that your utility is not an id Software product and id Software cannot and will not provide support for your product, nor for Doom after the data has been changed by your product; You may be required to include some *legal* text in your utility to make our lawyers happy; There may be more or some of the above may not be in the final document. It depends on my frame of mind at the time. :) . . . I am sorry to have to resort to the *post*," he concluded, "but . . . there is no other way to keep this process under control."

But control at id Software was all the more difficult to be found.

By the spring of 1994, id had a new answering machine message: "If you are calling to discuss some great idea you have on how you can make money with our product," it said, "please press five now."

As the Doom phenomenon grew, the big leagues began to take notice. Universal Pictures with Ivan Reitman, director of *Ghostbusters* and *Stripes*, optioned the rights for a Doom movie. Other companies, including George Lucas's LucasArts, began developing Doom-like games. Even Microsoft, the powerhouse of the industry, was entranced; the company saw Doom as the perfect program to flaunt the bold new multimedia features of its upcoming operating system called Windows.

To show off Windows's potential, Microsoft enticed John Carmack to port a short demonstration of the game. The company ended up using the game at the Computer Game Developers Conference to promote the power of the platform. "Microsoft is committed to delivering top-notch multimedia functionality in Windows," said Brad Chase, a general manager of the personal operating systems division at Microsoft. He said games were one of the "largest, most important categories of multimedia applications."

Soon, however, many began to marvel at how id might make companies like Microsoft or IBM look obsolete. Id had taken the shareware phenomenon and transformed it into a recipe for addiction. Doom was so compelling that people just *had* to have the full dose. Some dubbed it "heroinware." *Forbes* magazine published a gushing article titled "Profits from the Underground" about how id, in fact, was making companies like Microsoft obsolete. "Privately held id Software doesn't release financials," it read, "but from what I can flush out about the company's profit margin, it makes Microsoft look like a second-rate cement company." The writer calculated that id's estimated $10 million in revenues would give them a profit margin that would rival Microsoft's. "What happens to this kind of business when the data superhighway arrives? . . . No sales force, no inventory costs, no royalties to Nintendo or Sega, no marketing costs, no advertising costs, no executive parking spaces. This is a new and exciting business model, not just for games, and not even just for software, but for a host of products and services that can be sold or delivered via an electronic underground."

The mainstream media picked up the ball. *The New York Times, USA Today,* and *Variety*—the movie industry's trade magazine—published articles about the business and cultural breakthroughs of Doom. Journalists came to Dallas to see who was behind the phenomenon and reveled in the idiosyncratic world of long-haired gamers and souped-up $200,000 Ferraris. Id wasn't just a company that made a killer game. It was the portent of something new, something unseen: rich, young, creative guys who were bucking all the sensible routes of traditional business for this strange amorphous thing that, at the time, was not even widely known as the Internet. "Everyone is talking about the power of the information superhighway," Jay boasted to *The Dallas Morning News*. "We're the living proof." The industry needed a rock star, he realized; id was it.

Like any good rock stars, the company had an air of controversy. Because of the violence, China was considering banning Doom; Brazil, in fact, would later outlaw the game. Even Wal-Mart, which would be the major retail outlet for Doom II's release, was beginning to balk at the content. But just as Doom was becoming positioned as the next great scourge of violent games, a safety valve was pulled.

Since Senator Lieberman's federal hearings on game violence in December 1993, the industry had raced to find a response that would curtail the threat of government involvement. After another hearing in the spring of 1994, the result was the Interactive Digital Software Association: a trade organization representing all the major publishers joined for the purpose of self-regulation. By the fall of 1994, the IDSA had a voluntary system, the Entertainment Software Rating Board, which would assign ratings much as the movie industry did: T for Teen, M for Mature. The first game that would bear its mark would be Doom II.

Id not only escaped unscathed but found its bad-boy image further enhanced. The hearings had, ironically, heralded a new, meaner, more violent era in video games, and the gamers of the world couldn't get enough. Sega's Night Trap sold out around the country. With the ratings system in place, publishers felt freer to release edgier content. Even Nintendo joined in the party, making plans to release a version of Mortal Kombat II—gore and all. But no developer was positioned quite like id. Now, as the media and fans descended, all it needed was a face, someone they could pin their worship on. At id, there was no competition. When it came time for a lead singer of the band to emerge, John Romero wasn't only perfect, he was the only one who wanted the job.

"We're not worthy, we're not worthy, we're not worthy," the gamers chanted, bowing at Romero's feet. It was a scorching hot afternoon in Austin, Texas. Romero and Shawn Green were standing inside Austin

Virtual Gaming, a six-hundred-square-foot shop above a coffee shop on the main strip outside the University of Texas. Five Doom junkies from the school's zoology department and local high-tech companies had pooled their cash to open this place just a few weeks before. They figured they weren't the only ones in town hooked on id's demonic creation. So they networked a small fleet of personal computers with twenty-seven-inch screens and began charging gamers eight dollars per hour to deathmatch. The occasion this day was the game room's first official Doom tournament. And, to the elation of the few dozen gamers gathered around the red-pulsing monitors to play, Romero—one of the guys who *wrote* the game!—was here to fight.

Though few if any of the gamers had seen pictures of Romero, they figured he was the guy wearing the black T-shirt with the militaristic Doom logo on the front and the bold white words "Wrote It" on the back. The shirt was Romero's own modification. After id had printed up a bunch of promotional tees, he suggested they add the phrase "Wrote It" for their own. He even sent his mother a Doom shirt with the words "My Son Wrote It" on the back. (Carmack preferred his own favorite shirt—a yellow smiley face with a bloody bullet hole piercing the forehead.)

Romero had taken to wearing the "Wrote It" shirt everywhere—around the office, around town, around gaming conventions. The shirt had a Moses-like effect. Gamers would spot him in the shirt and do a celebrity double take, parting as he moved through the crowd. The brave few would venture forward with sweaty palms and shaky hands. It happened first outside a CompUSA when the clerk came sheepishly after Romero, who was getting into his yellow Testarossa, and asked for an autograph. Such displays were becoming a regular occurrence, especially when he donned the "Wrote It" shirt. Gamers began not only asking for autographs but literally falling to their knees and echoing the "we're not worthy!" refrain that *Saturday Night Live* characters Wayne and Garth bestowed upon rock royalty. The other guys at id couldn't believe it. In fact, they were embarrassed by it: *We aren't Metallica, we're gamers.*

But as the enigma around the company grew, the fans and media wanted more and more information about just who id *was*. In response, the guys created a news file that gamers could obtain by sending a message request or, in technical slang, "fingering" id's computers. They started posting regular updates about technical matters, but soon the news expanded into lifestyle, giving the skinny on, among other things, the status of Carmack's and Romero's Ferraris.

Fans began to build a sense of wonder about the company, which, as they discovered, was spilling over into real life. This was something new, as Jay described it — "nerd worship." And there was no one who liked being worshiped more than Romero. Not only had he printed up the shirts but he was starting to change his appearance, growing out his dark hair, wearing his contacts more often. But he didn't look at the bowing gamers as his minions. He saw them as his peers, his friends. Here were all these people, he thought as he looked down on their bowing skulls, who loved games as much as he did. As the Doom momentum built, after all, Romero was becoming as addicted to the game as his fans were. He and Shawn were now deathmatching on a regular basis, staying long into the night. When he wasn't playing Doom, Romero was talking about Doom. He was a regular attendant in the burgeoning Doom chat rooms and message boards and newsgroups, discussing the latest mods, deathmatch tourneys, and technical happenings. To the outside world, Romero *was* id.

This was as much the others' doing as it was his. The other owners had no interest in courting the fans or the press. Jay, id's "biz guy," did his share, but that came with the territory. When the press wanted to strut out one of the Doom gods, one of the guys who Wrote It, Romero fit the bill. And as Carmack, Adrian, and the rest readily acknowledged, Romero was *good* at it — funny, likable, bouncing off the walls with energy. He had been the company's biggest cheerleader from the moment he saw the Dangerous Dave in Copyright Infringement demo. When he hyped the company, it wasn't merely the hype of an owner, it was the hype of id's biggest fan.

The language of that hype was the language of deathmatch: confident to the point of egotism, inspired to the point of confrontation. Id was the ruler of the world, and Romero was quick to make everyone aware of just how great they were and how much greater they would become. *"The Plan,"* he posted online, "[is] to get the entire world running NeXTSTEP for development, get everyone connected on the Internet, and own a Testarossa TR512." Romero lashed out at the popular and emerging operating systems. "DOS blows. DOS-Extenders create developer *Hell.* Windows sux."

By the time he showed up in Austin for the Doom deathmatch in the summer of 1994, Romero was exuding white-hot game-god heat. With the fans bowing, a reporter descended on him and asked why he had come to this tournament. Romero puffed out his chest and said, "So we can beat everybody!" Romero and Shawn found their seats while others played. It was silent except for the sounds of fingers rattling on keys. But all that changed as the id guys began to play.

Romero hurled a few shotgun blasts into an opponent and yelled, "Eat that, fucker!" The sheepish guy on the other computer looked up in fear. Shawn knew that look—the look of gamer who had never heard true, unbridled smack-talk, just like he'd been the first time he had heard Romero insult him during a game. But now Shawn was a pro and joined right in. "Suck it down, monkey fuck!" he called, after firing a few blasts from his BFG. The gamers cowered. They would learn.

Romero savored the long drive back to Dallas in his Ferrari. Life was good for the twenty-six-year-old. He had been beaten down by his father and stepfather, picked himself back up, and now, after all this time, finally arrived. He really was the Ace Programmer, the Future Rich Person. He had mended his relationship with his parents, who now had a new perspective on their son's wayward days at the arcades. He loved his new wife, Beth, and sons, Michael and Steven, who, though still in California, could proudly call him their dad. He had become the man he had envisioned all those years before.

One night back at the office, Romero decided to share his feeling of success. He stepped into Carmack's office to find his partner, as usual, sitting at his PC with a Diet Coke. Since Doom's release, Carmack had immersed himself in side projects: programming conversions or ports of Doom for other game platforms, including the Atari Jaguar and the new console from Sega. Id was getting good money for the gigs,

$250,000 from Atari alone. But for Carmack it wasn't the cash that was intriguing, it was the opportunity to get back into the trenches.

This was what he truly loved: the work, the rolling up of the sleeves, the challenging of his intellect. And he at least somewhat appreciated the rush of fortune and fame; on a recent trip home he told his father, the renowned Kansas City anchorman, that he would soon be as famous as he was. Like Romero, Carmack had found peace with his parents, who now admired and supported his work—his mother played Commander Keen in her spare time. He had even gone out on a few dates with a woman whose parents owned a Chinese restaurant he frequented. Still, he was spending the majority of his days and nights at id. Nothing pleased him quite like sharpening his chops with low-level programming work. He would need the skills, he knew, when he went off to create his next big game engine.

But while he had been here, he was beginning to notice, Romero was gone: deathmatching, doing interviews, corresponding with fans online. Something was changing, slipping away. And the work, Carmack thought, was beginning to suffer. Doom II was falling behind schedule. While Romero was out being the company rock star, the levels that he had promised to create were not getting done. In fact, the company was now relying on other level designers—Sandy Petersen and a new employee, American McGee—to get the majority of the levels done. Out of the thirty-two levels of Doom II, Carmack noted, only six were shaping up to be Romero's.

Romero had his explanation—the levels he made simply took more time. But Carmack suspected something else: Romero was losing his focus. In addition to the interviews and the deathmatching, Romero was now acting as executive producer on an upcoming game by Raven, the company they knew from Wisconsin. Romero had approached Carmack at one point with the idea to milk the Doom engine for all it was worth. "Let's make some more games using our technology," he said. "Let's get some stuff out there because we can get some money off of this. And Raven's a good group that would be perfect for licensing the engine and making a great game that we can publish." Carmack agreed but without enthusiasm. How much bigger did they need to get?

For Romero, though, it wasn't just about getting bigger, it was about fun. He loved playing games. He lived for playing games. And there was no game that was more fun than Doom. The deal with Raven would give him more games to play. This night in Carmack's office, Romero spelled out his new life code: It was time to enjoy id's accomplishments. No crunch mode. No more bloodshot nights. "No more death schedules," he happily said.

Carmack remained quiet. The cursor on his monitor pulsed. In the past, Romero would have stayed here by his side, experimenting with the engine on screen, testing bugs until the sun came up. Tonight, Carmack watched the guy in the "Wrote It" shirt walk out the door.

ELEVEN

Quakes

Everyone has unfulfilled dreams. Maybe the dreams are too costly or time-consuming: fly a plane, drive a race car. Maybe they're too far-out: fight an alien space war, stalk a vampire. Or maybe they're illegal: streak through the suburbs, hunt down the boss with a sawed-off shotgun. But the dreams are there, nonetheless, animating minds every day. This is why there is a multibillion-dollar industry that lets people explore these fantasies the best way technology allows. This is why there are video games.

Of course, video games don't let people really *live* their dreams. They let gamers live a developer's *simulation* of a dream. The action is digital. It's confined to a computer or a television or a handheld device. Players experience it through their eyes, ears, and fingertips. But when they're done careening down the Daytona Speedway or storming an interstellar military base, they feel as if they've really been somewhere, as if they've momentarily transcended their sac of fat and bones, their office politics, their mounting bills. Games let them escape, learn, recharge. Games are necessary.

This belief has existed since ancient Greece, when Plato said,

"Every man and woman should play the noblest games and be of another mind from what they are at present." In the fifties, the anthropologist Johan Huizinga wrote that "play . . . is a *significant* function . . . which transcends the immediate needs of life and imparts meaning to the action. All play means something." He suggested a new name for the human species: "Homo Ludens," Man the Player. Marshall McLuhan wrote in the sixties that "a society without games is one sunk in the zombie trance of the automaton. . . . Games are popular art, collective, social *reactions* to the main drive or actions of any culture. . . . The games of a people reveal a great deal about them. . . . [They] are a sort of artificial paradise like Disneyland or some Utopian vision by which we interpret and complete the meaning of our daily lives."

By 1994 there was no more utopian vision of a game than the Holodeck. And the dream of this virtual world simulator on *Star Trek* was inching from science fiction to reality. Neal Stephenson's sci-fi novel *Snow Crash*, published in 1992, imagined the Metaverse—an alternate reality similar to the "cyberspace" envisioned in William Gibson's 1984 novel, *Neuromancer.* The Internet was taking off, capable of connecting humans into such a domain. Arcades buzzed with virtual reality games—unseemly machines with big, clunky headsets that, for about five dollars, immersed a player in a first-person polygon world. A new generation of programmers was devoting their work, their lives, to realizing the Holodeck. As John Carmack said, "It's a moral imperative that we must create this." His contribution would be Quake.

The development of every id game began with Carmack telling the other guys what his next graphic engine would be capable of doing. When Carmack first described his vision of the Quake technology, Romero nearly combusted. They had talked about doing Quake, after all, for years. The idea came straight out of their old Dungeons and Dragons games; Quake was the character Carmack had invented who possessed a powerful hammer, capable of demolishing buildings, as well as a supernatural conjuring object, Hellgate Cube, floating above his head. Id had first worked on a Quake game back in the early Commander Keen days but gave up because they felt the technology was not yet powerful enough to do their idea justice. Now, Carmack said, the time had come. The technology was ready to make the most convincingly immersive 3-D experience yet, the first fast-action, first-person game to support groups of players competing together over the Internet. Not only would Quake be id's most ambitious game yet but it could be the world's.

Romero exploded with ideas. "A full 3-D engine!" he said. "Hell, we can have forests and stuff. . . . The artifact that we talked about in Keen—the hammer of thunderbolts—that's going to be your main weapon in Quake. And you're going to have this transdimensional artifact, the Hellgate Cube, a cube that orbits your head, and it will just do things! It'll have its personality and its own programming to where you feel like it's a different entity; it'll attack people if you're good to it, if you're whacking on someone and taking damage off someone, then the cube feeds off of pain basically in a certain distance around it. So the more pain you do the happier the cube is, so it will start doing things for you, it will heal you when you get screwed up or it will teleport you somewhere else. And if you don't fight for a long time, it'll start damaging you or it would take off and maybe it'll come back one day."

Romero was so excited, he just *had* to share the news with all id's fans. "The next game is going to blow Doom all to hell," he typed. "Doom totally sucks in comparison to our next game, Quake: The Fight for Justice! Quake is going to be a bigger step over Doom than Doom was over Wolf 3-D (ya know—Doom = Pong)." Romero smacked his keyboard and uploaded the message to the Internet.

But with Doom II still in development, all the Quake talk began striking the other owners as premature. "Romero's going out and telling people what we're doing," Adrian lamented to Kevin and Jay, "even though we know that all our stuff is going to change, so there's no need to tell the public all these plans. Romero just likes all the attention, which is why he does it."

Jay, having been flamed by gamers on numerous occasions after id missed its promised deadlines for Doom, heard Adrian loud and clear. "Let's not talk about stuff at this point that's still projection," he told Romero. "Because if it doesn't come to fruition, there's backlash." Romero agreed but soon caved in once again. "Quake won't be just a game," he told *Computer Player* magazine, "it will be a movement." He had to be stopped.

Late one night in September 1994, Romero sat at his computer, tweaking the final sounds for Doom II. With the game near completion, he took it upon himself to polish the audio effects for the final enemy or "boss" of the game, called the Icon of Sin. To win the game, the player had to shoot the Icon—a hideous beast that spit out cubes that could spawn into other monsters—between the eyes.

Romero ran around in a special mode that allowed him to, for purposes of testing the game, pass through walls—effectively going behind the images the player would see in the game. He had just passed behind a wall in back of the Icon of Sin when he stopped cold. *Did I just see my own face?* Shrugging it off, he went on with his work, thinking maybe he had been there too long. But then, as he ran behind the beast again, he thought he saw his face once more. How weird, he thought, slowly creeping back. And then, to his shock, he saw it: a digital copy of his head, decapitated and bloody, writhing on a stick. "No fucking way!" he said.

Romero raced his character back around and fired a shot at the Icon of Sin, then followed the trajectory of the rocket: it sailed through the beast, through a back wall, into the hidden chamber, and smack into Romero's head—which would twitch in agony. Romero got the joke. The player thought he was winning the game by shooting the beast, but in fact he was shooting Romero. Romero *was* the Icon of Sin.

The next morning, word spread around the office that Romero had found the Easter egg and left one of his own. Adrian and Kevin booted up the final scene of the game and began firing off the rockets at the beast. All the while, they heard demonic sounds—like a backward track of a Judas Priest song—coming from the hidden room. The words were indistinguishable but, when reversed, perfectly clear: "To win the game," the voice bellowed, "you must kill me, John Romero." With another blast of the rocket, the Icon of Sin was dead.

On October 10, 1994, Doom II hit the Limelight. Limelight, a onetime church in New York City that had been converted into a gothic nightclub, was the site of the "Doomsday" press party for Doom II. TSI Communications, the high-powered public relations company hired by GTI to break id Software into the mainstream, used a sizable chunk of the game's $2 million marketing budget to convert the club into a hellish mansion of demons and gore. A holograph machine near the front door projected beasts from the game. The techno-rock soundtrack from the game pumped through the halls. A giant deathmatch arena constructed in the center of the church pulsed with Doom players who had been flown in for the event.

Reporters representing every paper from *The Wall Street Journal* to *The Village Voice* mingled through the crowd with awe and confusion. There was a growing fascination with computer culture and the Internet, buoyed by that month's release of Netscape Navigator: the new Web browser from the creators of Mosaic. Though many had heard about the underground success of Doom, they had never witnessed the strange new world firsthand. Even Audrey Mann, the publicist in charge of the event for TSI, was taken aback. Her company had long represented two of the heaviest hitters in the high-tech industry, IBM and Sony, but they had never faced the unique challenges that came with the id Software account. Launching Doom II brought a whole new vernacular to the PR industry, words like *deathmatch* and *frag* and *mods*. They debated the appropriateness of terms like *kick ass* in a press release. "How many ways can we say 'mutilate'?" they joked. But when they saw the response at the Limelight, they realized they had underestimated their client. "We didn't think it was worth a story," Audrey said. "We thought we were just launching a *game*."

Doom II, it was clear that night, would become not just a game but, in fact, a movement. Reporters who had previously ignored Jay's pitches about the company now besieged any id gamer they could corner. Protesters muscled in too. With violent films like *Natural Born Killers* and *Pulp Fiction* on the radar, Doom was perceived as yet another threat to the youth of America. During Jay's speech to the crowd, a man stood up in the rafters and screamed, "You should be ashamed for making such violent games that children can play!" Everyone fell silent, looking to Jay for a response.

"Sir," Jay said calmly, "I have two children, I would never do anything that would hurt them. To some extent we're creating the Three Stooges of interactive media with guns. If you look at this from the top down, this is more humorous than it is damaging." But the protester wouldn't relent, screaming about violence and Satan until finally Shawn Green, who was sitting next to Jay onstage, rose to the microphone and yelled, "Suck it down, dude!" The crowd laughed. Everyone, it seemed, was on id's side.

Six hundred thousand copies of Doom II were sold to retail stores for the initial release, guaranteeing that it would be among the bestselling games in history. The inventory was supposed to last a quarter. It lasted one month. After the Doomsday event, the mainstream media snowballed around the game. Anyone who'd missed the so-called Doom cult the first time around jumped on board, while the ones who had been hip the whole time trumpeted their pioneer status.

Journalists from all walks cooed over the game's immersion, the marketing scheme, the violence, the great American success story. "It's as close to virtual reality as you're going to get," gushed the *Chicago Sun-Times*. "Virtual Mayhem and Real Profits," headlined *The New York Times*. *The Economist* published an essay titled "Doomonomics," which academically explored how "the drippingly gory computer game took its creators from obscurity to riches. . . . [It's a tale that] holds a lesson of striking relevance to tomorrow's information economy." *The Red Herring* marveled that id had "an entire file filled with letters from VCs and private investors who are just dying to sink cash into [the company]" — yet the company was remaining staunchly and profitably independent.

Of course the millions of players who were *living* the game could give two flying fireballs about any of those things. What was really selling the game, they knew, was deathmatch. And the person who wanted to own deathmatch was DWANGO Bob.

DWANGO Bob, a.k.a. Bob Huntley, was a thirty-four-year-old who looked and behaved like a Texas version of the Woodstock emcee, Wavy Gravy. He'd gotten into the high-tech industry by producing interactive kiosks for gas stations throughout Houston. After some years, though, he began to burn out on the fumes. He was looking for something else, and he found it in Doom.

During the early part of 1994, the DWANGO guys were falling behind on work, staying at the office until 2:00 A.M., lying to their wives so they could play the game. Bob's partner, Kee Kimbrell, had become yet another blissful victim of Doom addiction. Bob pulled Kee aside one night and said, "If every machine is not clear of Doom, you're fired." Kee didn't have the nerve; instead of deleting the game, he renamed the file—so Bob wouldn't find it—and kept on playing. When Bob found out the truth, something clicked. *If these guys are this passionate about this game, maybe there's something to it.* Bob sat down for one round, and his life changed forever.

The thrill, he found, was in the head-to-head competition, playing against real live people over a local area computer network. With some research online, he realized he was hardly alone. Doom deathmatch was taking over lives: fans hijacked their office networks to play all weekend, threw their kids out of their basements to wire together their own arenas, and put off so many trips to the bathroom that at least one player (who had been consuming Ding Dong cupcakes during a marathon match) explosively defecated in his pants midgame.

How incredible would it be, Bob and Kee mused, if a gamer could just go out and pick up a game against random people who were far away—in some other house, some other room, some other state! What if there could be a computer hub or server that would turn the game into the virtual equivalent of a pickup basketball game on a neighborhood court—except that people could play together from anywhere in the world. Problem was, Doom didn't work that way, it supported only modem-to-modem play. This meant that, to compete, one gamer would use a modem to telephone another's computer; once connected, they could play against each other. Undaunted, Kee looked over at Bob and said, "You know, I think that we can get this to play over a phone line."

"Okay," Bob said, seeing dollar signs, "you've got six weeks. If you get it together, then I promise to get us an introduction to id Software." Bob was bluffing. He didn't know id from Shinola. But, seeing as that they were Texas boys, he figured they'd be easy enough to enlist. They weren't. His calls, like so many others, went unanswered. Five weeks later, Kee sped from his house on his bike to tell Bob the news. "I've got it!" he said, panting. "Give me ten minutes!"

Bob sat down at his computer while Kee banged away at his keyboard in another room. Ten minutes later Bob got the signal and booted up the program Kee had created. He saw a simple little interface that streamlined all the difficulties of multiplayer action. With this program, anyone could dial up through a phone and connect to a computer system that hosted the game. Instead of having to be in one place, someone could just dial a number, join a chat room, then click off to play three other people in Doom. "Okay," Kee said, smiling, "now we have to get ahold of id."

Bob lowered his eyes and broke the news. "Id's not talking," he said. "Hell, they ain't even answering the phone." He tried more faxes, letters, e-mails, but nothing worked.

Just as they were about to lose hope, Bob came across an article about the upcoming Doom II press event at the Limelight in New York. He called id's publicity firm. "I've got a big opportunity for id," he said, "and just *have* to get into the event." The guy on the phone told him people from all over the world were trying to get in. Forget about it. But Bob persisted and sweet-talked him down. "Okay," the guy finally relented, "if you want to fly up from Houston, I'll see what I can do." Bob hung up the phone and turned to Kee. "We're going to New York," he said.

Kee and Bob bought plane tickets with frequent flier mileage and booked a room at a Holiday Inn in New Jersey. With their last business in shambles, they were living off bread crumbs. They banked everything on their new service for Doom, which they had dubbed the Dial Up Wide Area Network Games Operation, or DWANGO. Hours before the event, Bob and Kee showed up at the club and met the guy from TSI. "Okay," he said hurriedly, handing them two T-shirts, "put these on."

Bob and Kee squeezed into the small black T-shirts, which had the militaristic Doom logo on the front and "contestant" on the back. The only way they could get in, the publicist told them, was to pose as contestants for the Doom deathmatch. Bob and Kee looked around. Behind them were dozens of skinny guys half their age in the same T-shirts. Bob gulped. Sure he and Kee had played Doom, but they sucked compared with the hard-core gamers. Now they were supposed to *play* the game against these champs on a stage *in front of the national press*? They thanked the guy, then snuck across the street to fuel up at a bar.

They stumbled back later to find the TSI guy screaming. "You missed the lineup! Hurry up. Get inside!" Bob was first up for battle. He got wiped out within minutes. Kee lost just as quickly. Games done, they went to find id. They ended up tracking down Jay Wilbur, who looked at these beer-soaked, middle-aged guys in tight contestant shirts and shrugged them off. "No time, not interested, go away," he said, and disappeared into the crowd.

Just as they were moping toward the door, Kee spotted Romero, with his unmistakable long, dark hair and Doom "Wrote It" T-shirt. They waited nervously for their break, then closed in. "We made this software!" Kee said eagerly. "You can dial in with your modem to a server and you can play other people over the modem! Here's the only disk we got! Guard it with your life!"

After the party, Romero told Jay about the disk. The DWANGO idea wasn't breakthrough—id had thought of it themselves but just hadn't gotten around to programming it; since Quake was going to be playable over the Internet, they had figured they would hold off on creating the multiplayer online feature. Anyway, Jay concurred, he certainly didn't want some bozos doing the job, not when they had companies like AOL and Time Warner calling. "Well," Romero said, "maybe I'll take five minutes and see what this disk does."

Back home in Texas, Romero popped the disk in his hard drive and dialed up the Houston number. After his modem whooshed, he saw a message on screen from Kee: "Come on, let's try a game." Next thing he knew, there they were—Kee in Houston, Romero in Dallas—playing a spontaneous pickup game of Doom II deathmatch. Romero picked up the phone. "That is fucking cool!" he said. "Cuz my whole thing is, I like staying up late and I want to play people whenever the fuck I want to and I don't want to have to wake up my buddy at three in the morning and go, 'Hey, uh, wanna get your skull cracked? Heh heh?' That's just not cool. And I want to do it 24/7. At any time. This is it! This is the thing that you can dial into and just play!"

But Carmack and the other owners weren't enthused. As far as Carmack was concerned, this smacked of yet another of Romero's diversions—like interviews, Raven, deathmatching—to distract him from the real work at hand, making games. Romero argued that if they could get online play going and further build the Doom community, it would surely help grow the company.

After having Jay negotiate a deal for 20 percent of the DWANGO revenues, Romero spent every night working on the project, which would be released with the shareware of Heretic—the game Romero had been overseeing for Raven. On December 23, 1994, he phoned Bob and Kee and said, "I'm fixing to upload this. Do you think you can handle it? Because when it hits it's going to overwhelm you guys." He was right.

News of DWANGO spread immediately through the burgeoning Doom fan base. By January 1995, ten thousand people were paying $8.95 per month to dial up to Bob and Kee's Houston server. People were dialing from as far as Italy and Australia. At this rate, DWANGO would break $1 million with just one server. They had to expand. And expanding wasn't that difficult to do. The guts of a DWANGO computer server was simply a computer and a few dozen modems with phone lines. All they had to do was buy the parts and strike deals with people across the country who would host the machines in their own homes or offices.

Bob, Kee, and Mike Wilson, a former daiquiri bar manager and childhood buddy of Adrian Carmack's, went on a cross-country spree to set up DWANGO franchises. It was a tantalizing pitch. For $35,000, DWANGO would set up a server and then let the franchisee rake in the cash. "It was," Mike said, "a guaranteed moneymaking machine."

Lawyers, programmers, musicians, people from all walks of life— including Adrian Carmack—snatched up the deals. The DWANGO guys put one in a private loft in New York, apartments in Seattle, warehouses in San Jose. They set up twenty-two servers in about four months. Every day, the guys would run to the nearest Home Depot to load up on shelving and cables, then hightail it over to install a new machine and walk out the door with $35,000. *Cash.* On one night they spent $10,000 at a strip club. The strippers were intrigued when they heard the guys made all this money selling deathmatch. Whatever that drug was, they figured, it must be some powerful stuff.

With the deathmatch fever and rising publicity, Doom II not only broke into the retail market but destroyed it. To Ron Chaimowitz's and GTI's delight, the game shot up the charts. A few months after its release, Romero and Jay cruised through the drive-through window of the local bank to deposit their first royalty check. The teller pulled the check out of the deposit tube and nearly collapsed. It was for $5 million. For that amount, she figured, the two guys in the Ferrari should at least have come inside.

By the time Romero returned to Austin Virtual Gaming for the next Doom tournament, he was no longer the only one screaming insults and punching walls. Deathmatch was now a way of life. The room brimmed with guys telling each other to "Suck it down!" and "Fuck a monkey skull!" There were broken keyboards and ripped-up mouse cords on the floor. One far wall was punched through to the core, the lingering wound inflicted by a frustrated gamer's fist. And, for the first time, Romero got beaten at his own game.

It wasn't the last time. Fueled by the success of DWANGO and Doom II, Romero deathmatched more than ever with his office mate, Shawn Green. One day in the summer of 1995, Carmack had enough. He was tired of Romero wasting his time, tired of hearing the screams, the profanity, the fists beating on the walls, the broken keyboards flying down by his door. So, unbeknownst to Romero, he plotted some revenge.

The next day Shawn came into Romero's office, beaming with confidence, and challenged Romero to a game. "Jesus, dude," Romero said, "yesterday I beat you down so hard. Come on, get in there, I'm ready any time!"

Everyone gathered around. Romero cracked open a Dr Pepper and began to play. He chased Shawn online, running through the levels, but to no avail. Shawn was annihilating him. Every time Romero ran behind him, Shawn spun around and unloaded a shotgun into Romero's face. "Fucking bullshit!" Romero screamed. "What's wrong with this fucking mouse?" He banged the mouse on the table, inadvertently spilling his soda. "Oh shit!"

Everyone started to laugh. "What?" Romero said, mopping the Dr Pepper from his leg. It was a setup, they told him. Carmack had programmed an option on Shawn's computer that enabled him to travel at ten times the average speed just by typing in a special little command. Romero looked around and, sure enough, there was Carmack, standing in the hallway. Carmack rarely laughed. But at the moment, he was visibly amused.

If deathmatch was a release from stress, work, family, and drudgery, it was a release that Carmack didn't need or, for that matter, understand. In fact, he had never really gotten the appeal most people found in hapless diversions. He would see things on television about drunken spring break beach weekends, and none of it would compute. A lot of people didn't seem to enjoy their work.

Carmack knew well and good what he enjoyed—programming—and was systematically arranging his life to spend the most time possible doing just that. Beginning with Doom, he had decided to adjust his biological clock to accommodate a more monkish and solitary work schedule, free from Romero's screams, the reporters' calls, and the mounting distractions of everyday life. He began by pushing himself to stay up one hour later every evening and then coming in one hour later the next day. By early 1995, he had arrived at his ideal schedule: coming in to work at around 4:00 P.M. and leaving at 4:00 A.M. He would need all the concentration he could muster for Quake.

The game, he quickly realized, was going to be a greater challenge than he had anticipated. His objective was to create an arbitrary 3-D world with Internet play. Carmack began the project as he often did, by reading as much research material as he could gather. He paid thousands of dollars for textbooks and papers, but everything was purely academic. There was no such thing as a computer program that could create an interactive, real-time, fast-action, 3-D gaming world. To create such an experience would tax not only every ounce of his skills but every drop of power a modern PC could muster. To make matters worse, for the first time at such a crucial moment in a game's birth, he felt his ally Romero was nowhere to be found.

It had been coming, of course, he thought. Though Carmack had considered Romero a better programmer when they met at Softdisk, he'd soon left Romero behind. At that point, Romero willfully took on other roles: developing the extraneous tools that he and Tom Hall could use to create levels of a game, conceptualizing design, plotting how id would rule the world. Through Doom, Romero had become the ideal collaborator for Carmack, someone who could sit by his side and knowledgably experiment with the new technology. With Quake, Carmack realized, he wanted both a programmer who could work with his engine and someone who could experiment with his early work. Romero had once assumed both roles. With the distractions of Doom's success, it seemed to Carmack, he would assume neither.

But, as Carmack discovered, there were others who were more than ready to fill the spots. For the programming, there was no one better in Carmack's mind than the veteran coder Michael Abrash. It was Abrash's book on power graphics programming for computers that Carmack and Romero had used to learn how to program the graphics for their earlier games. Since then, Abrash had become something of an icon in the programming world. In recent years he had led graphics programming for Microsoft, where he worked on their Windows NT operating system. But, like anyone who lived for graphics, he knew there was no better place to see results than in games. And there was no game that impressed him quite like Doom.

On a trip to Seattle to visit his mother, Carmack took Abrash out to lunch to tell him about his plans for Quake. The challenge, as Abrash heard it, was to increase cyberspace through 3-D graphics and a persistent online world—an alternate world that would live and breathe around the clock, waiting for players to cohabit. Abrash's blood pulsed. Like most graphics programmers, he often theorized about virtual worlds. When he read *Snow Crash* and the description of the Metaverse, he'd thought, I know how to do 80 percent right now—at least theoretically. There was no question in his mind that he was sitting across from a twenty-four-year-old who had the skills and confidence to make it happen. When Abrash mentioned how after a project he always wondered if he could do anything quite as good again, Carmack narrowed his brow and said, "I never wonder that. Mmm."

Still, when Carmack asked him to come work for id, Abrash said he'd have to give it some thought, since it meant uprooting his family. Days later, he got an e-mail from his boss, Bill Gates. Gates had caught wind of the id deal and wanted to talk. Abrash was shocked; a meeting with Gates was like a meeting with the Pope. Gates was aware of id. His programmers had been talking with the company about creating a version of the game for the upcoming Windows platform. But id was just a small company down in Texas, he told Abrash. Microsoft had plenty to offer, he said, and regaled Abrash with the interesting research the company was planning to pursue in graphics. Gates also mentioned how a Microsoft employee had gone to work for IBM, only to return eight months later. "You might not like it down there at id," he concluded.

Abrash chose Carmack over Gates. The potential at id was too great, he thought; he wanted to have a front-row seat to see that breakthrough virtual world, that networked 3-D world, evolve. Furthermore, he was touched by the subtext of Carmack's invitation. Carmack seemed lonely, Abrash thought, like he didn't have anyone who appreciated the beauty of his ideas.

Carmack soon expanded his own crew even more. He found an ambitious level designer who was especially eager to put his dreams into action. American McGee connected with Carmack not through games but through Carmack's other fetish: automobiles. Carmack met him one day in his apartment complex while American was under the hood of a car. Skeletal, chain-smoking, with grease-speckled glasses and a badly grown beard, American was a tightly wound auto mechanic. He spoke in fast bursts, like a race car driver jumping the gates, rushing forth, then going back and blasting out again.

American's blood was a strange fuel. Just twenty-one years old, he would often joke to his friends that he wanted to write an autobiography of dysfunction ironically titled "Growing Up American." Born in Dallas, American never knew his father and was raised by his eccentric mother, a housepainter. He was a highly creative, if not odd, only child. At school he would talk vividly to imaginary friends. He would stop in his tracks to draw a doorway in thin air, which he would walk through to get to imaginary places. He was also gifted in math and science, and took an early interest in computer programming, eventually getting accepted to a magnet school for computer science.

After living with a flurry of stepfathers, American's mother finally settled on a man who thought he was a woman. One day when American was sixteen, he came home from school to every kid's nightmare: an empty house. The only things left were his bed, his books, his clothes, and his Commodore 64 computer. His mother had sold the home to pay for two plane tickets and the fee for her boyfriend's sex change operation. American packed up his computer. He was on his own. To pay his bills, he dropped out of high school and took a variety of odd jobs, finally settling on a Volkswagen repair shop. In Carmack, he found someone who shared his interest in both cars *and* computers. When Carmack asked him if he wanted to work at id doing technical support shortly after Doom's release, he jumped.

The id office was palpably awesome, American thought; he could feel the momentum, these irreverent young guys riding a tidal wave. Particularly impressive was Romero. There was a real sense of magic to his work; it was like he was an architect, an engineer, a lighting person, a game designer, an artist all in one. Romero had an intuitive sense of how to surprise the player and make the game flow. On top of that, he seemed just plain cool—living large, driving the hot car, always joking, and, unlike Carmack, actually *enjoying* his fame and fortune. American and Romero too became fast friends. American never wanted to go home.

With Doom II, Romero and Carmack agreed to promote American to level design. American repaid the favor by emulating both Carmack's ruthless work schedule and Romero's ruthless sense of fun. In turn, he became the ultimate id prodigy. As a level designer, he had a fine aesthetic sense as well as a natural feeling for entertainment. In one level of Doom II he called the Crusher, he placed a cyberdemon in the middle of the room; when the player approached, a giant upper section of the room would come mashing down like a hammer. Romero thought it was hilarious. Carmack was equally impressed by American's long hours. By the end of Doom II, American had completed more levels than Romero himself.

As Quake's development began, American was not only id's hotshot young designer but Carmack's best friend. With Romero off working on his various projects, it was American who experimented with Carmack late into the night. Carmack began to open up to American about Romero. He said he didn't know what to do with Romero, whose passion for programming games seemed to be getting taken over by his passion for playing them.

Despite his empathy for Romero, American wanted to appease Carmack, so he said, "Yeah, I think Romero's slacking off too." As Carmack listened, his mood turned. *Who did American think he was?* He was no Romero. Carmack thought Romero, despite his flaws, was still the best level designer at the company. His levels were the best ones in Doom, and the best ones in Doom II. There was no reason he couldn't still be the best one for Quake. "Romero is a really strong finisher," Carmack said, "and until you see it, you're not going to understand."

Romero knew Carmack. He knew that, at the beginning of a project, Carmack went into research mode, and there was nothing much for him to do but experiment with other things until the engine was done. As Romero had already noticed, American had taken on the role of experimenting with Carmack late at night. He didn't think anything of it—better American than him.

Romero was too busy experimenting with the brave new world that Doom was continuing to spawn. DWANGO and deathmatching were in full tilt. Raven's game Heretic was doing so well that Romero was already overseeing the sequel, Hexen. He had the big vision in his head: a trilogy of games from Raven based on the Doom engine, concluding with the final project, Hecatomb. He had also begun overseeing a Doom-driven game called Strife by a local group of developers called Rogue Entertainment.

These games were fitting nicely into what he wanted to be id's master plan: squeezing every last drop of business and marketability out of Carmack's engines. Carmack's technology was getting more complicated and, as a result, taking longer to produce. *Why not use that time to pursue other projects?* Id didn't have to just be a company, it could be a gaming empire. Though Carmack had been skeptical, Romero felt that Heretic's success had proven his vision. As the Doom II phenomenon grew, the obvious way to build the company was to release more Doom product. The answer: cash in on the Doom mods.

Every home, office, or school had someone in the back who worked on computers; now that person was working on Doom mods. Since Doom II, thousands of gamers had begun modifying id's products and making them available for free online. Doom fans would communicate entirely over the Internet to create mods of the game—often never even meeting in person or, for that matter, talking on the phone. It was a virtual company complete with job descriptions, responsibilities, and monikers like Team TNT and Team Innocent Crew.

As a result, the mods were growing in sophistication. Among the most popular was a so-called total conversion of Doom II to make it look like the movie *Aliens*. There were deathmatch mods based on schoolyard games like Freeze Tag or King of the Mountain. People were replicating their offices, their homes, their schools. A student in England made a photorealistic version based on Trinity College. Another released one simply titled School Doom. "School is a hell," read the introductory text. "Nobody really understands why you spend your time by the computer. . . . You are being mocked. . . . You think about committing suicide, but then you realize it's not what you want to do. You should make the others suffer rather than yourself! . . . You will kill them all! You will burn the school building out of the map as if it never has existed. . . . Who cares if you are right or wrong! It's your destiny . . . it's your hell . . . it's your SCHOOL-DOOM!"

Such mods were taken to be all in good fun—*it was just a game*, after all. But some people were beginning to feel that the game had real-life applications. In Quantico, Virginia, in 1995, a project officer in the Marine Corps Modeling and Simulation Management Office named Scott Barnett created a modification called Marine Doom—complete with realistic military soldiers, barbed-wire fences, and marine logos. The game was perfect for training real-life soldiers in teamwork, Barnett's supervisors agreed. Barnett contacted id, who gave their blessing, though they thought the idea of someone using their game to train soldiers was a joke. But it was the real deal. The game made its way across the Net and would be used by the marines for years.

Id decided to jump into the game after discovering that Wizard-Works, a publisher in Minnesota, had released D!Zone—a collection of nine hundred user-made Doom mods (which id obviously did not own); the D!Zone CD-ROM had, remarkably, surpassed Doom II to top the PC games sales charts, earning millions of dollars. It was a source of great consternation in the office—this was exactly what people like Kevin Cloud had been afraid would happen. In response, Romero initiated deals with a variety of mod makers to put out id-approved collections called The Master Levels for Doom II as well as one sprawling team project, Final Doom. They also put out a retail version of the shareware product Ultimate Doom.

As the other projects grew, one question lingered on everyone's mind: *What about Quake?* Many had gotten caught up in the hype; American McGee, Dave Taylor, and Jay Wilbur had even been talking up the game themselves online. An industrious fan began collecting any sly comment made by a member of id and began putting them together in an online newsletter called *QuakeTalk*. Romero uploaded early pictures to the Net showing how the world was shaping up. "In the screens where you see some pink/purple sky," he wrote in an explanatory note, "you can just imagine the wind whistling in your ears. . . . You should see these screens in action. :)"

But back in the office by the middle of 1995, there was little to see. Work was proceeding chaotically at best. With Carmack and Abrash working on the engine, and Romero spending more and more time on other projects, the others were left to their own devices. After having found happiness in a recent marriage, Adrian Carmack was growing impatient with the lack of stability at work. He and Kevin, his now close friend and fellow artist, began churning out textures for the games based on gothic, medieval schemes as well as Aztec designs for a time-traveling portion of the game. Kevin also used the time to start learning how to create characters in 3-D, something they had never done before. Adrian, frustrated by the increased game technology, left the character work to Kevin, who began to wear down from the mounting challenge.

The newer ranks felt frustrations of their own. American and the other guys thought Quake was beginning to flounder. Romero, their project leader, seemed more interested in leading his own life than in leading them. When pushed at one point to create a design document for Quake, he grudgingly responded with a two-page sketch. The rest thought it was a lazy attempt. But, as Romero was quick to explain, independence had long been id's modus operandi. They never had a design document, never wrote anything down; the only person who'd tried was his old cohort Tom Hall, and it got him fired.

The guys at id responded by resenting both Romero *and* Carmack. Romero was off being a rock god. Carmack was off being a tech god. And everyone else was left out to dry. Something had to change. Months were passing, and Carmack's engine was nowhere close to being done. The Wolfenstein engine had taken only a couple of months. Doom had taken six. Already Quake's engine was passing a half year of development with no end in sight. Forget about the promised release date of Christmas 1995, they resolved. From now on if people wanted to know the completion date of an id game, the reply was "When it's done!"

TWELVE

Judgment Day

Alex St. John was sitting at his desk at Microsoft when he got the e-mail from Bill Gates about Doom. Word had it that that there were 10 million copies of the shareware installed on computers — more than the company's new operating system, Windows 95. Microsoft had spent millions to promote the Windows 95 release in August 1995, blanketing the country with ads that asked "Where do you want to go today?" Gates wondered how this little company in Mesquite — the same one that had seduced Michael Abrash — was outperforming him with some *game.*

In the e-mail, Gates asked Alex, the chief strategist for Microsoft's graphics division, if he thought he should buy id Software outright. Alex, a large redheaded man with a quick wit and easy laugh, couldn't help but chuckle. By 1995 everyone, it seemed, wanted a piece of id.

Doom imitations were flooding the shelves and topping the sales charts: Dark Forces, a *Star Wars*–themed shooter from LucasArts; Descent, a free-flying shooter from Interplay; Marathon, a Macintosh game from a small company called Bungie. Even Tom Hall, who had always wanted to do deeper games at id, had been corralled into doing a shooter called Rise of the Triad for Scott Miller's company, Apogee.

The games were now a part of the cultural lexicon. Doom was featured on television shows like *ER* and *Friends*. It was in a Demi Moore movie. It was novelized in a series of books. Hollywood was developing a Doom movie. The marines were making a Doom training mod. Even Nintendo—the goody-goody empire that had long battled over video game violence—was porting the gory hit to its new home video game platform, the Nintendo 64. Yet all the while id had developed the enigmatic reputation of being staunchly independent. "I don't think you'll be able to pull off buying id," Alex wrote back to Gates, "but Doom could certainly be valuable to us."

Alex had been addicted to id's games ever since Wolfenstein 3-D hit the Microsoft campus in 1992. Doom was being played so frequently around the company that he equated it with a religious phenomenon. Microsoft's employees worshiped the game, not only for its addictive qualities but for its enviable technical feats. The buzzword in the industry was *multimedia*, and no one had seen a multimedia display for the computer quite as impressive as Doom. Since Microsoft was embarking on a battle to rule the emerging age of multimedia with its new operating system Windows 95, Alex thought it was time to enlist Doom in the fight.

But a *game*, as he knew, was far from his boss's idea of what multimedia really meant; in Gates's mind, multimedia meant video. Apple was gaining ground with its QuickTime video-playing software, and Gates wanted Microsoft to respond with a similar program. Alex didn't agree with this direction. The real multimedia applications of the future, he argued, were in games. Another competitor, Intel, he pointed out, was pursuing its own solutions, and if Microsoft wanted to maintain its foothold, it needed to prove that Windows 95 would be the best game platform in the business.

Earlier attempts at games for Windows, however, had left Gates with a bad taste. For Christmas 1994, the company had shipped a game based on Disney's *The Lion King* with one million Compaq computers. At the last moment, Compaq had changed its hardware, which caused the million games to trigger a million system crashes. The problem, Alex surmised, was that there was no technical solution that would allow a game in all its multimedia splendor to play safely and effectively on a variety of machines. As a result, game developers were steering clear of Windows in favor of DOS, the old operating system that Microsoft was trying to put out to pasture. If Microsoft was going to convince the masses to upgrade to Windows 95, it needed the game developers to come on board.

So in early 1995, Alex and his team developed a technology that made sure a game would run on Windows no matter how a computer's hardware might change. The technology was called DirectX. With DirectX, developers could make games without having to worry about a *Lion King*–like fiasco and, in turn, pledge their support to Windows. But Alex knew that game developers were a highly skeptical bunch. There was no better way to convince them to use this new technology, he figured, than to show them a version of Doom running on Windows with DirectX.

Id, he quickly discovered, was less than interested in taking on the job of programming a Windows version of Doom. The company had already turned away Apple and IBM because Carmack didn't want to spend time doing ports. And Doom was already running fine on DOS—and being played by plenty of people—so why bother? Furthermore, Carmack—long an advocate of giving away source code for the greater good of the technology—seemed almost disdainful of Microsoft's proprietary stance. Alex assured him that id would not have to lift a finger; Microsoft would port the game itself. Carmack agreed.

WinDoom, as the version was called, was showcased at the Game Developers Conference in Silicon Valley in March 1995. Microsoft spared no expense, renting out the Great American Theme Park to unveil its goods. As the lights dimmed in the auditorium, the audience of gamers began chanting, "DOS! DOS! DOS!" in defense of Microsoft's established platform for games. But as WinDoom began playing on the large screen, a hush of reverence fell over the crowd. The age of Windows and DirectX had begun.

The next and most formidable step was to come: selling Windows as a gaming platform to the public. Despite Doom's success, most casual gamers still viewed computers as geeky things, full of weird bugs and cryptic command requirements that plagued DOS games. Now was the key moment, Alex knew, for Microsoft to put up or shut up.

On the strength of the WinDoom demo, he had managed to enlist several companies to create games for Windows 95 using DirectX. They just needed to make a big splash in time for Christmas 1995. With a demonic game like Doom as its showcase, what better way to make a splash than a Halloween media event? It would be a bash like no other, filled with hundreds of reporters from gaming to mainstream publications. This would be their chance to see what Microsoft was all about in the multimedia age. The event would be called, appropriately, Judgment Day.

Alex couldn't have called id about the party at a better time. The company had just brought on a new colleague who was the epitome of a party guy: Mike Wilson. A childhood friend of Adrian Carmack's from Shreveport, the twenty-four-year-old had finished his stint working with DWANGO Bob. The rise of the Internet had put an end to DWANGO's spree; gamers had no reason to pay to play when they could do it for free online. But for Mike, life was a party that never died. With long blond hair and a surfer's ease, he was a free spirit who had done everything from manage a daiquiri bar to sell Jesus wallets in a local country and western store. Though he wasn't a big gamer, he could see that games were the new rock 'n' roll, and the guys at id, the new rock stars.

Mike loved the idea of Judgment Day. Alex was going to convert Microsoft's cafeteria and garage into a sprawling haunted mansion. More than thirty of the biggest game developers, including Activision, LucasArts, and id, would be invited to create their own sections of the mansion. Mike's eyes widened, imagining what demonic fun id could have with such an assignment. Why not invite the top Doom gamers from around the world for a giant deathmatch tournament—the first ever!—to be held right at the show? The plan was set. "It's now official," Mike declared in a press release. "We are leading Microsoft down the highway to Hell."

Alex didn't have much trouble connecting with Mike's devilish attitude. Despite all his work on DirectX, he still felt like Microsoft was treating his project as "skunk work." On one occasion, he received a call from an incredulous superior who simply said, "Tell me why I shouldn't fire you." Judgment Day would show them all the answer.

But to succeed, he knew that he needed to unveil not only the games but the man himself: Bill Gates.

Alex's requests to feature the CEO at the Halloween event, not surprisingly, were turned down. Gates had other things to do, he was told. But Alex persisted and managed to persuade Gates's public relations lackeys at least to have him record a video address for the crowd. On the day of the shoot, Gates met Alex in the Microsoft video studio, flanked by anxious PR representatives, who began dictating how the shoot was going to proceed. Gates, noticing Alex's clear dismay, cut them off.

"So what do I need to do for this video?" Gates asked.

Alex took a deep breath. Then he handed Gates a shotgun.

Halloween came one night early at Microsoft, on October 30, 1995. The party was in full swing. A Ferris wheel spun outside. A circus tent offered beer and barbecue. A three-story-tall makeshift volcano bubbled up red light. Over at the microphone, Jay Leno, master of ceremonies for the night, entertained the crowd. But the real action was happening underground, in the garage that had been converted into a haunted mansion. There, the deathmatch competition Mike Wilson had organized was under way.

Twenty elite gamers had been flown in and were competing under a giant screen that showed the game. The two top contenders—a stealth Asian American teenager nicknamed Thresh and a Floridian beach bum nicknamed Merlock—twitched over their PCs as they fought. The crowd gathered around them, cheering and taunting. Thresh won the match and was besieged by fans and reporters. "Oh my God," Jay Wilbur said to himself, looking on in disbelief, "this is a *sport*."

Alex St. John, dressed as Satan, was busy chasing Mike Wilson through the red lights and fog. He found him in a corner, sucking down beers with one gamer dressed as Jesus and another as the Pope; Mike and his wife came as the blood-soaked antiheroes of the movie *Natural Born Killers*. Alex told them that he had seen the id installation and he thought it was hilarious. But, he said, Microsoft's PR people were less than pleased. How were the press — or, for that matter, the Microsoft execs — going to react?

As the media and execs started making their way through the mansion, the displays seemed innocent enough. Activision was promoting an adventure game called Pitfall Harry and had built a little jungle scene in which passersby could swing on a makeshift vine. In another room, a company called Zombie had a metal sphere that shot blue electric bolts through the air. But the id installation had a bit more in store: an eight-foot-tall vagina.

Gwar, the scatological rock band that id had hired to produce the display, had pushed their renowned prurient theatrics to the edge. The vagina was lined with dozens of dildos to look like teeth. A bust of O. J. Simpson's decapitated head hung from the top. As the visitors walked through the vaginal mouth, two members of Gwar cloaked in fur and raw steak came leaping out of the shadows and pretended to attack them with rubber penises. The Microsoft executives were frozen. Then, to everyone's relief, they burst out laughing.

Not everyone else, however, was getting the joke. Onstage, a band of Mike's friends called Society of the Damned was screeching through a dissonant set of industrial rock. No sooner had they launched into an abrasive track called "Gods of Fear" than the Microsoft PR people decided they'd had enough. Two security guards stormed the stage and demanded that the band members conclude their set. Alex saw the commotion and lumbered over, his face as red as his Satan costume. "These guys are the guests of id Software!" he barked. "*The* id Software! The guys who made Doom! Any friends of id's are friends of Microsoft." But the guards weren't having it and unplugged the sound system.

As the lights fell, a video screen lowered above the stage. It was time for the main event. The crowd cheered as footage of Doom's familiar corridors began to roll. But it was not the Doom soldier chasing the demons, it was . . . Bill Gates. Microsoft's fearless leader was superimposed running inside the game in a long black trench coat and brandishing a shotgun. Gates stopped running and addressed the crowd about the wonders of Windows 95 as a gaming platform, a platform that could deliver cutting-edge multimedia experiences like Doom. But no sooner had he begun than an imp monster from the game jumped out and, through a voice-over, asked Gates for an autograph. Gates responded by raising his shotgun and blowing the beast into gory chunks. "Don't interrupt me while I'm speaking," he said, then finished his speech. At the end, the screen went black with blood, only to be replaced by the familiar Microsoft logo and the phrase "Who Do You Want to Execute Today?"

This is it, Alex thought, I'm going to be fired. He went to retrieve the video, but it was gone. He could keep his job, he learned; Microsoft was keeping the tape.

The news was spreading fast.

> Subject: ROMERO is DEAD
> > I heard on the Newsgroup that John Romero was in a car accident?
> > Is he OK?

Could it be? John Romero—twenty-eight-year-old Ace Programmer, Rich Person, the Surgeon—dead? According to the gossip online, his fly yellow Ferrari had gone careening off some Dallas highway in one final joyride. It wouldn't have been the first ill fate of an id sports car. Just weeks earlier, a $500,000 custom Doom Porsche race car—complete with the game's logo emblazoned on the fire-red hood—being financed by Carmack and built by Bob Norwood had been mysteriously stolen from his lot. Maybe Romero was suffering some curse.

In reality, Romero was very much alive. He had just returned from inspecting the house he was having custom built: a $1.3 million nine-thousand-square-foot Tudor mansion with a six-car garage, video game arcade, and two limestone gargoyles guarding the door. Now he was sitting at his desk in Suite 666 overlooking his pristine car in the lot. The rumors were a fitting coronation, the game-god equivalent of the Beatles' "Paul is dead" legend. But Romero took exception to the implication that he would perish by his own ineptitude. "Uh, no. I'm not dead," he wrote online in response. "I don't wreck cars or myself."

Not everyone in the office would agree. By November 1995, Quake was nowhere near completion, and factions were more vocally blaming Romero. With Carmack still immersed in making his engine, the rest of the company felt like they had nothing tangible to pursue. The artists, Kevin and Adrian, were tired of churning out all the fantasy textures without a clear plan. The level designers, American and Sandy, were bored twiddling around with rudimentary game sections. Beyond the basic concept of a fantasy game and a big hammer weapon, there wasn't much to go on. Whenever they asked Romero for direction, he would just spew out his generalizations and leave them to fend for themselves. What kind of project director was that?

In Romero's mind Quake was coming along just fine. Carmack was busy working on what he knew would be the next killer game program. There was no reason to rush Engine John. The rest of the company had to just be patient and get ready to throw on the great game design. The best thing they could do was find ways to be productive. Romero chose to spend this time by immersing himself in side projects that he felt would have direct benefit to the company.

But he could sense that they wanted to blame him for not getting the game done, that he wasn't doing enough work. They viewed his detachment, his flipped bit, as a sign that their resident rock star was spinning, if not crashing, his wheels. Their attitude was starting to piss him off. So what if he was going home at 7:00 P.M.? He had a wife. He was building a home. He was making a *life.* And he deserved it. Now that id finally had some more employees to take up the slack, he should be able to take it easier. If the company were hurting, he could understand the complaints. But the company was doing well, in no small part thanks to his multiple projects. And if he wasn't going to oversee these projects, who was?

Yet Romero was neither seeking nor finding empathy. One night Sandy Petersen decided he had had enough. He stormed into Carmack's office and shut the door. "I think John's a really good designer," he said, "and I think that he's currently not properly organizing Quake.

I've been at a big company where games get organized, and I know how it's done and he's not doing it. He's not a project manager, he doesn't know how to do it, and the game's not gonna come together unless he changes some things."

Carmack hit the reply button in his head and spewed out what was now his rote response to this complaint: "Romero works like a demon at the right time," he said, "and it'll all come together." Then he spun around in his chair and went back to work, no good-byes, no conversation ender, no nothing. Typical, Sandy thought. Carmack had long behaved this way, unconcerned with the conventional etiquette of how to begin, continue, and conclude a dialogue with another human being. But these days it was growing worse. One afternoon Michael Abrash told Carmack about how his daughter had finally gotten into a good school after considerable effort. It had meant a lot to Michael, but all Carmack had to say in response was "mmm"; then he spun around to his desk.

Carmack could feel that he was drifting off into space, further and further away from things that he could talk about with *normal* people. He couldn't connect with anything that was stirring around him: the office politics, happy hours, MTV. His world was Quake. His days were Quake. His nights, his life. He was working eighty-hour weeks easily, fully immersed in his nocturnal schedule. People would see him walk in, grab a Diet Coke from the fridge, then make a beeline to his office. The only action they'd see would be the occasional pizza delivery person knocking on his door.

And yet, despite his best efforts, Carmack for the first time in his life felt like nothing was falling into place. Quake was requiring him essentially to reinvent everything. Little from Doom could be extended into Quake's 3-D world. Doom supported four players in deathmatch in somewhat tricky network mode, but Quake would support sixteen people easily over the Internet. Doom had a limited three-dimensional perspective, but Quake would deliver full-blown immersion, allowing players to look in *any* direction and see a convincing virtual world. The most frustrating consequence was his engine's inability to draw a complete visible world or, in technical terms, a potentially visible set. As a result, the world of Quake was filled with holes. Carmack would be running down a hallway of the game only to find it abruptly end in a hideous blue void. There were blue voids in the floor, in the walls, in the ceilings. His virtual world was Swiss cheese.

Consumed by this dilemma, Carmack's thoughts began getting all the more abstract. His mind filled with geometric forms, floating and spinning at his command as he tried to separate them, assemble them, organize them. He didn't dream about girls in bikinis at spring break like many guys his age; he dreamed about the relationship of two polygons in space. He would stumble home at 4:00 A.M., and the visions wouldn't leave him. One night, he sat on the edge of his bed watching coded messages travel down to his arm, instructing it how to move, grip, release. This isn't the way it works in real life, he thought. I must be having a weird dream. He awoke in a cold sweat. There was no escape, not even in sleep.

Though Carmack rarely felt—let alone cracked from—pressure, Quake was beginning to break him. He started lashing out at his employees. One day, Jay suggested they talk about getting software patents for their game technology. "If you guys ever apply for software patents," Carmack barked, "I quit, that's it, end of discussion." Everything grated on him: the distractions of business, the politics of emotion, the laziness—at least in his mind—of others. "You always leave early," Carmack said one evening as Sandy was walking out the door. Sandy was stunned; he was putting in eleven-hour days at least, but his days started at 9:00 A.M., whereas Carmack didn't even get in the office until 4:00 in the afternoon. "I don't leave early," he said. "You're just not here when I'm here."

Carmack didn't relent. He began firing off disciplinary e-mails. First, he banned deathmatching in the office. Then he sent out grades. Everyone in the company was given a letter grade based on his performance: Sandy got a D, Romero a C. Carmack wasn't through. One night he dragged his desk outside his office and planted himself to work in the hallway—the better to keep an eye on everyone around him. Employees began living in fear of their jobs and staying later and later, trying to keep up with Carmack's relentless pace.

The fun, they felt, was being sucked out of the company. The tension was so thick that people started to complain about Carmack too. Romero wasn't the only one with the ego; Carmack was off in his own world, refusing to come down. Soon nothing, not even the most tempting distraction, could lighten the situation. One afternoon Carmack was sitting in his office when he heard a woman's voice down the hall asking if someone had ordered a pizza. Romero replied, "No, I didn't order a pizza." She asked again, "Did you order a pizza?" Someone else said, "Uh, no." Carmack heard his door open. "Did you order a pizza?" the woman asked. He spun around to see an attractive young woman, topless, carrying a pizza box. The stripper was a practical joke arranged by Mike Wilson in an attempt to lighten the mood. "No," Carmack told her flatly, "I didn't order a pizza"; then he too went back to work. "Boy," the stripper said, "you guys are boring as hell!" Then she walked out the door.

All Carmack wanted was to be left alone to work or, even better, just be cast adrift, left as a hermit. The only person who had any empathy for him, it seemed, was Romero. One night Romero pulled him aside. "Dude, I know you're being hard on yourself," he said, "but you can't be superhuman."

To some extent, Carmack thought, Romero was being reasonable. They could certainly work hard without requiring people to work the death schedules of the past. But Romero's attitude was indicative of something deeper, something much more telling. After all these years, all the late nights, the collaborations, Romero was pulling himself out of the trenches of code for the ether of fame and notoriety. Where *was* Romero when he needed him to work, experiment, lead by example? Off building his mansion and being a celebrity!

Carmack knew what he had to do. He had to prove that Romero was slacking. And he knew just how. He wrote a program that would create a time log whenever Romero worked on his PC. According to the results, his partner wasn't working much. When he confronted Romero with the data, his partner exploded. "You're only doing that so you can fire me," Romero snapped.

Well, Carmack thought, yeah!

After all his speculation, Carmack now had his proof—*scientific* proof—that Romero was not only not working but becoming toxic. With that evidence in hand, he didn't feel the least bit of remorse when he arrived at his conclusion: Romero needed to be warned, officially warned, to shape up. He was talking too much to the press, talking too much to fans, deathmatching too much in the office, and now the rest of the company was suffering. Carmack approached Adrian and Kevin and said, "We need to put Romero on record that he is about to be fired."

Carmack had a habit of being abrupt, they knew, but this statement took them aback. "No, no, no," Adrian said. "I don't want to do that, he's a friend of mine, a partner. He'll come back around."

But Carmack insisted and, as was becoming the pattern, Kevin and Adrian did what Carmack wanted. There was no question in their minds—or the others' at id for that matter—that Engine John was their key man. As Mike Wilson said, "If he takes his ball and goes home, the game's over." A meeting was called in November 1995. The owners solemnly gathered around the black conference table behind the black Venetian blinds. Carmack sat at the head of the table, as usual. "You're still not doing your work," he told Romero, "and you absolutely need to do all of this or you're going to be fired."

Romero was indignant. "I work as much as anyone else," he said. "I'm here all the time."

Carmack looked to Kevin and Adrian for help, but Adrian was just staring at the floor. "Well," Kevin said in Romero's defense, "John does come in and do his work."

Carmack was flabbergasted. He thought Kevin and Adrian were going to support his argument. Everyone knew that, if it came down to it, he couldn't fire Romero by himself—he needed their vote too. For now, they agreed to give Romero a so-called smackdown bonus, a lower bonus than usual to tell him that he had to get his act together on the game. Whatever, Romero thought; he didn't need the cash right now and, when the game was finally done, he knew he'd prove them wrong.

By Thanksgiving, however, nothing had changed. The game was still far off track. Carmack called another meeting, this time for the entire company. "There's no proof of concept for game design," he declared. Everyone concurred that the game was taking forever. There was no cohesive plan. American McGee finally made the inevitable suggestion to abandon Romero's ambitious idea of a hand-to-hand combat game for something more simple. "I think it will be better," he said, "if we make a game with rocket launchers and stuff like that."

"Yeah," Sandy said, "let's do Doom III, and the next game we'll do something innovative."

Romero was floored. First the smackdown bonus, now this? Who the fuck were these guys? What did they know? They had never worked on a new game from start to finish. They didn't understand id. "Every id game proceeded just like this before!" he said. "Carmack makes a revolutionary engine, *then* we put a revolutionary game design on top of it. Let's just get the engine done, then we can make this really cool game idea that no one's seen before. Quake is going to be better than Doom; even if we just slap Doom on this new engine, it'll still be a hit. We need to go beyond that and put the original great game idea that no one has done on top of this new engine and create something that's as big as Doom was when it came out."

But the ball was rolling. Newer guys like American began arguing passionately against Romero's fantasy design. They felt they couldn't be creative because there was nothing to work with. There were two paths in the road. They could just stick with Carmack's technology and create a lean, mean game that could be done in a reasonable amount of time. Or they could go with Romero's design and end up God knows where. They should just do another Doom.

At first, Adrian and Kevin seemed to take Romero's side. "Holy crap, guys," Adrian said. "We've done a shitload of work here." They had spent nearly a year churning out art specifically designed for a medieval fantasy, *not* a futuristic marine game. And after all that work, they were just getting to the fun part: putting blood on the walls, making specialized areas. "Just because some of you guys haven't gotten anything done," Adrian snapped, "there's no reason to scrap the project. If we switch games, it's going to take us another *year* to get to the point where we are right now. We're not talking about an easy change."

The others didn't seem to care. As they continued to argue against Romero's ambitious design, Romero watched Carmack in disbelief. Oh my God, he realized, Carmack agrees with them. He's giving validity to the idea of not doing a revolutionary game design. Romero burst. "We're already slaves to technology in this company," he said, "and at least we can do what we can to make a great game on top of it like we did with Doom. Now these guys just want to slap out a game using the Doom stuff? We can still make a great game if we take the time to program it."

Carmack could see both sides. But there was a key flaw in Romero's argument: he had nothing to support himself. The only workable levels of Quake that existed were the high-tech Doom-style ones coming from American. If Romero had created an amazing fantasy world, that would have been a different story. But, in Carmack's mind, Romero had done practically nothing. Clearly their old ambitious idea for Quake—the one that went back to the lake house in Shreveport—was misguided.

"You have to give yourself the freedom to back away from something when you make a mistake," Carmack said. "If you pretend you're infallible and bully ahead on something, even when there are many danger signs that it's not the right thing, well, that's a sure way to leave a crater in the ground. You want to always be reevaluating things and say, Okay, it sounded like a good idea but it doesn't seem to be working out very well and we have this other avenue which is looking like it's working out better—let's just do that."

That was when it really hit Romero: We're not of a single mind anymore. We're not an agreeing entity. He couldn't believe that Carmack wasn't saying, "Calm down guys, you'll see, it's going to be a bad-ass game." As much as Carmack thought Romero had stopped being a programmer, Romero thought Carmack had stopped being a gamer. The fact that Carmack was listening to these guys showed that he was actually worried, that he didn't have the faith in the big ambitious game anymore, that he didn't have the faith in Romero.

After hours of arguing, Romero threw in the towel. "Okay," he said, "I'll redesign the whole game with Doom-style weapons and we'll get it out." But to himself he said something else entirely, words that echoed the statement he had uttered long ago to Carmack at Softdisk, the day he saw their future, their destiny. This is it, he thought, I'm gone.

Despite Quake's new direction and a release date that would now surely slip into 1996, id's publisher, GTI, cashed in heavily in December 1995. Sales for Doom II in the United States would eventually top the $80 million mark. The game sold overseas as well, with another $20 million from Europe, 30 percent of which came from Germany—a country that had banned the game from its shelves. Meanwhile all of id's old games were continuing to sell, as were the spin-offs. Ultimate Doom, which was essentially a retail version of the Doom shareware, was bringing in over $20 million in the United States. And Raven's games, Hexen and Heretic, were doing just as well, accounting for nearly another $20 million.

Buoyed by the success, GTI began striking deals with other developers, including Midway, creators of the lucrative Mortal Kombat series; the arcade magnate Williams Entertainment; and WizardWorks, a publisher of budget games. With Doom's help, computer games had skyrocketed GTI's sales from $10 million to a projected $340 million in just two years. When the company went public in December 1995, it was the largest venture-capital-backed IPO of the year, even ahead of the Internet browser company Netscape. "[GTI] came out of nowhere to conquer a host of competitors," declared *Crain's New York Business*, "and become the country's third largest interactive entertainment company." It was valued at $638 million.

But the success was by no means endearing GTI to id. When GTI offered that year to buy id for $100 million, id declined. The publisher was a shitty company, the guys thought, and they didn't want to sell id to people they didn't believe in. Furthermore, they felt too frazzled to make any kind of rational business decision. Money wasn't exactly a problem either. In 1995, id's earnings had doubled to $15.6 million, and they would surely continue to rise. With the overhead still low, the owners were each making millions. Id also thought GTI was claiming too much credit for the success of Doom II. The guys didn't like how GTI was throwing around its money at so many other unworthy companies. At the urging of Mike Wilson, id's increasingly brash biz guy, they decided to use Quake as a way to bring GTI down.

The weapon: shareware. In most publishers' minds by the end of 1995, shareware was a thing of a past, a cute way to distribute software that was losing its relevance in the increasingly big business of video games. So when id negotiated to retain shareware rights for Quake, GTI's Ron Chaimowitz didn't think much of it. He would regret that choice. Mike pitched the id guys on a new way to capitalize on the shareware plan. Instead of just distributing Quake shareware over the Internet for free, id could sell a CD-ROM containing both the shareware and an encrypted version of the full game. Someone would buy the shareware for $9.95, then could call up id directly and pay $50.00 for the code to unlock the complete game. As a result, id, despite not owning the retail publishing rights to Quake, could succinctly cut GTI out of the equation.

Though Carmack had reservations, the rest of the company was more than eager to embark on an even more radical experiment in self-publishing. The deal was hatched. Ron Chaimowitz read about it in the newspaper. Wilson—that prick! he thought. He's an immature kid who doesn't know how to deal in a professional manner! But id had every right to do the deal, even though it was not a move anyone had ever imagined. There was nothing GTI could do to stop them.

As 1996 rolled around, not only was id at war with GTI but it was at war with itself. The decision to abandon Romero's design for Carmack's technology created incinerating pressure. The company was in perpetual crunch mode, trying to get the Doom-style shooter done by March. Carmack, feeling like he was the only one running the ship, decided it was time to turn up the heat. For weeks he had been working out in the hallway to keep an eye on everyone else. But now he suggested they tear the walls down.

The decision was made, ostensibly, because the company had long been talking about doubling its work space. With the purchase of a suite next door, they could begin the remodeling right away. Carmack saw this as a key opportunity to get everyone out of isolated offices and into one big communal work space while the renovations would be done. Reluctantly, they agreed to the new arrangement. They called it the war room.

They had no idea how messy the war room would be. Within days, walls began crashing around them, blanketing the area in plaster dust. They lined tables up against the windows and piled on their computers, sitting by each other with barely enough room to grab a soda without knocking elbows. Carmack and Romero sat side by side. To get all their computers networked they had to run cables through the ceiling and bust out the acoustic tiles to rope the wires down to their machines. Shades drawn, lights low, long gray cables stretching from the ceiling to their desks, it looked as though they were all sitting *inside* a computer's dark web of wires. There was nowhere to go without getting caught.

Without the privacy of personal space, the tension began to mount. They worked eighteen-hour days, seven days a week. They had to listen to their music on headphones. At any given moment a visitor might walk in to find a room full of guys quietly typing with headphones on their ears. Romero had taken a liking to instrumental video game soundtracks—available as Japanese imports. He popped one in and bitterly slipped on his headphones. This is not the id of the past, he thought, the id of "let's make a great game together and have fun." This is the id of "shut up and work."

Competition rose within the ranks. With Romero vulnerable, aspiring designer American McGee jockeyed for supremacy. But now even he had competition: Tim Willits. Tim had the distinction of being the first employee drafted from the Doom mod community. He had discovered the game while studying at the University of Minnesota. At the time, the twenty-three-year-old was a hardworking computer science major who lived at home with his parents—his father, a pipe fitter, his mother, a radiation technician. It was a competitive household, and Tim frequently butted heads with his sister—a graphics design major at the university. Short and balding with an occasional nervous stutter, he overachieved as best he could, not only signing up for ROTC but volunteering to slip into a life-size rodent costume to portray the school mascot, Goldie Gopher, at football games and events.

On a lark one day, Tim downloaded this game a lot of kids were talking about called Doom. Though he had played games before, he never had the sense of entering a world. But here, his actions affected the world; he could move doors, trigger buttons. He was amazed at the size of the place he had entered, the scope of this strange new universe. Tim began experimenting with the hacker-made Doom level-editing programs that were floating around the bulletin board services. He started to get recognition for some of the levels he had made and uploaded. Soon enough, he got the ultimate response: an e-mail from id.

Tim was hired by American to work on the id-produced title Strife. But as Quake began to grow, he was brought in to help the team. Tim immediately aligned himself with Romero and started learning as much as he could about the art of level design. In the war room, he sat at Romero's side. He proved himself to be not only highly skilled but highly efficient, able to complete a level design in record time. Soon Romero found himself competing just to keep up with Tim's output. Carmack immediately began to show appreciation for Tim's work. Though he still considered American his close friend, American felt left out to dry.

Long enamored of Romero's rock-star lifestyle, American started living the life himself. This came after id struck a deal with Trent Reznor of the industrial rock band Nine Inch Nails, a die-hard Doom fan, to provide the music and sound effects for Quake. Overseeing the project, American began to change his look: shaving his beard, styling his hair, dressing in black. He felt increasingly disconnected from Carmack, who, despite having originally approved of his work on Quake's music, now seemed only to chastise him for not spending more time making levels for the game. For American, it was the beginning of the end. Even his best friend at id, Dave Taylor, had left to pursue his own game company. American had never felt more alone. His days as id's wonder boy were over.

It didn't take long to find out who had replaced him and Romero. Carmack abruptly announced one day that Tim's levels would have the coveted honor of being the opening levels of the shareware release—

players' first taste of Quake. Everyone was silent in disbelief. It was an insult to Romero, who they all assumed would get that distinction. But the backlash had been coming. Since the meeting to change Quake's direction, Romero had seemed to distance himself even more from the project.

"What?" Romero said. "I'm the lead designer!"

"That's my decision," Carmack replied. "Tim's levels are more cohesive." Romero, as always, was quick to let the bad vibes go and wished Tim well. As far as everyone was concerned, Carmack had just passed the torch.

It was late one night in January when Romero picked up the phone in his Tudor mansion and dialed the number of Tom Hall, his ex-partner at id. The two had rekindled their friendship some months before with no hard feelings. Romero knew that Tom wasn't happy at Apogee. Tom had been running into the same old problems he'd had at id, feeling like he wasn't able to implement his own creative ideas. Apogee started doing business under the name 3D Realms, making games that would one-up id Software. Their first release, Duke Nukem 3D, was in fact doing just that. The game was like a comic book version of Doom set in a realistic modern-day world. Players would shoot through abandoned porno theaters and strip clubs. There were even strippers. Though Carmack hated it, feeling that its engine was "held together with bubble gum," the gamers bought it in droves. People were dubbing it the "Quake killer." Tom, however, was stuck working on another project for 3D Realms called Prey that was barely getting off the ground. Romero's call couldn't have come at a better time.

"Dude," Romero told him, "the same thing that you ran into at id just happened to me." He explained how he had been trying to push Carmack into doing something new and creative but Carmack just wanted to play it safe and do the same old Doom game over again. Romero had even suggested splitting the company in two, with Carmack leading a technology side and him leading a design side, but the suggestion went over with a thud. "I'm going to leave after Quake," he concluded. "What do you think about starting another company? It'll be a company where any kind of design we want to do, that's what we make. Technology has to work with *our* design, not the other way around. How would you like to have a company where design is law?"

"That," Tom said, "would be a dream."

[idsoftware.com]
Login name: johnc   In real life: John Carmack
Directory: /raid/nardo/johnc Shell: /bin/csh
Never logged in.
Plan:

This is my daily work . . .

When I accomplish something, I write a * line that day.

Whenever a bug / missing feature is mentioned during the day and I don't fix it, I make a note of it. Some things get noted many times before they get fixed.

Occasionally I go back through the old notes and mark with a + the things I have since fixed.

--- John Carmack

= feb 18 =====================================

*   page flip crap
*   stretch console
*   faster swimming speed
*   damage direction protocol
*   armor color flash
*   gib death
*   grenade tweaking
*   brightened alias models
*   nail gun lag
*   dedicated server quit at game end

+ scoreboard
+ optional full size
+ view centering key
+ vid mode 15 crap
+ change ammo box on sbar
+ allow "restart" after a program error
+ respawn blood trail?
+ −1 ammo value on rockets
+ light up characters

As life in the war room pressed on, Carmack took it upon himself to let gamers know that, yes, id really was moving along with its work on Quake. So he decided to upload his daily work log, or, as it was known, a .plan file, to the Internet. .Plan files were often used by programmers to keep each other informed of their efforts but had yet to be exploited as means of communicating with the masses. But id's fans had suffered months, years, of Romero's unsubstantiated hyperbole, Carmack felt, and it was time that they saw some hard data.

After weeks of all-nighters, Carmack and his programming partner, Michael Abrash, had finally tackled the problem of Quake's strange blue gaps. The world was coming together. Carmack would spend minutes on end just looking down into a corner of a room in the game, just walking around in the virtual world and feeling, The world is solid, it's really there. On February 24, 1996, there was enough of Quake in place for id to upload a test deathmatch level to see how it worked on gamers' various machines. Gamers had been clamoring online for months to get a taste of id's new creation. There was so much anticipation and speculation, in fact, that websites specifically devoted to Quake news began to surface.

After the test, however, the reviews were not entirely flattering. Players were keen on the prospects for deathmatching online but complained that the game was dark, sluggish, nothing like the fast-action world of Doom. The criticisms were not unfounded. These Doom-like features had had to be sacrificed in order to accommodate Quake's meticulous 3-D rendering engine. But the gamers weren't sympathetic. "While not bad for a 'test' version," posted one player online, "there are

still many rough edges that have to be worked out . . . there is still a
lot missing that is needed to make this game truly rule."

Dejected by the response, the id team went about the laborious task
of stitching together their disparate work. Over the sixteen months
since the game began, the level designers and artists had been off in
their own worlds, and the results showed. Romero's levels looked medieval, American's were futuristic, Sandy's were strange gothic puzzles. Though there were many staples of id's trademark dark
humor—such as the zombies who would rip chunks of flesh from their
asses and hurl them at the player—the game needed cohesion fast.

Halfheartedly, the guys came up with a story they'd throw in
Quake's manual: "You get the phone call at 4:00 A.M. By 5:30 you're in
the secret installation. The commander explains tersely, 'It's about the
Slipgate device. Once we perfect these, we'll be able to use them to
transport people and cargo from one place to another instantly. An
enemy code-named Quake is using his own slipgates to insert death
squads inside our bases to kill, steal, and kidnap. The hell of it is we
have no idea where he's from. Our top scientists think Quake's not
from Earth, but another dimension. They say Quake's preparing to un-
leash his real army, whatever that is.'"

Whatever, indeed—they all felt. But the vehicle was there, and they
went about inserting slipgates throughout the game, little gray static
doorways that would lead players through the strange different worlds.
The final months of Quake became a blur of silent and intense all-
nighters, punctuated by the occasional crash of a keyboard against a
wall. The construction had turned the office into a heap. The guys were
taking their frustrations out by hurling computer parts into the dry-
wall like knives. Even good press couldn't boost their spirits. *Wired* descended on the office for its highest honor: a cover story on id. But the
guys could have cared less, showing up three hours late for the photo
session. The cover showed Carmack in front of Romero and Adrian
staring into strange colored light with the headline "The Egos at id."
The story ordained Quake "the most anticipated computer game of
all time."

By June, the endless days and nights finally gave way to a finished
product. But the occasion of uploading the shareware to the Internet

barely resembled the glory days of Wolfenstein 3-D and Doom. When Romero showed up to ready the game on Saturday, June 22, 1996, he was alone. He walked down the halls, past the old id awards, the Freddy Krueger mask, the Doom plastic shotgun. So it had come to this. No Carmack. No Adrian. No Kevin.

Romero took refuge with the fans, heading into a gamers' chat room that teemed with id fans. He phoned Mark Fletcher, a Doom addict who had become one of Romero's friends. He wanted someone there with him that night who really understood the games, who would appreciate this moment. At 5:00 P.M. he tapped the button on his keyboard and sent Quake to the world. It felt weird, he thought, that none of the other guys were here with him, but it all added up. They weren't gamers. They didn't even *play* games anymore. They were broken.

"Okay," Carmack said, "we can't put it off any longer." Shortly after Quake's release, he sat in a Mexican restaurant called Tia's having lunch with Adrian and Kevin. Romero's time was up. He was clearly not pulling his weight. It was time to let him go.

The thought made Adrian physically sick. This is Romero we're talking about. But he knew he was at a crossroads. Either Romero was going to have to leave or Carmack was going to dissolve the company. There was no middle ground. Kevin agreed. It was hard to let someone go, especially given that Romero was one of the founders of the company, someone who'd contributed so much to their success; but there was no alternative.

The chasm between Carmack and Romero was too wide. Both of them had their views of what it meant to make games and how games should be made. Carmack thought Romero had lost touch with being a programmer. Romero thought Carmack had lost touch as a gamer. Carmack wanted to stay small, Romero wanted to get big. The two visions that had once forged this company were irreparably tearing it apart. And though Adrian and Kevin had, on so many occasions, sympathized with Romero's goals, they had once and for all to choose which John to follow.

Romero, unbeknownst to them, was making plans of his own. On the way to work that morning, he had dialed up Ron Chaimowitz at GTI to discuss a possible publishing deal for the company he wanted to start with Tom Hall. This wasn't going to be any ordinary game company, he said, this was going to be a Big Company, unrestrained by technology; design would be law.

The next day at id, Romero was beckoned to the conference room. Carmack, Adrian, and Kevin sat around the table. Adrian stared at the floor. Kevin was silent. Carmack finally spoke. "We're still not happy with how everything's going, you know," he said. He reached for a piece of paper and handed it to Romero. "This is your resignation. You can sign it."

Romero, despite all the warnings, all his plans, felt nothing but shock. "Wait," he said, "don't you mean *a year ago* that I wasn't working? Because these last seven months I've been killing myself! I've been killing myself to make Quake!"

"No," Carmack said, "you're not doing your work! You're not living up to your responsibilities. You're hurting the project. You're hurting the company. You've been *poisonous* to the company, and your contribution has been negative over the past couple years. You needed to do better and you didn't. Now you need to go! Here's a resignation and here's a termination! You're going to resign now!"

I don't want to be here, Adrian thought, staring more deeply into the carpet, I don't want to be here, I don't want to be here. Despite the fact that both Carmack and Romero were each somewhat justified, he knew there was no way out.

But then everything stopped. Romero fell quiet. Deep inside him, the bit began to flip, as it had so many times in his life: he would not let this get him down just like he hadn't let anything else — his father, his stepfather, his own broken families, and now his own broken company. I was making plans to go start a company with Tom anyway, he reminded himself. I guess I'll go now. He wasn't bowing out from a fight, he was starting his new life. Romero signed the form, handed it to Carmack, and headed out.

By the time Romero got to the door, Carmack assumed his ex-partner had convinced himself that he had been planning on doing this for a long time, that he had been stifled creatively and was off to bigger and better things. In the space of forty feet, he thought, Romero had re-designed history. Carmack didn't watch him go with sadness or nostalgia. He watched him go with relief.

Two days later, Romero posted his first and last .plan file at id. "I'm going to jump on this .plan bandwagon just this once," he wrote for all the world to read online. "I have decided to leave id Software and start a new game company with different goals. I won't be taking anyone from id with me."

The next day, Carmack posted a .plan file of his own. "Romero is now gone from id," he typed. "There will be no more grandiose statements about our future projects. I can tell you what I am thinking, and what I am trying to acomplish [*sic*], but all I promise is my best effort."

The old deathmatches were over. A new one had begun.

THIRTEEN

Deathmatch

In a dark room pulsing with blood red shadows, Stevie "Killcreek" Case sat at her computer, twitching her body as if she were repeatedly and intentionally sticking her toe in a light socket. "Doh!" she yelped, leaping her soldier on the screen through a static-filled teleporter gate, only to see him rematerialize in an unanticipated blizzard of nails. Or, as she described the style of this particular death, "Tele-fragged!"

It was January 1997, minutes away from the online gaming underground's unofficial Super Bowl. Like the few dozen others convulsing throughout this University of Kansas flophouse, Stevie—an ebullient twenty-year-old with a short brown bob—had been practicing two sleepless nights for the match between her team, Impulse 9, and their rivals, who had driven eight hours from Michigan, the Ruthless Bastards. Their contests were part of the burgeoning international subculture of clans: organized groups of gamers who played—and lived—Quake. Like those of the hundreds of thousands of other Quake addicts, their wars were usually over the Internet. But on this tornado gray day in Lawrence, Kansas, the country's best were settling the score in the flesh.

On one level such passion came down to the beautiful nightmare of the game itself. Despite id's internal problems during the game's development, Quake was heralded for its breakthrough graphics and visceral experience. *USA Today* gave Quake four out of four stars, calling it "bloody amazing." A reviewer for *Computer Gaming World* gave it ten out of ten, saying it was "a towering programming feat that goes beyond immersive to make you feel like you're there in a combat environment." *Entertainment Weekly* said, "Quake delivers the most carnage you can revel in without having to deal with actual jail time. No wonder bored office workers across the country love it." Even the actor Robin Williams praised Quake on the David Letterman show.

Though gamers enjoyed the single-player experience—hunting down monsters through the twisting 3-D mazes—what they *really* enjoyed was deathmatch. As the first game designed specifically for multiplayer team competition over the Internet, it allowed up to sixteen people to compete in paintball-like teams, hunting each other down in a wild panic to kill or be killed. "Football with guns," as a player named Dr. Rigormortis put it. In addition to competing over the Internet, gamers schlepped their computers to each other's homes and wired them together into a local area network, or LAN, so they could fight in person. These so-called LAN parties—which began casually with Doom—became the offline social nexus for the online gaming world.

Within days of Quake's release, fans in chat channels and newsgroups began forming clans with names like the Breakfast Club, the Revolting Cocks, Impulse 9, and the Ruthless Bastards. By August there were about twenty clans with up to twenty players each. Two months later there were close to a thousand. A group of women calling themselves the Clan Widows started a webpage support group. It was the dawn of cybersports.

And it didn't take long for the moguls to cash in. "Electronic games are the extreme games of the mind," said an entrepreneur behind a chain of virtual reality arcades in New York, Chicago, and Sydney, "so, let's bring the cyberathletes into arenas and elevate this to a spectator sport": big screens, Quake matches networked from around the world, beer, prizes, the works. His prediction of star players competing with

Nike logos tattooed across their knuckles wasn't crazy. One clan, Dark Requiem, hustled a webpage ad from a joystick maker. Thresh, winner of the Judgment Day tournament, received a sponsorship from Microsoft. The kids who were always the last ones picked in gym class lineup could be the next Michael Jordans. Michael Jordans who might look something like _fo0k (pronounced "fook," like "spook"), the coleader of the Ruthless Bastards.

The twenty-seven-year-old with a tiny soul patch beard led his clan to the top of the ClanRing league, a feat accomplished by only one other team at that point, Impulse 9. Since Quake's debut, _fo0k had been spending his evenings in East Lansing, Michigan, buried in his parents' basement, a windowless computer game mission control filled with twisted piles of joysticks and keyboards, mammoth speakers, a scattering of NBA video game cartridges. The only art on the walls was a black velvet portrait of Jesus, which _fo0k found funny because the nose resembled the end of a double-barrel shotgun, one of the weapons in Quake.

Video game images had been burning into _fo0k's consciousness ever since Space Invaders, he said, "first melted my mind." At the time, _fo0k was just Clint Richards, a competitive new kid on the block escaping into the fantasy worlds of sci-fi novels and the Atari 2600. After seeing *Star Wars* a few dozen times, he decided his life's ambition: "to fly to other planets and battle aliens." Contrary to most kids, he never gave up. Following a stab at rock god fantasy in a "disco punk" band called Shampoop, Clint found a more stimulating environment to live out his childhood dream: Quake.

Using the handle _fo0k (a satire of self-conscious hacker typescript) and a high-speed modem hustled from his job as a cable installer, he cofounded the Ruthless Bastards, a team of Doom junkies who became his closest friends. Though _fo0k said he probably wouldn't be hanging out with some of the younger, geekier clan members if it wasn't for the game, their friendships, he said, ran deep. The last time he stopped to check the clock, he was plugging in six hours a night.

Despite the camaraderie, _fo0k, like most players, rarely spoke to his "brothers" in person or on the phone, preferring instead the anonymity of the Internet's chat channels, the locker rooms of Quake. At any time, day or night, he could log on and trash-talk his way into a pickup game. "The Internet is my real home," he said. "At work, I'm sentient, but I find myself walking around in a daze, because I'm so bored with the usual stuff: my job, meeting people who aren't interesting. When I get home and start shooting the shit with the guys and start playing, that's when I get excited."

Although he was well known online for his wit and skills, _fo0k readily acknowledged the absurdity of being underappreciated, if not unknown, everywhere else. "The mainstream just sees them as little games," he said. "Sometimes I think I'm wasting my time, but I guess this is my chance to play rock god for five minutes. Everyone wants to be remembered. I'm really good at video games, so maybe this is how I can do it. . . . In some future Olympics," he joked, "the weight-lifting team will be standing there and right next to them: a bunch of weird-looking guys with big bulging foreheads."

_fo0k wasn't the only id fan with big dreams. One of his chief competitors in Impulse 9, the legendary game grrrl Stevie Case, was just beginning to transform her life through Quake. Stevie was among the leaders of a new generation of young women who were defying the stereotype of the adolescent boy gamer. Raised in the small town of Olathe, Kansas, the daughter of a social worker and a schoolteacher, she'd always had a strong competitive nature. She took to sports early on, becoming the first and only girl on the neighborhood T-ball team — much to the distress of the local dads, whose boys she regularly beat. By high school, Stevie had been voted athlete of the year and parlayed her popularity into becoming student government president. An exceptional student, she was among those flown to the White House to meet President Clinton. She wanted to be a politician.

Once enrolled at the University of Kansas, she overachieved even more — committing herself on the fast track to law school. She earned straight A's, ran for student government. She became a member of Mensa. Then Quake took hold. She was dating a guy, Tom "Entropy" Kizmey, who was deep in the throes of the game's grip. But unlike the women online who despaired over their men's obsessions, Stevie was eager to compete. Quake was everything that a woman was not supposed to be: loud, violent, aggressive. It was also creative: programmed to be even more extensible than Doom, thus giving rise to even more elaborate modifications. Stevie wanted it all. Soon enough she found herself at the top of her boyfriend's clan, Impulse 9, facing off in the ultimate showdown with their rivals, the Ruthless Bastards.

As the countdown on the screen began that day, Stevie slipped on her headphones and began nervously clicking her mouse. "You okay, honey?" asked her boyfriend, ready at a computer beside her; reflected in his screen, he resembled a hydrocephalic Emilio Estevez. Stevie gave him the thumbs-up and said, "I'm fine, hon." Down the hall in the Ruthless Bastards' room, _fo0k sucked the last of his cigarette and reached for the keyboard. "Okay, brothers," he said, "let's win."

But when the dust cleared, Stevie and her clan had clocked _fo0k's Bastards, making Impulse 9 the undisputed champions. Leaning back at her PC, Stevie slipped off her headphones and ran her hand through her hair. Victory felt good. She was powerful, supreme, connected with the gamers of the world, even the baddest of them all—her hero, John Romero. I'm not a lawyer, I'm not a politician, I'm a gamer, she resolved. And I'm going to Dallas.

The only place that wasn't in the throes of Quake deathmatch as 1997 arrived, it seemed, was a tiny company in Texas: id Software. No one was screaming or cursing, or smashing keyboards into the ground. With the renovations complete, the war room was divided into a suite of small private offices. The pool table had been sold, the Foosball shipped away. Everything was, if not respectable, respectably quiet. And everyone in the company knew why: John Romero—Ace Programmer, Current Rich Person, Deathmatch Surgeon—was gone.

American McGee felt Romero's absence from the moment he walked by his old office and saw the empty chair. Romero, even with his problems, had always bridged the gap between the owners and the employees. And there was no one who could even remotely take his place. Carmack didn't take into account that he had let go more than just John Romero, American thought. He had let go the soul of any video game company: the fun.

American wasn't the only one feeling gloomy. Quake's shareware retail experiment had proved disastrous. In theory, id was going to cut out retailers by allowing gamers to buy the shareware and then call an 800 number to place an order and receive a password that would unlock the rest of the game. But gamers wasted no time hacking the shareware to unlock the full version of the game for free. Worse, all the mundane aspects of distribution and order fulfillment were spinning out of control. In a desperate measure, id tried to put the brakes on the retail shareware, but it was too late. They were stuck with almost 150,000 CDs sitting in a warehouse.

Mike Wilson, id's biz guy, put the burden on their publisher, GTI—forcing them not only to absorb the inventory but to increase id's royalty before releasing the full version of Quake into the retail market. For GTI's Ron Chaimowitz, it was just more of the kids' audacity. Id had even made him wait to release the retail version of the game until it could rake in as many sales as possible through the shareware; Ron didn't get the game until *after* the lucrative holiday season, and by that time the shareware debacle had left its scar. Sales were good—with 250,000 units shipped—but not a phenomenon like Doom II. Id decided its days with GTI were over. Ron was disappointed but, with his company doing fine without id, his attitude was Good riddance.

Mike and his cohort Jay Wilbur had another plan: turn id into a publishing empire, beginning with their next game, a sequel to Quake called Quake II. "We don't need GTI," Jay said to the owners. "We don't need Activision, we can do this all on our own. We can keep the benefit, but we need an organization to do that. In order to do that right, we need to hire more people. And that can be id publishing, here, there, or yonder. It can be a completely separate company whose charter is to completely handle our product."

Kevin and Adrian were intrigued by the idea but knew it was Carmack's decision. Even though they were now the majority owners, there was no question about who was really in charge. Carmack's technology had long been the heart of id—with Romero out of the way, it was completely unfettered. The last thing Carmack wanted to do now was spoil the company by turning it into an empire—that had been Romero's wish, not his. Despite Carmack's battles with his mother's conservative fiscal ideals, he himself had become quite the conservative businessman. As long as he was in the company, he told Adrian and Kevin, id was going to stay small and let a new publisher, like Activision, handle their next game.

With Romero gone, Carmack felt happier than he had in some time. No more grandiose statements about stuff they were working on. No more all-night deathmatching. No more poison. Now, with the other guys beginning work on Quake II, using the existing graphics engine, he was free to experiment—no deadlines, no pressure, just pure immersive learning.

Carmack's first project was to explore the burgeoning hardware for 3-D computer graphics. In the past, only arcade machines had been designed specifically to improve or accelerate 3-D graphics. With robust computer games like Doom and Quake, however, start-up companies saw an opportunity finally to bring 3-D acceleration to home machines. This would be done by putting powerful graphics processing chips onto special cards that could be inserted into an existing PC. One manufacturer, called 3Dfx, convinced Carmack to port a version of Quake in a programming language called OpenGL, which could run with its debut line of Voodoo 3-D accelerator cards. Carmack completed the task in a weekend and uploaded the OpenGL version to the Web for free.

The hard-core gamers flipped at the results, which made the game at least 20 percent faster and smoother. Once they saw 3-D acceleration, they would never go back, and they eagerly spent the few hundred dollars to upgrade their machines. Other game programmers, as was becoming protocol, followed Carmack's lead and programmed for 3Dfx's cards. More card manufacturers jumped into the game. A new high-tech industry had begun. The success buoyed Carmack's other pet project, Quakeworld, a free program he wrote and distributed to improve Quake's multiplayer capabilities. With OpenGL improving Quake's graphics and Quakeworld improving Quake's networking, the game had never looked or played better.

But Carmack's hard work couldn't save id from the reverberations of Quake's stressful development. Before long, id began to hemorrhage employees. It started with biz guy Jay Wilbur, who quit after his four-year-old son asked him, "How come all the other daddies go to the baseball games and you never do?" Programmer Michael Abrash soon followed suit, returning to the structure and sanctity of Microsoft. Level designer Sandy Petersen, who had been on the skids with the management since clashing over Quake's design, was let go. Mike Wilson, marketing whiz, and Shawn Green, tech supporter and death-match fiend, gave notice: they were going to work for Romero.

The gaming community, already reeling from the split of Carmack and Romero, became ablaze with speculation until Carmack finally addressed them in an unusually personal and lengthy e-mail interview. "Lots of people will read what they like into the departures from id," he wrote, "but our development team is at least as strong now as it has ever been. Romero was pushed out of id because he wasn't working hard enough. . . . I believe that three programmers, three artists, and three level designers can still create the best games in the world. . . . We are scaling back our publishing biz so that we are mostly just a developer. This was allways [*sic*] a major point of conflict with Romero—he wants an empire, I just want to create good programs. Everyone is happy now."

Romero hit the highest button inside the gilded elevator of the Texas Commerce Building—fifty-five floors of bankers, lawyers, and oil moguls in the heart of downtown Dallas; now a twenty-nine-year-old gamer was bound for the top. Romero had been called here abruptly late one night by his real estate agent, who said he *had* to see this amazing penthouse that had become available. He was skeptical. Since leaving id to open his own company, he had seen dozens of spaces, but nothing was right. And there was *everything* at stake.

Romero was essentially starting from scratch. Though he'd received an undisclosed multimillion-dollar buyout from his partners at id (*Time* magazine estimated his net worth to be $10 million), the terms required that he relinquish all rights to id products and royalties—no more money from Doom or Quake. More important, Romero was on a mission. After years of feeling repressed by Carmack's shackles, he was finally free to pursue *his* vision of what a game, a game company, and, ultimately, a life could be. Not only was that vision big but it was everything that id Software was not.

"At id, the company was rolling in millions of dollars and we just had walls," Romero lamented. "It was the whole Carmack idea of 'I don't need anything on my walls, all I need is a table and a computer and a chair' instead of 'Okay we've got a lot of money, why not make it a really bad-ass office?'" Romero's new office wouldn't only be a fun place to work, it would be where a gamer could show the press, family, and friends that *games* had built an empire and that the empire would be the ultimate place to make more games.

When the elevator doors finally opened into the penthouse, it felt as though Romero was standing on top of the moon. The two-story, 22,500-square-foot loft seemed to spill into the stars. The space was bare but surrounded by a wraparound window view of the city and a seemingly endless sixty-foot arched glass ceiling. Anywhere Romero spun, he saw the kaleidoscopic twinkle of lights—evening lights from below, the celestial bodies up high. It was raw, waiting to be designed. Romero imagined a room full of pillows, a Vegas room with slot machines, a "Break Shit" room where you could just go around destroying things!

But there were problems, the agent explained. The space was so big and windowed and close to the sun that it was extremely difficult to air-condition. It was also expensive: $15 per square foot, or roughly $350,000 per month. For these reasons and the fact that the space was just too weird for tenants like Paine Webber, Texas Commerce Bank, or the Petroleum Club, the penthouse remained empty. No more, Romero said, eyes gleaming. "This is amazing. There is nothing like this. This is it," he declared. "*This* is a game company." He named it Dream Design.

With his old friend and sidekick Tom Hall, Romero pitched the Dream to eager publishers. Neither technology nor Carmack would be his ruler. In fact, he would simply license the Quake engine—which id had agreed to do—and make a game around it. He would have three designers, working on three games at a time in different genres. And he would give each designer a large enough staff to get the jobs done quickly. It wouldn't be just a game company, it would be an *entertainment* company. And the mantra of anything they produced would be loud and clear: "Design is law," Romero said. "What we design is what's going to be the game. It's not going to be that we design something and have to chop it up because the technology can't handle it or because some programmer says we can't do it. You design a game, you make it and that's what you do. That's the law. It's the fucking *design.*"

His terms for publishers were brash: $3 million per game with a 40 percent royalty, plus, he wanted to keep all the intellectual property rights as well as rights to port his company's games to other platforms. Companies balked but didn't back away. This was the age of vanity game development houses. Sid Meier, legendary designer of Civilization strategy games, had his own company, Firaxis. Will Wright, creator of the bestselling SimCity series, had his company, Maxis. Richard Garriott had Origin; a former employee of his named Chris Roberts would spawn off his own, Digital Anvil. After the success of Wolfenstein, Doom, and Quake, Romero was not just famous, he was bankable. Publishers flew him and Tom out first-class, putting them up in thousand-dollar-a-night suites in Beverly Hills and whisking them around in limousines to the best restaurants in town. The two felt giddy with the freedom and sense of possibilities. They washed away id's baggage with champagne.

With Romero planning to do a shooter and Tom a role-playing adventure game, Dream Design needed one other designer for balance. That person would be Todd Porter, who was then heading up a Dallas developer called 7th Level. Todd, whom Romero had met through an old Softdisk friend, seemed energetic, upbeat, and, most important, a gamer, a *real* gamer—a veteran Apple II guy. The thirty-six-year-old had originally gone to school to be a minister. But preaching, he discovered to his dismay, was as much about business as it was about spirituality. He didn't like the pressure he felt to have to land a sweet spot in some big church. So he dropped out of school and used the money to buy a computer.

With his parents divorced, Todd had to do what he could to provide for the family. He moved to Iowa to study business. He took a brief stint as an exotic dancer with the stage name Preacher Boy. With the money he saved, Todd refined his programming skills and eventually landed a job with Richard Garriott's Origin company in Austin. He soon left to found his own company with an artist, Jerry O'Flaherty, in Dallas. Tough times forced him to sell out to 7th Level, however, and his dreams of his own company seemed dashed. That was, until Romero walked in. Todd told Romero he had the business sense that would round out the team. Romero felt Todd indeed had a knack for selling the company. Plus, he could bring on Jerry, who could head up the art department. Over lunch at McDonald's, the four gamers agreed to join forces. They took notes on a napkin.

All they needed was a name. Dream Design wasn't good enough, Romero decided; he wanted something more original, something short, punchy, powerful, scientific, intelligent. Tom suggested Ion. The competition had better watch out, a friend quipped, "or they're going to get caught up in an Ion storm." Ion Storm it would be.

On Christmas Eve, Ion Storm closed a publishing deal with Eidos Interactive. Eidos was a British company that had been founded on the riches of South African gold mines and had recently scored a hit with a female-led shooter, kind of a sexy variation of Indiana Jones, called Tomb Raider. They were looking to develop more brand names; Romero was already among the biggest. They agreed to almost all Ion's terms: $3 million per game, but they offered to pay another $4 million for console rights. They also wanted to have an option on Ion's next three games, making it potentially a six-game deal. In total, it valued Ion Storm at $100 million.

With the money in place, Romero, Tom, and Todd sketched plans for their dream games. Tom began cobbling together ideas for a sprawling and comedic intergalactic adventure game called Anachronox. Todd announced plans for a strategy title about body-snatching slugs called Doppelganger. And Romero outlined his ultimate title ever, an epic first-person shooter that would take its name from the mystical sword Carmack had tantalized him with in their Dungeons and Dragons game long ago. It was the weapon for which Romero had risked everything—the dreams of his partners, the fate of Carmack's game; he had made a deal with the demons to get the sword Daikatana. That time, it led to the end of the world. This time, it would lead to his conquering it.

In Daikatana, the player would become Hiro Miyamoto, a Japanese biochemical student in twenty-fifth-century Kyoto who must save the world from Kage Mishima, an evil scientist who has stolen the Daikatana (Japanese for "big sword")—a magical blade invented by Miyamoto's ancestors. Using the sword's time-traveling powers, Mishima is altering history to his own corrupt ends, such as hijacking the cure for an AIDS-like disease. Faced with Hiro's threat, Mishima sends the young warrior on a wild, time-traveling goose chase between Kyoto, ancient Greece, dark-ages Norway, and post-apocalyptic San Francisco. For added drama, Hiro is teamed with sidekicks, the Shaft-like Superfly Johnson and the beautiful, brainy heroine Mikiko.

Daikatana embodied Romero's greatest ambitions. Every polygon of these grandiose worlds would have to be coded from scratch, interacting seamlessly with the characters and action. In addition to the complex nuances of the artificially intelligent characters, the game would require over one hundred unique levels and monsters spread throughout what were essentially four games—roughly four times the size of Quake. Romero had spent years making games almost completely on his own. But for John Romero's Daikatana, as the game was officially named, there was no way to do everything himself, as he would have preferred.

Romero proceeded to fill the ultimate gaming company with the ultimate gamers. Mike Wilson hoped finally to exercise all the outlandish marketing schemes he could never pull off at id. Shawn Green, Romero's old deathmatch partner from id, was ready to help with coding. After Romero put the word out on the Internet, rabid Doom and Quake fans swamped Ion Storm's e-mail server with résumés and mods. Romero handpicked his favorites, figuring that any who could wow him with a fresh character or monster or level had a place in his dream posse. Romero, after all, was once just like them: flipping burgers, eschewing sleep, school, and relationships to make and play games. So what if all these young dudes never actually *worked* in the business before? If they had the passion, the predisposition for crunch, that was qualification enough.

By early 1997, hard-core gamers who had been living and breathing Romero's games for years were road-tripping to Ion Storm's temporary offices to work—and deathmatch—with their mentor. Brian Eiserloh, who had achieved notoriety in college for his nude Doom hacking parties, took a job after sending in an application essay written in the form of a medieval short story. Will Loconto gave up his gig in the industrial band Information Society to be Ion Storm's sound designer. Sverre Kvernmo, a star mapper from the Doom community, left his home country of Norway to become Romero's lead level designer. These weren't hard sacrifices for them to make. "We were all starstruck by the Romero phenomenon," Sverre said.

Few were more struck than Stevie Case. Stevie was the University of Kansas Quake fan who had become known as one of the sharpest-shooting players on the scene. During a pilgrimage to Dallas, she'd managed to score a deathmatch with Romero. She lost, but just barely, and challenged him to a rematch. The next time around, Romero got clocked. As penance, he uploaded a Web shrine in Stevie's honor. Later he offered her a job.

Stevie and the other gamers weren't the only ones enamored. The press rejoiced over the vision of Ion Storm. Anyone who visited the temporary office was treated to the spirit of a *real* game company. Deathmatching wasn't just permitted, it was celebrated. At any given moment, Romero and dozens of others would be screaming obscenities while hunting each other down in Quake. Working with id's former PR company in New York, Mike regaled the press about an office that, when built out, would be "the Willy Wonka Chocolate Factory of Gaming!"—complete with an in-house movie theater, a massive game room, and a specially designed area of networked computers made specifically for deathmatching. *Time* named Romero among the country's top fifty "cyber elite." *Fortune* anointed Ion Storm one of the country's twenty-five "cool companies."

Eidos sent the Ion Storm owners on a whirlwind champagne and limousine press tour, which Mike cheekily dubbed the "No Excuses" tour, since these were game designers who were finally in the position essentially to put up or shut up. Mike described the group as the "Fab Four" of gaming, which pleased the guys to no end. Todd even suggested they take a picture of them crossing Abbey Road. But, behind the scenes, everyone knew who this company was about: John Romero.

Ion painted itself as the place of freedom and dreams, while id was the out-of-touch oppressor. It was about not just two companies but two visions: design versus technology, art versus science, Dionysus versus Apollo. "Id is a technology-oriented company," said Mike Wilson, "whereas our main focus is to indulge our artistic sensibilities. At id, by the time the 3-D engine was finished, there wasn't enough time to work on aspects of the game. We didn't think this was a well-balanced approach."

Romero agreed. "After I left," he told *Wired News*, "the mood at id turned dark and gloomy. . . . No more plans to expand the company; no one to confront Carmack on important issues. I want to create more types of games with no limits on creativity, and I want as many resources (i.e., people) as I need to get the job done. That is why I left." Romero told *The Times* of London that within two years Ion Storm would surpass id as the market leader. "It's going to happen," he said, "and it'll be great."

Carmack was pulling into the parking lot of id's black cube office building when he heard the crash. It was a terrible sound, the sound of his cherry-red Ferrari F40 getting swiped by a pickup truck. No sooner could he react than the truck peeled out of the lot and into the blur of traffic nearby. Carmack inspected the gruesome damage, then stomped upstairs and vented in a .plan file. "Words cannot do justice to how I feel right now," he typed. "If anyone knows a tall white male in the dallas [*sic*] area that now has red paint and carbon fibre [*sic*] on their tan pickup truck, turn the bastard in!"

Among the respondents was John Romero. "The F40 got hit," Romero posted online. "Carma."

This wasn't the first snipe from Romero. Every day, it seemed, someone from the office would wander in with some new outrage Romero had told the press. It was bad enough that he kept deriding id as an out-of-touch technology company. Worse, the id guys thought he was claiming sole credit for their success. Even Romero's official press release broadly credited him with being "responsible for the programming, design, and project management of the [id's] games." And journalists eagerly and lazily picked up the refrain, calling Romero "the creative talent behind [id]" and "the man responsible for creating the blockbusters Doom and Quake."

Such comments were becoming the talk of id. Though they knew the press was often misleading, Romero sure didn't seem to be taking an active role in trying to *correct* the misconceptions. It quickly became fashionable in the office to bash Romero and Ion Storm. American posted a .plan file mocking Romero's claim of having made id. Adrian and Kevin grumbled about how they were going to sink Romero's ship. But no one took up the war like id's new artist and Carmack's new friend, Paul Steed.

Paul was the antithesis of a computer game geek. Tough, muscular, inscribed with tattoos, Paul had been abandoned by his father and spent a transient childhood up and down the Eastern Seaboard. He had an early interest in computers but gave it up for other pursuits. "Either you stay up all night chasing that program you want to write," he said, "or you stay up all night chasing girls. For me, women won out." Though talented, he grew into a volatile, confrontational personality, eventually getting thrown out of military school for a classroom brawl. He retreated to the computer world and took a job as an artist for Origin. The job at id was a dream, Paul thought, when he was presented with the offer. He didn't know he'd be walking into a war.

Paul didn't know much about John Romero, other than that id's estranged cofounder kept making surprise visits to Suite 666, as if he still wanted to be friends. Romero's visits angered the staff, particularly Kevin and Adrian, who resented him behaving as if he were not trashing id in the press. "Why is that fucker coming over here all the time?"

Paul would hear them complain. Finally, Paul spoke up. "Fuck Romero and his company!" he said. "Let's just show up in his office and see what happens!"

The next day Paul, Adrian, and Kevin paid a visit to Ion Storm's temporary office space near downtown Dallas. Romero was surprised to see them but showed them around nonetheless. Paul noticed that one of Romero's artists seemed to be using an antiquated program to create his animations. So he came back to id and questioned Ion's direction in a public .plan file. The comment ignited what became known as the .plan wars. Id and Ion employees began disparaging each other on a daily basis. Romero eventually jumped in, sending Paul a cheeky e-mail asking him if he'd endorse Daikatana on the back of the game's box. Paul showed Adrian the e-mail and suggested he retaliate. Adrian was more than happy to give Paul his blessing. "Dude," Paul wrote to Romero, "don't fuck with me because I'll grab you by your ludicrously long hair and kick your ass back into the Doom days where you wish you were."

Carmack, up until this point, had stayed aloof. But as the competitive bile built in the office, even he felt himself getting swept up in the fervor. So, in what he described as "an experiment in mood manipulation," Carmack decided to feel what it was like to take the gloves off. He chose quite a forum for his first public salvo: *Time* magazine. In an interview for a two-page profile of Romero, Carmack set the record straight that, contrary to his ex-partner's frequent assertions, Romero didn't quit, he was fired. "After he got rich and famous, the push to work just wasn't there anymore," Carmack said. "He was handed his resignation." He scoffed at Romero's ambitions for fame and fortune, saying, "There's only so many Ferraris I want to own." And he added that there was "no chance" Romero would fulfill his promise of finishing Daikatana in time for Christmas.

Romero retorted in the same story that "id was too limiting, too small, small thinking," which did little to quell the id-Ion deathmatch. The skirmish became even more public with the approach of the Electronic Entertainment Expo, the video game industry's massive annual convention, where companies demo their latest, greatest games. Id had every confidence that its showing, Quake II, would not only outshine John Romero's Daikatana but crush it.

Since work had begun on Quake II in September 1996, it had been shaping up to be the most cohesive and technologically impressive id game yet. The idea had come from a 1961 World War II movie called *The Guns of Navarone,* in which the heroes must take out two giant enemy guns that reside in a mountain fortress on a remote island. It was the perfect theme, the guys at id thought, something that could give their game not just a militaristic milieu but a narrative, a purpose—which had never really been in an id game before. In Quake II, players would be cast as marines doing battle on the evil planet of Stroggos, where mutant Stroggs have been hoarding human limbs and flesh to build a lethal race of cyborgs. The object: take out the Stroggs before they conquer humankind. To do this, players would have to take out the weapon protecting the alien species, the Big Gun.

The technology would bring this world to life. Though Carmack didn't consider his new engine nearly as great a leap as Quake, it was still going to be formidable. Most significant, Quake II would run with either software or hardware acceleration. This meant that someone running a new 3Dfx card could get exceptional special effects—colored lighting, smoother surfaces, a more fluid, cinematic feel.

Under the leadership of Kevin Cloud, who was always the most diplomatic and organized of the owners, id's troop took on its own militaristic approach. With the deathmatching days over, the long hours proceeded with quiet intensity. The Shreveport swamp band of the past—Tom, Romero, Jay, Mike—was replaced with a regime that fulfilled Carmack's conservative vision, including a new CEO—Todd Hollenshead, a former tax consultant at Arthur Andersen—and Tim Willits, the company's new lead designer.

Carmack uncharacteristically effused. "I doubt I can convey just how well things are going here," he posted on June 16, 1997, in his .plan file, just before attending the Electronic Entertainment Expo, a.k.a. E3. "Things probably look a little odd from the outside, but our work should speak for itself. I have been breaking into spontanious [*sic*] smiles lately just thinking about how cool things are (of course, that could just be a sleep deprivation effect . . .). We have a totally kick-ass team here. We are on schedule. (no shit!) We are doing a great product. Everyone watch out!"

The 1997 E3 convention in Atlanta was not just devoted to video games, it *was* a video game. Stepping inside the main floor was like walking into the heart of a machine: flashing lights, pounding rock, skateboarders, and the ubiquitous "booth babes"—actresses, models, and strippers who dressed up like video game vixens and pressed the gamers' eager flesh. The babe of the moment was Lara Croft, protagonist of Tomb Raider. As lines of attendees with plastic bags of giveaway toys lined up to play games, the Laras worked the floor. But they couldn't compete with the real star of the show, the long-haired guy walking through the halls and leaving a trail of bowing gamers in his wake.

"We're not worthy, we're not worthy, we're not worthy," the gamers cooed to John Romero or, as he was lately referring to himself, God. Romero had accepted the divine moniker as a tongue-in-cheek descriptor of himself in his .plan file, but it wasn't entirely a joke. As far as the press and fans were concerned, Romero was a rock god. He was everywhere: *Computer Gaming World, The Wall Street Journal, Fortune* — on covers, in color, regal. In an ad for a joystick, Romero wore a crown and flowing red robe to give, as the tag line declared, "The Royal Seal of Approval." "If you want to crack skulls with the big boys," Romero's quote read, "the Panther XL is the weapon of choice." His publicity stills featured him sitting in a nine-thousand-dollar medieval chair he had bought for his Tudor mansion.

Romero looked more royal than ever. He was dressing in tight-fitting designer shirts, jewelry. He had let his hair grow out so that it flowed to the middle of his back. His mane had become so renowned that, in an online interview, he dispensed his own ten-step plan for grooming: "I always flip my hair over in front of my face and look at the floor while using a brush and hair dryer to slowly dry all my hair. Brushing downward while drying will help straighten your hair and completely drying it will make sure it doesn't kink up or curl up."

Walking through the kaleidoscopic floor show of E3, Romero

buzzed and beamed as brightly as the games around him, but he was not there to preen. He was there, as everyone in attendance was keenly aware, to unveil a demonstration of Daikatana. From the day production began in March 1997, Romero had promised the game for a Christmas 1997 release, which meant that, by now, it would be nearly halfway to completion. Romero thought this was more than doable since he had assembled such a large team—eight artists versus id's two, for example—to get the job done. Though Carmack had publicly expressed skepticism, the gamers and press were frothing at the bit. They had reason to feel piqued. Between the rock 'n' roll showmanship of Mike Wilson, the hyperbolic confidence of Romero, and the multimillion-dollar vested interest of Eidos, Ion Storm had pulled out all the stops to hype the game. And, with one ad in particular, a lot of people thought they had finally gone too far.

Earlier in the year, on the suggestion of Mike Wilson, Romero had agreed to an ad that would emulate the cheeky bravado of deathmatch smack-talk—the very language Romero had helped define. But when he saw the words in print, he felt a tinge of hesitation. "Are you sure about this?" he asked Mike.

"Yeah," Mike said, "don't be a pussy."

Romero agreed. The ad ran in all the major gaming publications in April with simply these words written in black against a red background: "John Romero's About to Make You His Bitch." Underneath was the tag line "Suck It Down!"—a phrase Mike had recently trademarked. The ad achieved its intended effect and then some. Gamers were not only provoked, they were pissed. Who did Romero think he was? Had all this fame gotten to his head? But they were willing to give him a chance, to see if his game would really be, as he was promising, the coolest one planet Earth had ever seen. Since it was coming from the ego at id, the Surgeon of Wolfenstein, Doom, and Quake, they certainly wanted to believe. At E3 they were ready for their first chance.

The Daikatana demo was front and center in the Eidos booth, right alongside promos for the much-anticipated Tomb Raider sequel. The demo of the game's Norway level was made especially for this event. And gamers crowded around the screens to see it. Gone were the dark mazes of Doom and Quake. Instead, scenes were outdoors, with blankets of snow covering little Norwegian cottages, teasing glimpses of ancient Greek temples. Gamers were complimentary but not ecstatic. When Romero wandered over to id's booth, he found out why.

He pushed his way through the crowd to see the demo of Quake II. His face filled with yellow light as his jaw slackened. *Colored lighting!* Romero couldn't believe what he was seeing. The setting was a dungeonlike military level, but when the gamer fired his gun, the yellow blast of the ammunition cast a corresponding yellow glow as it sailed down the walls. It was subtle, but when Romero saw the dynamic colored lighting, it was a moment just like that one back at Softdisk when he saw Dangerous Dave in Copyright Infringement for the first time. "Holy fuck," he muttered. Carmack had done it again.

Romero thought Quake II was the best thing he had ever seen on a computer. By programming the game specifically to take advantage of hardware acceleration, Carmack had forged a true thing of beauty. Colored lighting brought the world magnificently to life. This was the next wave, Romero knew; Carmack's game was also, alas, his competition. The difference between his game and id's was like that between a piece of paper and a color TV set, Romero thought. There's no way in hell Daikatana can come out against this, not the way this looks.

Part of Romero's license deal with id was that he could upgrade to use their next engine, but he'd never anticipated the leap would be so great. Now he knew he had to scrap all the existing work on Daikatana and redo the game using the Quake II engine. But there was a problem: id's contract specifically stipulated that a licensee couldn't *use* the new engine until id's game was on the shelves. This meant that Romero would not get the Quake II engine until after Christmas. He would have to finish Daikatana using the existing technology, then spend about a month, he estimated, converting it when he got the Quake II engine.

Carmack's technology had once again forced him to change his plans.

Later in the show, the gamers made their way to the *other* main event: the Red Annihilation deathmatch tournament sponsored by id. In the middle of the floor was the grand prize: Carmack's cherry-red Ferrari 328. "I bought my first Ferrari after the success of Wolfenstein 3-D," Carmack told the press. "Doom and Quake have bought three more. Four Ferraris is too many for me. Rather than sell off one of them or stick it in a warehouse, I'm going to give it back to the gamers that brought it to me in the first place. The king of this Quake deathmatch is going to get a really cool crown."

More than two thousand gamers had been competing online for the right to be one of the sixteen flown to E3 to compete. Everyone was gathered for the finals, which came down to Tom "Entropy" Kizmey, the sharpshooting clan member of the University of Kansas's Impulse 9, and Dennis "Thresh" Fong, winner of the first official death-match event, Microsoft's Judgment Day. The two sat onstage in front of Carmack's car, which bore the license plate IDTEK1. With the crowd cheering, they battled as their match played out on a large overhead screen. Thresh could see the reflection of the Ferrari in his monitor as he closed in for his final slaying, winning the deathmatch thirteen kills to one.

Carmack walked onstage and handed Thresh the keys. "So how are you planning on getting the car home?" he asked. "I don't know," Thresh said. "I guess I'll ship it." Carmack came back a half hour later and handed Thresh five thousand dollars in cash to cover the costs.

As the crowd cleared, Romero wandered up to see who was around from id. Just because they were competitors didn't mean they couldn't be friends. He found Carmack and a couple of other id guys gathered near some computers. They talked about the event, and then it was suggested that they have a go at deathmatching each other. Romero beat everyone until it came down to just him and Carmack.

The Two Johns sat at their machines and faced off. It was funny how the games had taken on such different meanings over the years. They'd played Super Mario back in Shreveport, when the world was full of possibilities and id was just an idea from the deep. They'd played F-Zero, the hovercraft racing game, in Wisconsin to escape the cold and dream of the race cars they could someday afford to own. They had played Doom, that very first deathmatch, which foretold the fame and fortune to come. And now they were competing for the first time in

Quake—the game that had finally torn them apart. In all those long months of development, they had never played each other.

On cue, they were off—blasting rocket launchers at each other through the halls. No sooner had it begun than Romero, the Surgeon, made giblets of Engine John. This match was over. The next one would take place in an even more challenging arena: the one where Quake II and Daikatana were destined to meet. And this world guaranteed competition—and surprises—of its own.

FOURTEEN

Silicon Alamo

Brother Jake stood behind the bar of the Horny Toad Cantina in Mesquite mixing up another Big Fucking Gun. One part Rumplemintz, one part Midori, with a splash of blue curaçao, the BFG was a drink he'd concocted in honor of his favorite weapon from Doom. It was the least he could do, considering the cantina was right across the highway from id's office. The toxic green cocktail was the unofficial toast of Dallas, the new capital of the video game gold rush.

By the summer of 1997, Dallas had become to gamers what Seattle was to musicians in the early 1990s; id was Nirvana. In the five years since the Two Johns had rolled into town with a Pac-Man machine in the back of their truck, the game developer community there had more than tripled. The growth extended to Austin, where just as many were popping up around Richard Garriott's flagship company, Origin. *Time* called the Texas gamers the "New Cowboys." *Wired* called them "Doom babies." *The Boston Globe* dubbed the state's video game renaissance "the new Hollywood."

A more appropriate name would have been Silicon Alamo, because the crux of the rush was first-person shooters. Between Doom, Quake, and Scott Miller's hit Duke Nukem 3D, shooters had spawned a multi-million-dollar cottage industry and dominated the video game charts. This fulfilled the dream that id had set out to accomplish back at Softdisk: to make the PC a viable gaming platform. Of the $3.7 billion generated in 1996 from interactive entertainment software, nearly half—$1.7 billion—was from PC games alone. "The PC gaming boom," declared *USA Today*, "has helped the industry bounce back."

With the prospects of id's and Ion's fame and fortune, a new generation of companies were arising around Dallas. Rogue and Ritual, spawned respectively from id and 3D Realms, specialized in making so-called mission packs, add-on levels for Quake. Ensemble Studios, empowered by the addition of id's Sandy Petersen, created one of the bestselling strategy games of all time, Age of Empires. Terminal Reality, founded by ex-Apogee members and the creator of Microsoft's groundbreaking Flight Simulator engine, devoted itself to a range of multiplatform gaming products. The Cyberathlete Professional League was trying to turn live deathmatching events into the gaming version of the NFL.

Id did much to increase the community by licensing out its technology. In addition to Ion Storm, other companies were now paying close to $250,000, as well as royalties, to use the Quake engine. Though id would profit from some of its competition, there was more on the rise. Soon the gaming press began speculating about the "Quake killers" that would or could knock id from its perch. Duke Nukem 3D had already received much acclaim. Valve, a Seattle-based company founded by some former Microsoft employees, had licensed the Quake engine to make Half-Life, a game that had previewed at E3 to a favorable response. Unreal, a shooter created by Epic, the North Carolina company discovered by Scott Miller years before, had demoed as well to laudable reviews. Then, of course, there was Daikatana. With all these games due sometime over the next year, as well as id's own Quake II, the Silicon Alamo showdown promised to be one of the best shoot-outs in years—if only those involved could survive the battles brewing in their own companies.

The race was on. Carmack was behind the wheel of his Ferrari F40, burning down the drag strip as the Porsche 911 stormed up behind him. It was a bright sunny day in Ennis, Texas. Carmack had decided to rent out this country racetrack for a little company competition. It was a fun way for everyone to flex the power of the sports cars the games had afforded them. This wasn't the only track they had been visiting of late. In a pinch, Carmack had once called the mayor of Mesquite and asked him if he would shut down the local airport long enough for the company to have a few little drag races. The mayor was happy to oblige. Carmack, after all, had donated tens of thousands of dollars of equipment, including bulletproof vests (which some gamer on the force stitched with Doom patches), to the local police. He deserved consideration.

The drag races weren't the only contests in town. Though Quake II was the favorite shooter at E3, the pressure inside id was mounting. Carmack had absolved himself of his competitive mood manipulation test—determining that such motivation didn't suit his circuitry—but the rest of the guys were hardly resigned. Other companies' shooters, even id's own licensees, became regular subjects of ridicule. When the first demo of Half-Life came through the doors, many insisted it would do nothing less than fail.

The company, like Quake II, had grown militaristic and serious. For some, all the fun and humor seemed to have been sucked out of id, not just figuratively but literally—with the most fun people—Romero, Mike, Jay, Shawn—all out the door. In place was real-life competition that had begun against Romero and now spread among themselves. American and others blamed Carmack, who sequestered himself in his office, for passive-aggressively encouraging the conflict.

One of the main sources of distrust among the employees was id's competitive bonus structure. Every quarter or so the owners would meet to assign a dollar amount to each employee. They would then split up a bonus payment based on those decisions. One quarter someone might get $100,000; the next, $20,000. The owners admitted that it was an arbitrary and imperfect plan, but it was the only one they could surmise. As a result, the employees realized that the easiest way to get the higher bonuses was to outwit, outplay, and outsmart each other. It was a business deathmatch.

With Romero out of the picture, the competition had only grown more fierce. Though American had been the golden boy during the early days of Quake, those days were over. Carmack had turned cold, American thought, making him feel like he was never sure if they were really friends. For Carmack, American was just another casualty of self, someone with talent who'd lost his drive and focus, like Romero. As a result, Tim Willits, American's old adversary, swiftly moved into favor, triggering rampant infighting.

More and more, Carmack wanted to grab his laptop and disappear into a hotel room in some strange state. All he wanted to do was code. That was all he had ever wanted. The problems at id, he thought, were precisely the kinds of problems that he could avoid by keeping the company small, the team tight. "For any given project," he posted in his .plan file online, "there is some team size beyond which adding more people will actually cause things to take longer. This is due to loss of efficiency from chopping up problems, communication overhead, and just plain entropy. It's even easier to reduce quality by adding people. I contend that the max programming team size for id is very small."

With Romero gone, Carmack's life could aspire to the elegance of his code: simple, efficient, lean. This was how he would lead his company. This was how he would make his games. He would not succumb to internal pressures or grand aspirations that would lead to infinite delays. He would deliver. And on December 9, 1997, he did just that.

"**Oh my god.** Quake 2 is the most impressive game I've ever played on a computer. . . . What game have you played lately that was better than Quake 2? I predict the answer is none." Among the most gushing reviews — and there were many — of Quake II was this one from Romero. He posted it on December 11 in his .plan file two days after the game was released. Romero had burned through nonstop for forty-eight hours, completing the entire game in one long twitch. He had reason to be excited.

By licensing the Quake II engine, Romero was assured that he could implement all the tricks of the game—including colored lighting—in Daikatana. Not only was he making what he thought was the most ambitious shooter ever created but he would be able to do it using the most ambitious engine ever created. It was finally like the ultimate collaboration—a marriage of technology and design that Romero could never achieve at id. And now, best of all, no one—not Carmack, not anyone—could get in the way.

Or so he thought. The burgeoning troops of Ion Storm were grumbling with discontent. It had begun when Ion released the "bitch ad" in April. Just as that backlash was stinging, the company went to E3 in June 1997 with what many thought to be a shabby demo of Daikatana. Romero seemed more interested in playing games and courting the press, they thought, than in telling them what they needed to do to realize his game. And the game, as a result, was feeling further and further from completion.

Unlike Romero, most on his staff didn't like the idea of switching Daikatana to the Quake II technology. In fact, they *hated* it. Romero seemed to have no idea how much work it was going to take just to implement the bare essentials of his four-hundred-page Daikatana design document. He wanted sixty-four monsters! Four time zones! A game four times the size of Quake! They'd have trouble meeting the new March 1998 deadline without the pressure of switching technologies. Now how were they going to handle this?

They weren't the only ones with suspicions after E3. Eidos was not pleased to find out that Ion Storm's flagship title was now going to miss the Christmas season. But the Eidos executives were willing to give Romero the benefit of the doubt. Romero assured them, as he assured his staff, that the game would be pushed back only a few months. "Bodies plus manpower," he said, was going to be the formula of success. The company already had eighty people, and it was still growing. *With all those people at work, of course the work would get completed. Just look at what we did at id with barely thirteen guys!* Eidos had no choice but to take his word, since he was managing the development of the game without intervention on their part. For all they knew, the game really *was* just a few months from hitting the shelves. And they were willing to do whatever it took to help make that happen.

What that took was money. After less than a year, Eidos's original $13 million deal—which was supposed to fund all three games—was starting to dwindle away. Eighty people on staff meant eighty salaries and, with two computers per person, 160 state-of-the-art machines with twenty-one-inch monitors. The office renovations were now approaching the $2 million mark. In all, there was no end in sight. Something had to be done. Mike Wilson, Ion's marketing whiz, had a plan.

Ever since his days at id, Mike had dreamed of running his own publishing company. And he'd made this dream clear to Romero and the other owners of Ion the moment he came on board. They even nicknamed the plan Ion Strike, which would be the self-publishing wing they'd start once they finished their obligation to Eidos. Mike couldn't believe that Romero, unbeknownst to him, had signed not a three-game deal with Eidos, as he had expected, but a deal that gave them the option on three more. This meant that Ion received $13 million for its first three games and, when presented with the next three game ideas, Eidos could decide whether to fund them as well. The faster they burned through the options, the faster they'd get their cash and be on their way to Ion Strike. The time now was to burn.

The first deal made to cash in on this plan was to acquire Dominion, which Todd Porter had begun at 7th Level. The game was languishing at Todd's former company, and he convinced the other owners that it was the perfect fit for Ion. They could simply buy it for $1.8 million, and it would take him only six weeks or so to get it out the door. Then he'd finish the game he was originally planning to do, Doppelganger. They made the deal. But it was only the beginning.

In September 1997, Romero had heard through the grapevine that a game designer named Warren Spector was looking for somewhere to go. At forty-one years old, Warren was a well-regarded veteran of the industry. The son of a dentist and a reading teacher in New York, he had grown up intellectual and academic. While pursuing a doctorate in radio, television, and film at the University of Texas at Austin in the late 1970s, Warren fell in with the town's burgeoning community of science-fiction authors and gamers, eventually taking a job with Richard Garriott's company, Origin. Games, for him, were not just diversions, they were the closest thing to artificial reality.

"There's never been a medium in the history of mankind that can literally put you in another world," he said, "we're stuck here." But, with the right balance of story and technology, a good game can get close. "This is the only medium ever that lets ordinary people travel to other worlds. . . . I am never going to fly a World War I biplane. I'm never going to visit a space station. I'm never going to be a super spy. But when I play one of these games, I am."

As id popularized what he thought were mindless first-person shooters, Warren worked on more literary first-person games, which he termed "immersive simulations." Titles like Ultima Underworld, Thief, and System Shock relied more on a player's intellect and stealth than on the trigger finger. Romero thought he'd be a perfect fit. Warren signed on to head up his own development team in what would become Ion Austin. He set to work on an idea for *his* own dream product—a sci-fi counterterrorist game that would be a most realistic and gripping immersive simulation. The title was Deus Ex. When Romero's public relations company tried to pull Warren into the fray, however, he was quick to draw a line in the sand. "I will never say the words 'suck it down,'" he told them, "and I don't want to make anybody my bitch. We're going to be the classy part of this company, just get ready for it."

Mike Wilson was less than concerned about how he himself was coming off. At a video game industry trade show in England in September, he called a meeting with the executives of Eidos and presented them with an outline of Ion Storm's *next* three games. "Here they are," he said, "take them or leave them." Mike had squeezed publishers in the past, particularly with the Quake shareware deal that essentially cut out GTI and the retailers. The Eidos executives didn't even discuss the plan. Who the hell did Mike think he was? Ion Storm was already behind on their first three titles, and now they wanted to talk about their *next* three? No deal was struck.

Todd Porter told the other owners that after the meeting he received a call from the Eidos CEO threatening to strangle Mike. Todd, who had long been against the idea of burning through the Eidos options, complained to Romero and Tom, but to no avail. They were too immersed in their games, he thought, to tend the store. So he decided to tend it himself. He didn't like what he found. Mike and the chief operating officer, Bob Wright, he thought, were recklessly spending cash without keeping clear tabs.

But while Todd was moving in against them, Mike was taking similar steps against Todd. Easygoing and fun-loving, Mike had quickly become something of a mentor to the young gamers at Ion Storm. And they were opening up to him about their increased dismay. Todd and his Dominion team were a pain in the ass, they said; so were Jerry's artists. A culture clash was emerging. While Romero's team was composed of young gamers from the Doom community, Todd's and Jerry's teams were older and more removed. Todd had hired a few PhDs; few of Romero's gamers had even graduated from college. Worse, Todd's guys didn't know the game that had made Ion Storm possible. Romero's crew was shocked that a guy from Todd's team didn't even recognize Doom when it was being played on someone's machine.

After hearing these complaints daily, Mike decided something had to be done. In October he took Romero and Tom to a bar and told them the things that their own staffs had been afraid to say: everyone hated Todd. Dominion, despite his assurances, was taking longer than six weeks and wasn't looking too impressive. Todd didn't fit in with the company. He was wearing business suits to work, for Christ's sake. They agreed to let Todd go.

The next week, on the elevator to tell Todd the news, however, Romero backed down. "Man, I can't do it," he told Mike. "I don't feel like we've given him a chance, and we're just firing him because everybody hates him. We should just talk to him and lay down some ultimatums and offer to help him." Mike was shocked. Romero had flipped his bit again. But Mike didn't realize just what the implications of that flip would mean. The next month Mike was called into a meeting himself. The owners, particularly Todd, had had enough *with him*. Eidos was calling every day and saying how much they couldn't stand working with him. And they had discovered some problems: without the owners' knowledge, Wilson had borrowed company money to buy a new BMW. Furthermore, the self-publishing deal was just too out of focus. Ion Storm didn't need to publish games, Romero said, it needed to *make* games. And if Mike was dead set on being a publisher, then Mike would have to go. He went.

With Mike out of the picture, Romero could buckle down and lead his team to the completion of the task at hand. By February 1998, he got what he had been waiting for: the Quake II code. It was the stuff that would enable them to put the completion of Daikatana into high gear. But when Romero opened the file, he took one look at the code and froze. Oh my God, he thought, what had Carmack done?

"Do you have some aspirin?" Carmack asked his friend, as they walked into a casino in Las Vegas.

"Do you have a headache?"

"No," Carmack said, "but I will soon."

It was February 8, 1998, and Carmack was about to put his brain to the test: counting cards in blackjack. This had become something of a new fascination of his. "Having a reasonable grounding in statistics and probability and no belief in luck, fate, karma, or god(s), the only casino game that interests me is blackjack," he wrote in a .plan file. "Playing blackjack properly is a test of personal discipline. It takes a small amount of skill to know the right plays and count the cards, but the hard part is making yourself consistantly [*sic*] behave like a robot, rather than succumbing to your 'gut instincts.'" To refine his skills before the trip, Carmack applied his usual learning approach: consuming a few books on the subject and composing a computer program, in this case one that simulated the statistics of blackjack dealt cards.

His research proved successful, netting him twenty thousand dollars, which he donated to the Free Software Foundation, an organization of like-minded believers in the Hacker Ethic. "Its [*sic*] not like I'm trying to make a living at [blackjack]," Carmack wrote online after his trip, "so the chance of getting kicked out doesn't bother me too much." It didn't take long for him to find out just how he'd feel. On the next trip, Carmack was approached by three men in dark suits who said, "We'd appreciate if you'd play any other game than blackjack."

The others at the table watched in disbelief. "Why are they doing this to you?" a woman asked.

"They think that I'm counting cards," Carmack said.

"They think you can *remember* all those different cards?"

"Yeah," Carmack replied, "something like that."

"Well, what do you do?"

"I'm a computer programmer," he said, as he was escorted out the door.

Casinos weren't the only places Carmack sought escape in February 1998. His old desire for monkish seclusion brought him rather spontaneously one day to a small, anonymous hotel room somewhere in Florida. Despite the glowing reviews and great sales of Quake II, the stress of the office had finally proven too great: all the infighting, the bitching, the moaning, the real-life deathmatches between the increasingly dissatisfied staff. Things had gotten so bad that they even worked their way into the game. A secret level created by Tim Willits contained portraits of each id member on the wall. Each portrait triggered some type of animation that, in Tim's mind, reflected the personality of the staffer: Carmack's disappeared into the floor when anyone approached.

Now Carmack had vanished for real — sequestering himself in this faraway hotel room for a week. Pizza boxes littered the floor. The phone didn't ring. The door didn't open. The only distraction was when his throat dried out so much that he had to venture outside for another Diet Coke. He had even bought a special laptop for the occasion: a Dolch portable Pentium II system with full-length PCI slots — just roomy enough for his Evans & Sutherland OpenGL accelerator. Ostensibly, he had come here to research what he was calling his Trinity engine, a new leap of a graphics system that he would develop while the rest of the team churned out a mission pack for Quake II. But when he arrived back in Mesquite the next week, he found himself as well with an uncommon need to reflect in a .plan file he posted online:

Name: John Carmack
Description: Programmer
Project: Quake 2
Last Updated: 02/1998 03:06:55 (Central Standard Time)

Ok, I'm overdue for an update.

The research getaway went well. In the space of a week, I only left my hotel to buy diet coke. It seems to have spoiled me a bit, the little distractions in the office grate on me a bit more since. I will likely make week long research excursions a fairly regular thing during non-crunch time. Once a quarter sounds about right.

I'm not ready to talk specifically about what I am working on for trinity. Quake went through many false starts (beam trees, portals, etc) before settling down on its final architecture, so I know that the odds are good that what I am doing now won't actually be used in the final product, and I don't want to mention anything that could be taken as an implied "promise" by some people.

I'm very excited by all the prospects, though.

Many game developers are in it only for the final product, and the process is just what they have to go through to get there. I respect that, but my motivation is a bit different.

For me, while I do take a lot of pride in shipping a great product, the achievements along the way are more memorable. I don't remember any of our older product releases, but I remember the important insights all the way back to using CRTC wraparound for infinate [*sic*] smooth scrolling in Keen (actually, all the way back to understanding the virtues of structures over parallel arrays in apple II assembly language . . .). Knowledge builds on knowledge.

I wind up catagorizing [*sic*] periods of my life by how rich my learning experiences were at the time.

My basic skills built up during school on apple II computers, but lack of resources limited how far and fast I could go. The situation is so much better for programmers today—a cheap used PC, a linux CD, and an internet account, and you have all the tools and resources necessary to work your way to any level of programming skill you want to shoot for.

My first six months at Softdisk, working on the PC, was an incredible learning experience. For the first time, I was around a couple of programmers with more experience than I had (Romero and Lane Roath [*sic*]), there were a lot of books and materials available, and I could devote my full and undivided attention to programming. I had a great time.

The two years following, culminating in Doom and the various video game console work I did, was a steady increase in skills and knowledge along several fronts—more graphics, networking, unix, compiler writing, cross development, risc architectures, etc.

The first year of Quake's development was awesome. I got to try so many new things, and I had Michael Abrash as my sounding board. It would probably surprise many classically trained graphics programmers how little I new [*sic*] about conventional 3-D when I wrote Doom—hell, I had problems properly clipping wall polygons (which is where all the polar coordinate nonsense came from). Quake forced me to learn things right, as well as find some new innovations.

The last six months of Quake's development was mostly pain and suffering trying to get the damn thing finished. It was all worth it in the end, but I don't look back at it all that fondly.

The development cycle of Quake 2 had some moderate learning experiences for me (glquake, quakeworld, radiosity, openGL tool programming, win32, etc), but it also gave my mind time to sift through a lot of things before getting ready to really push ahead.

I think that the upcoming development cycle for trinity is going to be at least as rewarding as Quake's was. I am reaching deep levels of understanding on some topics, and I am branching out into several completely new (non-graphics) areas for me, that should cross-polinate [*sic*] well with everything else I am doing.
There should also be a killer game at the end of it. :)

The good mood didn't last. Like Romero at Ion Storm, Carmack was discovering that the glory days of a small team and easy chemistry were gone. In their place was a palpable atmosphere of bitterness and dysfunction. The tension between Tim, American, and the other level designers had reached a boiling point. Adrian and Kevin were battling with Paul Steed. They disliked each other too strongly to work closely together on the mission pack, Carmack realized. The solution: build the next game around the company's animosity. Quake III would be a deathmatch-only title, using most of his ideas for the Trinity engine, that would allow the map designers to work in complete isolation from each other.

Carmack's idea did not go over well. Adrian was vocally upset with yet another marines and shotguns shoot-'em-up game. He felt like they had been making the same title for years, and he wanted something different. So did American. Paul agreed, lobbying to do a title that had more of a story, more characters, more freshness. He drafted a long design document detailing a story for the game. Carmack shot it down, saying that story was not important. Even Kevin, long the ultimate team player of the group, expressed his dismay, telling Carmack that if he wanted to do this game he'd have to find a different project manager. This was Carmack's company now more than ever. Quake III would be Carmack's game.

For American, it was the beginning of the end. He was called into a meeting with the owners and told that he was being fired for not performing. Carmack thought American had served his purpose but had now gone the route of Romero. When American wanted more of an explanation he was told, ultimately, that it was because no one liked him. Typical, he thought. It was indicative of what the company had become since Romero had left. There was no balance anymore.

He wasn't the only one feeling newfound empathy for Romero. Even though Paul Steed had never worked with him, he was beginning to think that firing Romero had been a terrible mistake. "Romero is chaos and Carmack is order," he said. "Together they made the ultimate mix. But when you take them away from each other, what's left?"

The emerald green elevator doors slid open on the penthouse of the Texas Commerce Building. In February 1998, Romero stepped out to see at last the completed renovation of his Willy Wonka factory. Everything he had imagined was there: the game room with the vintage arcade machines, the Foosball, the pool table. A deathmatch arena with shiny twenty-one-inch monitors wrapped around a fine oak kiosk. A bank of twelve television sets flashing MTV. A maze of corrugated steel cubicles that resembled a level of a game. A kitchen overflowing with candy and junk food. And, wrapping around and on top of the 22,500 square feet, windows that scraped the clouds. Romero took it all in and had one thought: Holy shit, we gotta fucking make some great games.

They needed to make great games because the expenses, Romero knew, were even greater. The office renovations had cost over $2.5 million. Dominion, which was supposed to have taken only six weeks to complete, had eaten up more than $3 million. The original $13 million was gone, and Eidos was now sending in cash on a monthly run rate. Between the lease, the salaries for the nearly one hundred employees, and the other expenses, the bills were nearly $1.2 million per month.

But there was another problem, a *big* problem: Carmack's Quake II code. The engine was completely different than what he had expected. All this time he'd had his programmers preparing Daikatana in a way that would make it easy to switch over to what he assumed Carmack's new engine would require. But it turned out that Carmack had trashed his expected direction and instead produced a structure of code that caught Romero completely by surprise. It certainly wasn't done to dupe Romero into a delay, it was just Carmack making his own idiosyncratic, intuitive leap—a leap that, once again, cramped Romero's grand designs.

"This is going to take a while," Romero told Eidos and his staff. "This code is jacked." Completing Daikatana for his promised March 1998 deadline was impossible, but Romero thought they could turn it around in a few months. Others weren't so confident, lobbying him to forget about competing with id's technology and just release the game using the original Quake engine. "You can't keep up with Carmack," said Romero's lead programmer, "so why even try?" But Romero wouldn't waver. His ambitions only grew larger.

Later that month, Romero told the gaming press that Ion Storm was going to begin work on Daikatana II. Co-owners Todd Porter and Jerry O'Flaherty initiated a plan of their own: to launch a comic book division within the company using the artists of Jerry's who had worked in that industry. The owners approved the plan to hire up a staff and release a comic book for each of the company's games as, essentially, free public relations. When Eidos got wind of the plan, however, they immediately shut it down. "You guys are supposed to be making games," they said. "Why should we pay you to make comics?"

Even the glass ceiling they toiled beneath became a problem, specifically, a nightmare of light. Next to vampires, no one hates the light as much as gamers; there's nothing worse than a big, bad glare blinding down on a computer screen. Nobody could work. The architects were immediately called in to install stylish spoilers on top of the cubicles. But they proved hardly dark enough to suit the gamers' finicky tastes. Instead, they caravanned to Home Depot and returned on a mission. They whipped out the staple guns and fastened thick sheets of black felt over every cube in the office. They didn't just work in the shade, they worked in the black. To get into their cubes, they had to part their drapes of felt like photographers entering miniature darkrooms. It became an awesome and ironic sight; walk through the glass dome of gamers' paradise and all one saw were rows of caves.

By the spring of 1998, the mood around the company was growing similarly black. Despite their working in what felt like perpetual crunch mode—twelve-hour days, six days a week—Daikatana was nowhere near being done. Many felt the project was out of control. One guy produced a series of levels that proved unusable. An artist created a graphical icon for an arrow in the game that was a thousand times the appropriate size. Factions within the Daikatana team began breaking apart. Even Romero's most devout fans—Will Loconto, Sverre Kvernmo, and about a half dozen others—began getting more clandestine, opting out of rambunctious deathmatches and keeping to themselves. Others started lashing out. One employee was found alone at his desk, screaming. Romero fired him.

But more were concerned about Todd Porter's and Jerry O'Flaherty's increased sense of ownership. The two, they felt, were running the company into the ground. Todd had been showing up more frequently at Daikatana meetings, making what they thought were fruitless suggestions about how to alter the game. Meanwhile, Dominion was a shambles, to their minds, a sorry-looking title that was, unfortunately, going to be Ion Storm's first release. They soon took action.

On May 13, Sverre, Will, and six other members of Romero's team asked Bob Wright, Ion's chief operating officer, whom they had perceived as an ally back when he was working closely with Mike Wilson, to join them for lunch. They had an ultimatum for Romero, they said—Todd and Jerry had to go or they would walk out the door. Bob urged them to put their complaints in writing.

Word about the meeting leaked back to Tom Hall—Bob had told the guys that he could help them to finance their own company if they did quit or get fired. Tom called Romero. It was bad timing. Romero was out of the office with his wife, Beth, who had just given birth to their first child, Lillia. He had been on something of a roll in his family life, having convinced his ex-wife, Kelly, to move with his boys, Steven and Michael, to Texas so he could see his sons more often. Before long he was right there by their side—playing games. The birth of his daughter was supposed to be a joyous day. But there was another fate in store.

"What the fuck?" Romero screamed when Tom told him about Bob's interference. "That's it. Bob fucked with my team. He's gone."

Bob was fired the next week, but this didn't begin to quell Ion's burgeoning problems. The company once again had a disappointing showing at E3, which took place the last week of May. Competing shooters, such as the recently released Unreal and the upcoming Half-Life, garnered most of the attention, as did id's upcoming game, Quake III. When Ion Storm's Dominion hit shelves the following week, it flopped. Another fantasy-based strategy game, StarCraft, had been released to rave reviews just a couple months before and made Todd's title look stale. Not only did it die in the marketplace but it confirmed to the already bitter gaming community that all might not be well in Romero's dream factory. And that community, the very people who had grown up on Romero's games, bit back.

On game sites with names such as Evil Avatar, Shugashack, Blue's News, and Daily Radar, players had a feeding frenzy around Ion Storm. "All talk, no game," a typical post read. "Reasons I Won't Buy Daikatana," read another. A comic strip online lampooned Romero with long hair saying, "Hi . . . I'm here to tell you that Daikatana will be great. You guys know I'm good for it. Like Doom! You remember Doom? I did that! And Quake, right? That was me too! Design is law!" The final frame showed that Romero was, in fact, pitching a hot-dog seller to get a free meal. "Nice try John," the vendor replied. "No game, no wiener."

Another death rumor surfaced. This time it came after a photo of Romero in a morgue with a bullet hole in his head leaked onto the Web. Gamers joked that he'd killed himself after losing a Quake game to Carmack. But when a gaming magazine online issued—and later retracted—a report that "sources at Ion Storm" confirmed Romero's demise, gamers went ballistic. Still reeling from the bitch ad, they resented what seemed to be another publicity stunt—despite the fact that the leaked photo had actually come from an upcoming *Texas Monthly* magazine article about Ion Storm.

The biggest blow came on September 30, when a scribe named Bitch X posted on a site called Gaming Insider broke news of a plan by Eidos to buy Ion Storm. For months now, the owners had been in talks with their publisher to hatch some kind of bailout plan. The idea had started back in May, with Eidos buying 19 percent of Ion Storm's equity for $12.5 million in exchange for forgiving the $15 million advance; Ion's royalty would be lowered from 40 to 25 percent as well. Bob Wright would even sue the company, alleging that they'd fired him specifically to cut him out of profiting from the Eidos deal.

Months later the deal was still being negotiated. How Bitch X knew, no one could surmise. When, over the next couple of weeks, the Bitch talked of various firings and e-mails at Ion Storm, the guy who ran Ion Storm's website told the owners, "Either people who are no longer with the company know a whole lot more than the people who are here, or we've got a leak that the *Titanic* can sail through."

No one admitted to leaking the news, so Romero tried unsuccessfully tracing employees' e-mail activity to see who might be sending information to the sites in question. But the damage was done. The company grew rife with suspicion and distrust. The employees began to grumble quite loudly about Ion Storm's financial future. From the beginning, they had expected to be cut in to some kind of royalty or bonus or ownership. And the more rumors spread, the more depression set in. Romero confronted his lead programmer, Kee Kimbrell—who had cofounded DWANGO—one day for playing too many games and not getting his work done, a complaint whose irony didn't go unnoticed.

"What the fuck, dude?" Romero said. "You stopped working. And we need to get this game done. It's serious, you know." Kee told Romero he was worried about the business; he had seen a spreadsheet of Ion Storm's financials and had been hearing rumors that Eidos was going to shut the company down. Romero exploded. "Rumor! Rumor! Rumor! Rumor! Rumor! Bullshit!" he said. "You don't understand business, don't try to fuck with business stuff. You don't understand the deal that we have with Eidos. You don't understand a lot of things. You're letting it affect the way that you are not working and you're bringing other people down and all this shit." But Kee wouldn't back down, and Romero fired him on the spot.

It would get worse. Employees began walking out the door, not to return. The deal with Eidos fell apart just as it was about to be signed, due, in no small part, to the increased delays and chaos within the glass walls. With the failure of Dominion and the need to keep Ion afloat,

Todd relinquished plans to work on Doppelganger and immersed himself in his new position as CEO. Romero, he thought, was too nonconfrontational. So Todd hired an auditing firm to make sense of Ion's hemorrhaging financials. Despite knowing that his own aggressive style could alienate those around him, he felt obliged to get the Daikatana team back into shape. But it was to no avail. Romero refused his suggestions to cut the game. And the employees only became more embittered at Todd's increasingly vocal lashings. They resented the fact that one day, while they watched a building go down in flames nearby from their perch, Todd exclaimed, "We're not paying you to watch a building burn."

By the fall, Ion was headed for a conflagration of its own. On the evening of the November 18, Romero was taken out to P. F. Chang's for dinner by Stevie Case and a couple of other trusted employees. Since Stevie was hired, she had remained loyal to Romero, providing solace and perspective during the increasingly hard times. "We heard a rumor," she said, "that your entire Daikatana team is going to leave tomorrow." Romero remained defiant. "Fuck them if they're going to leave," he said.

The next day Romero and Tom were called into the conference room, where they found the Daikatana team waiting. "We can't keep working under these conditions," they were told by Will Loconto. "We don't think this game is ever going to get done, so we're going to go and start our own company."

Romero wandered back through the maze of cubicles and sat down at his desk, where he would remain long after the sun came down on the glass tower. Everything is bullshit! he thought. Why did I hire these people? It shouldn't have been this big. This was too many people, too much money. It should have been just me and Tom and a small team of people with a common goal. It should have been like the way it was when we weren't biz guys. We were just gamers.

FIFTEEN

Straight out
of Doom

As gamers came, RebDoomer wasn't unique. He loved first-person shooters, especially Doom and Quake. He stayed up late at night, deathmatching over the Internet. He made amateurish mods—an arena space based on a hockey rink; a boxing ring for hand-to-hand combat—and traded them with friends online. "Whatsup all you doomers out there!" he typed to them. "REB here, bringin you another kick-ass doom2 wad! This one took a damn long time to do, so send me some bloody credit man!"

Offline, he wasn't finding much camaraderie at all. He was deeply troubled at school: the jocks, the jokes, the feeling of being a pariah. He began keeping increasingly angry journals, venting his desires for revenge. Finally, one day he set up a video camera in his basement, then sat in a reclining chair holding a bottle of Jack Daniel's and a sawed-off shotgun in his lap. Looking into the camera, he described his plan to go on a shooting spree through his high school. "It's going to be like fucking Doom," he said. "Tick, tick, tick, tick. Ha! That fucking shotgun is straight out of Doom!"

On the morning of April 20, 1999, Eric "RebDoomer" Harris and his best friend, Dylan "Vodka" Klebold, strapped themselves with bombs and shotguns and went on a rampage through their Littleton, Colorado, school, Columbine High, leaving fifteen people, including themselves, dead. The event, which played out on live television, galvanized the country. Parents, teachers, politicians, and children wanted to make sense of the ultimate senseless act. They were looking for something to blame.

At 5:15 P.M. on April 21, 1999, Steve Heaslip, the editor of a game news site called Blue's News, uploaded a message. "Several readers have written in reporting having seen televised news reports showing the Doom logo on something visible through clear bags containing materials said to be related to the suspected shooters. . . . There is no word yet of what connection anyone is drawing between these materials and this case." As the killers' Doom books, Doom games, and Doom fantasies surfaced, the connection was made soon enough.

In the weeks following the tragedy, Doom became emblematic of how violent media were inspiring real-life violence. The Simon Wiesenthal Center issued a report suggesting the Eric Harris had reconfigured Doom in a "dry run" of the real-life killings. Similarly without substantiation, others began reporting that Harris had created a mod based specifically on Columbine High. *The Washington Post* described the world of Doom deathmatching as a "dark, dangerous place." *Newsday* wrote about how playing Doom can "widen the hole in any kid's soul." David Grossman, a former army ranger, became a media darling for his views on games as "murder simulators." Even President Clinton chimed in, quoting Grossman in a radio address and adding that "Doom . . . the very game played obsessively by the two young men who ended so many lives in Littleton, make[s] our children more active participants in simulated violence."

Once again, violent games and their associated pop culture—black clothes, heavy metal, gory films—were under attack. The mayor of Denver asked promoters to cancel a concert by Harris's and Klebold's alleged favorite band, Marilyn Manson. Schools banned trench coats. Disney World and Disneyland pulled violent games from their arcades. But none took the call to arms like the senator who had initiated the country's first investigation into violent games six years earlier: Senator Joseph Lieberman.

In an April 28 statement, he called for a new investigation into the scourge. "My hope," he said, "is that such a summit would persuade the nation's top cultural producers to call a cease-fire in the virtual arms race, to stop the release of ultraviolent video games and movies and CDs that romanticize and sanitize extreme forms of violence and teach our children that killing is cool—the very material, such as Doom . . . that several of the school gunmen murderously mimicked down to the choice of weapons and apparel."

Without any sensible counterpoint, the press and politicians— many of whom had never played such games—were left to draw their own conclusions. Ellen Goodman, in her nationally syndicated column, asked, "How many of us accept as 'normal' boy stuff the video games that we are now told are virtual training sessions for military de-sensitization?" She didn't seem to know or care that the military didn't use the games to desensitize, they used them for team building.

Good Morning America corralled a friend of the teenage killers who led the viewers through a game of Doom. "There's more to learn from Eric Harris's computer game," the reporter intoned. "Watch closely as we enter the secret rooms he created." There were bodies hanging from the ceiling, images, he implied, that Harris had created; in fact, they were the original B-movie effects of the game. "This is like walking through somebody's nightmare," the reporter declared. "Did it ever strike you that, Hey, this is a little strange, this guy really likes all this blood and shooting and violence?" His friend replied, "Never." He was just a gamer.

And these were just *games*. It was an obvious point among the people who actually played Doom and Quake but one that seemed strangely to elude everyone else: games were make-believe. In video games, no one *really* got hurt. But when it came to violent play, people had a history of linking fantasy with reality, as the author Gerard Jones explored in his book, *Killing Monsters: Why Children Need Fantasy, Super Heroes, and Make-Believe Violence.*

As Jones noted, an influential study in 1963 found that children who watched films of a person punching an inflatable clown doll later beat up such a clown toy more aggressively than kids who hadn't watched the film. The conclusion: exposure to violent media caused real-life violence. In reality, of course, the kids were just punching inflatable clowns; they were not running to the local circus and pummeling Bozo. Rather than blame violent media, Jones argued, adults needed to understand the role make-believe violence plays in human development: "Exploring, in a safe and controlled context, what is impossible or too dangerous or forbidden . . . is a crucial tool in accepting the limits of reality. Playing with rage is a valuable way to reduce its power. Being evil and destructive in imagination is a vital compensation for the wildness we all have to surrender on our way to being good people."

Researchers since the 1980s had been finding positive effects of video games; a report in the *Journal of American Academic Child Psychiatry* argued that games not only didn't inspire aggression, they released it. An academic study in England would find that gamers "seemed able to focus on what they were doing much better than other people and also had better general co-ordination. Overall there was a huge similarity with top-level athletes. The skills they learnt on computers seem to transfer to the real world." In Finland, researchers used computer games to help treat children with dyslexia.

And, despite all the studies that attempted to link violent media with aggression, the conclusions remained suspect. "Violence in film, in video games, in music lyrics is disturbing to us all," Dr. Stuart Fischoff, founder of the Media Psychology lab at California State University in Los Angeles, said in an address to the American Psychological Association later in 1999, "but because two phenomena are both disturbing and coincident in time does not make them causally connected . . . There is not, I submit, a single research study which is even remotely predictive of [events like] the Columbine massacre."

Murderers, after all, had proven that they could find inspiration in anything—the White Album, *Taxi Driver, Catcher in the Rye.* How many acts of violence had the Bible inspired? After Columbine, however, few had the nerve or the knowledge to defend games. Jon Katz, a writer for *Rolling Stone* and the tech community Slashdot, posted several essays that assailed the media's stereotypes of geeks and gamers. "This is so crazy and hysterical," he told the *San Francisco Chronicle.* "The real issue should be how teenagers get their hands on machine guns and bombs—not about a Web site and video games." Others offered backhanded defense at best. "Violence has always been a big thing in the U.S.," wrote *Time,* "and there are good constitutional reasons why we can't legislate that out of our entertainment products. But the video-game industry makes only what it can sell. And as long as gore is what we're buying—for our kids and for ourselves—gore is what they'll give us."

The politicians, however, weren't going to wait for the people to decide matters for themselves. Sam Brownback, a Republican from Kansas, made a speech on the Senate floor, saying, "The video game 'Quake,' put out by . . . id Software, the same company as the producer of 'Doom,' consists of a lone gunman confronting a variety of monsters. For every kill, he gets points. As he advances in the game, the weapons he uses grow more powerful and more gory—he trades in his shotgun for an automatic and later gets to use a chain saw on his enemies. The more skilled the player, the gorier the weapons he gets to use. Bloodshed his reward."

By June 1999, the White House had stepped up to the plate. During a press conference in the Rose Garden, a dour-faced President Clinton stood holding up an ad from a gaming magazine that promoted a game as "more fun than shooting your neighbor's cat." "We ought to think twice," he said, "about the impact of ads for so-called 'first person shooter video games,' like the recent ad for a game that invites players to—and I quote—'Get in touch with your gun-toting, cold-blooded murdering side.' "

With that, he ordered a federal investigation to determine whether gaming and other entertainment companies were guilty of marketing violent products to children. The industry's assertions that games were being made, in part, by and for adults didn't ring true. "It's hard to argue with a straight face that the games were made for adults in the first place," he said. Three days later Senators Lieberman and John McCain announced a solution: the Twenty-first Century Media Responsibility Act, a formidable bill that would establish a standardized rating system for movies, music, and video games. If the bill passed, retailers who sold violent games to minors would face ten-thousand-dollar fines. No one in the games industry opposed ratings; they already had their own voluntary Entertainment Software Rating Board. But, of course, they bristled at standardization and government involvement. The message from Washington was loud and clear: Rethink violent games or else.

It was 1:34 A.M. in Suite 666, days after the Columbine shootings. Carmack sat at his desk behind the black windows in the black night, cursor blinking on his computer, awaiting a response. He thought over his words carefully. Writing his .plan updates was becoming increasingly laborious because, as Carmack knew, everyone seemed to be hanging so much on what he said. "Some of you," he finally typed, "are busy getting all bent out of shape about this."

Carmack was talking about the gaming community's reaction to id's announcement that the first test of their next game, Quake III Arena, would be released for Macintosh, not Windows. In the gaming world, this was usually as big as the controversies got. But while Carmack turned his attention to his plan, describing the pros and cons of the new Macintosh systems, he couldn't avoid the *other* controversy. Finishing his update, he pushed himself away from his desk and walked down the hall to get a Diet Coke and a snack. "Hey," he said, passing the police officers in his lobby, "do you guys want anything to eat?"

The cops were the most obvious sign of Columbine's impact on id. They had been hired to stand guard shortly after the first wave of hate calls and hate mails started flaming into the office. Miss Donna, receptionist and id mom, would pick up the phone to find a raging protester on the other end of the line asking *what in God's name this company had done.* Soon there were journalists hanging around outside, trying fruitlessly to get a word from one of the many long-haired guys walking from their sports cars into the jet black cube. After a hateful protester was found outside screaming, a few of the newer members of the id staff pleaded for security during the late hours. Carmack and the other owners relented but felt it was an overreaction. "Oh," they said, "this happens all the time."

In fact, it had happened only eight days before the Columbine shootings. On April 12, 1999, the parents of three students killed in a 1997 school shooting in Paducah, Kentucky, had leveled a $130 million lawsuit against entertainment companies, including id Software, whose violent products, they said, had inspired the fourteen-year-old murderer, Michael Carneal—a fan of Doom and Quake. And, of course, it had happened long before that: the Wolfenstein controversies in 1992, the Mortal Kombat hearings in 1993, the Doom bans to follow—not to mention the Death Race arcade outrage in the 1970s, or the Dungeons and Dragons hysteria in the eighties.

As long as these guys had played games, there had been the detractors, the lawsuits, the sensationalism, but nothing quite as powerful as the one-two punch of Paducah and Columbine. Because of the Paducah lawsuit, id's lawyers strongly advised the owners and employees to remain quiet. The staff obliged, but Carmack felt frustrated that he couldn't tell the world what he thought. As a result, the media storm brewed and brewed, with no word from the people who had made the games. But Carmack knew exactly what he would say.

"The succession of the two events did not necessarily mean that something more significant was happening or the trend was increasing. It was just the odds. This life event, like every other, could be broken down to mathematics. If you've got any event that has this random chance of happening, eventually after a certain time, there are going to be multiple occurrences of it quickly after another." Carmack wasn't worried that there was suddenly going to be some secret link exposed between games and murder; disturbed people are disturbed people, pure and simple.

Id's games weren't about *really killing someone,* Carmack knew, they were just extensions of childhood play. "Deathmatch was tag," he said. "Doom was cowboys and Indians with better special effects. We build games that we think are going to be fun. All the games we enjoyed like Defender and Robotron were all about running around and blasting things. The gore and graphics just make an already challenging and interactive game more visceral. It makes people jump and sweat and be tense. It's an *okay* game if you're sitting saying, 'Okay this is fun.' But our definition of a good game is something that's going to be gripping and exciting."

Were these violent games being marketed to kids? "Of course teenagers like our games," Carmack said. "To say that our games are targeted only for eighteen-year-olds and older is ludicrous." But the thing that people weren't getting, he thought, was that id wasn't targeting anyone. All the way back to Softdisk, they had made games not for an audience but for themselves. They made games they wanted to play that no one else was making, games that, as fate would have it, would appeal to millions of others. As Carmack returned to his desk, he went back to work on a game that was going to be id's most gleeful shooter yet: Quake III Arena. But, after Columbine, would people want— would the market allow—his or Romero's games again?

John Schuneman gripped his bowling ball tighter as the talk turned to Doom. Romero's stepfather, now in his sixties, had been coming to this bowling alley more frequently since retiring, and he could usually count on relaxing with a good game. But not today. The people next to him, like millions across the country, were talking about the horrific events at Columbine High School. *Kids today, they're being corrupted by these violent video games like Doom.* Schuneman's heart raced again as they spoke. He stepped over to the group. "We can take it outside anytime you want," he said, curling the ball at his side. He didn't want to hear any more trash about Johnny's games.

He wasn't the only one. Romero himself couldn't believe the way people were harping on Doom, a game that was *six years old.* It just showed how clueless the politicians had become. It was just the same old crap from the same old people. And Romero was tired of the blame. Those kids were defective, he thought, so don't blame it on my game. Don't blame the games. Blame the fucking parents.

From his own experience, of course, Romero had strong opinions about just *how* parents could screw up their kids. And now, at the age of thirty-one, with three kids of his own, he had become more self-aware of where the violence in his games came from and the effect the violent games could have. He was a fucked-up kid making fucked-up games to deal with the fucked-up physical and emotional violence he'd experienced when he was young. He liked the violence in his games, just as he liked the violence in his Melvin comics. There was no question—the violence in his games did have an impact on him at least: he'd scream and curse and break keyboards, but he never confused fantasy and reality. He didn't even know how to fire a gun in real life.

But because he thought violence in games could have an effect, Romero thought that even more responsibility should rest with the parent. For that reason, he supported ratings on games, as did most of his peers. Ultimately, the responsibility shouldn't be the game makers' or the politicians'. The parents should decide when their kids were mature enough to play a game like Doom. Romero had long relished the day he could sit down with his boys, Steven and Michael, and play through the worlds he created. They were ready for that day, Romero decided, when they were eight.

After Columbine, though, Romero kept these opinions to himself. He wasn't being sued like id, but why say anything anyway? You talk to journalists and they're going to take what you say and twist it any way they want into their story and it will only end up looking bad. The last thing Romero wanted was more bad press. Even before Columbine, after all, he'd been getting more than his share.

The avalanche of trash talking—in the press and in the community—broke the moment the eight members of the Daikatana team, or, as they became known, the Ion Eight, had walked out Ion Storm's emerald doors a few months earlier, in November 1998. No sooner did Romero lose the core of his team than news broke that the Ion Eight had formed a new company, Third Law, which was under contract to create a first-person shooter based on the rock band Kiss for the Gathering of Developers—the independent-minded publisher started by Mike Wilson after his departure from Ion Storm. It was a double slap to Romero's face. He felt backstabbed by Mike and burned by the team he trusted. It was like the Softdisk mutiny in which Romero and the rest had jilted Al Vekovius. Only this time Romero was the boss getting screwed.

But Romero, as usual, didn't wait long to change moods. And this time he had someone to help speed his recovery: Stevie Case. Throughout all the darkness at the company, Stevie had been a beacon. They had much in common: two misfit kids who'd found a home in the fantasy life of video games. And, like Romero, Stevie had radically reinvented herself. Inspired by Ion Storm's creative atmosphere, the small-town girl with the student government bob had transformed her image. She stopped eating meat, went to the gym, lost fifty pounds, bleached her hair. She ditched the sweatshirts for midriffs, the baggy jeans for leopard pants. She used her video game salary to buy breast implants. In the space of a year, she had gone from model tomboy to *Playboy* model—the magazine, hearing her story, paid her to pose. After the Ion Eight left, she became Romero's lead designer.

She also became his girlfriend. Just as he engaged to get Ion back on track, he separated from his wife, Beth—not long after she had given birth to their daughter, Lillia. Once again Romero had grown dissatisfied with his marriage and overwhelmed by the pressures of being a Rich Person and Game God. After all the years of assuring everyone—his fans, his friends, his family—that he could do it *all,* he had finally realized he could not manage both an empire *and* a family. His ex-wife, Kelly, had made this point clear when, to Romero's dismay, she moved back to California with his boys. Ultimately, he gave in to the truth: he was married to his games. With Stevie, the first woman in his life who shared the passion, it was a three-way affair.

As his personal life changed, Romero put his energy into rebuilding his team, hiring a few old friends and picking up some help from Tom Hall's squad. Though Daikatana was in need of an overhaul, the end was in sight. The Quake II engine conversion was complete, they announced in early January 1999. A producer Romero had hired to organize Daikatana proudly told the press that "come hell or high water, the game will be done on February 15, 1999."

Or so the team hoped. Days later they would receive the worst blow of bad press yet: a scathing cover story called "Stormy Weather" in the city's free weekly paper, the *Dallas Observer.* The seven-thousand-word story explicitly detailed how "the place where the 'designer's

vision is king' has turned into a toxic mix of prima donnas and personality cults." More shocking, the article was based on internal e-mails.
They now appeared in print and online for the entire world to read.

The result, inside and outside the company, was devastating. Suddenly all of Ion's internal affairs — from Mike Wilson's BMW financing
to Romero's interest in "burning" through Eidos's options — was public.
Internet sites traded the story as fast as Doom shareware, reveling in
how the Surgeon of deathmatch, the one who was going to make them
his bitch, was finally getting his due. Romero tried fitfully to determine
the source of the leak. He blocked access to game gossip sites and even
tried, though unsuccessfully, to sue the *Observer* to reveal its sources. All
he found was that his partner Todd Porter had accidentally posted his
e-mail file on the company computer network and that *anyone* within
Ion could have copied them.

By the time the Columbine blow came, a few months later, Romero
couldn't have been beaten down any worse. His company was a laugh-
ingstock. His game was once again delayed, with no end in sight — having sailed past the promise for a February 1999 release. It now was in
danger of buckling to technology once and for all, with id Software already deep into the Quake III engine. When a deathmatch demo of
Daikatana was released in March, gamers thought it looked dated.

The dream of the Big Company seemed to be proving too big after
all, too loose, too high, too ambitious. All those things Carmack had be-
rated him about — the hyperbole, the lack of focus, the dangers of a
large team — had come back with a vengeance. Even Eidos, Romero's
publisher, agreed. In return for their sinking by now nearly $30 million
into the company, Romero had to change his ways once and for all. As
the Eidos president, Rob Dyer, put it: "Shut up and finish the game."

Id Software was once again in the spotlight at the E3 convention in Los
Angeles in May 1999, but this time for all the wrong reasons. Coming
only one month after the Columbine shootings and the Paducah lawsuit, the show became a feeding ground for the media's increasingly
sensational investigation of video game violence. Of all the companies

the reporters wanted to interview, there was none higher on the list than the creators of Doom and Quake.

This wasn't going to be easy. No one, it seemed, wanted to talk about the events. In his opening remarks, Doug Lowenstein, president of the Interactive Digital Software Association—the group that was created in response to Senator Lieberman's 1993 hearings on game violence—tried to set the tone. He pointed out that only 7 percent of the five thousand games released were violent enough to be rated Mature. Nevertheless, he added, the game industry was in fact growing up. This was not for kids. The IDSA reported that 54 percent of video gamers were over eighteen, with 25 percent of these older than thirty-six; the age of computer gamers was even higher, with 70 percent over eighteen and 40 percent of them over thirty-six. Together, U.S. gamers were spending nearly $7 billion that year alone—more than Americans spent on movie tickets. "For those of you who are here to focus on violence," Lowenstein said, "I submit that you're missing a much bigger story about what it is that makes interactive entertainment the fastest-growing entertainment industry in the world."

The reporters responded by rushing over to id's booth for comments on Columbine, to no avail. Any journalist who muscled up to one of the gamers from id was abruptly intercepted by a PR representative, who would refer him or her to the publisher, Activision, who would refuse to say anything at all. These weren't the only gamers laying low. Raven, id's old friends from Wisconsin, showed their violent shooter, Soldier of Fortune, only behind closed doors; the same was true for one of the year's other hotly anticipated shooters, Kingpin. For id, however, the controversy was the least of their difficulties. With Quake III Arena, the game they had come to demonstrate, they were having enough problems.

The trouble started the moment Carmack had announced the previous year that the game's design would be deathmatch only. In light of the success of Half-Life, a shooter in which story was everything, the free-for-all plan sounded heretical, if not out of touch. Others bristled at the notion that id's next title would be, essentially, its most elitist ever: not just suggesting that a player had a high-end machine but requiring it by making the game compatible only for players who had 3-D graphics cards installed.

The fans weren't the only ones in doubt. After the office dysfunction that had surrounded Quake II, the energy level heading into Quake III was at an all-time low. The old battles that Carmack had endured with Romero had been supplanted by the rest of the team. Inspired by Half-Life, everyone, it seemed, wanted a more ambitious design. But no matter what they came up with, Carmack shot it down. For Adrian, it was just more of the same: further proof that after all these years since their lake house in Shreveport, id had become Carmack's company. Adrian felt frustrated, wanting to do something, *anything*, that was different. It was a criticism that was starting to bubble up in the community as well: id was rehashing the same game over and over without any consideration for story and design. But Adrian resigned himself to go along. What was he going to do, he thought, fire John Carmack?

As work began on the project, the dissolution only festered. Carmack's intention to create a game that allowed the members of his company to work in, essentially, isolation proved a bit too isolationist. As he churned out early versions of the Quake III engine, the mappers and artists felt adrift, with no direction on what to pursue. Left to their own devices, they simply created their own little worlds, worlds that clearly didn't relate to or complement each other.

Carmack grew increasingly frustrated. Here he was, creating the most powerful graphics engine the company had ever seen, and no one on his staff seemed to be taking advantage of the opportunities. No one was pushing the technology, pushing the design, pushing *him*. Though Carmack never came out and said that he pined for the days of Romero's giddy experimentations, it was clear to him that something was missing. The magic of the self-motivated id Software team was gone.

By February 1999, the staff had had enough. Carmack clearly had no interest in managing the day-to-day affairs of the game. They wanted a producer. So Carmack called Graeme Devine. Graeme was a prodigy in gaming history. At sixteen he was expelled from high school in England because he was spending too much time programming games for Atari. He later moved to the United States to cofound

Trilobyte, the company that produced one of the bestselling and most technologically impressive CD-ROMs of the early nineties, 7th Guest. Graeme and Carmack had struck up a programmers' relationship along the way, corresponding often about the latest in coding. Now that it was time to bring on help for Quake III, Carmack thought of Graeme, whose own company had recently gone under. Graeme was more than happy to come on board, but he was surprised at what he found.

When he asked the fourteen people what they thought the direction of the project was, he got fourteen different answers. The night before his first day, three of the newer guys took him out for a coffee at Starbucks in Mesquite to prepare him for the bloody arena he was about to try to tame. "They are going to tell you that you have power," one explained, "but you will not have any power. They may say something's okay, but they will override your decisions." They warned Graeme of what to watch out for: the mind games, the politics, the people to distrust. Graeme wasn't swayed. "Everything's going to be okay," he assured them. "Don't worry. Things will change."

Nothing did. Graeme discovered that the egos at id were stronger than he'd surmised. Though people felt like they were working without direction, at the same time no one wanted really to be told what to do. To make matters worse, a fundamental ingredient of the game—the bots—was missing. Bots were characters controlled by the computer. A good bot would blend in with the action and flesh out the scene like a robotic extra, as well as interact with the player. For Quake III, a deathmatch-only game, bots were essential for single-player action. They were implicitly complex because they had to behave like human beings.

Carmack had decided, for the first time, to delegate the job of creating these bots to another programmer in the company. But he failed to follow up. Once again, Carmack incorrectly assumed that everyone was as self-motivated and adept as he was. He was wrong. When Graeme struggled to rein in the work, it was discovered that the bots were completely ineffective. They didn't behave at all like human beings. They behaved, basically, like bots. The staff began to panic. By March 1999, they had reason to be scared.

At the Game Developers Conference in San Jose, id employees got their first look at Unreal Tournament, a new game by Epic, the creators of the 1998 shooter Unreal. Epic had quietly become formidable competition. Tim Sweeney, Epic's lead programmer, was revered. The company had even employed two former id guys: Jay Wilbur and Mark Rein—the "probationary president" from the Wolfenstein days—to handle business affairs. Unreal was a surprise hit, bringing, like Half-Life, more of a cinematic story feel to the genre. But their new game took id by even greater surprise. Unreal Tournament was a deathmatch-only multiplayer game, just like Quake III.

Epic, some thought, had flat out stolen id's idea. They resented the fact that Carmack, as usual, had been so open about the company's direction in his .plan file. But Epic denied stealing anything, saying that they had been on that track long before Carmack had announced it in his plan. The animosity and competition nevertheless remained. And, with Quake III so disorganized, not to mention the heat of Columbine, there was no reprieve.

Despite positive reviews of the game at E3, id began to fall apart. Two respected young employees—Brandon James, a level designer, and Brian Hook, a programmer—quit in frustration. Adrian separated from his wife, whom he had married during the height of Doom's success. Kevin, always the conciliatory owner, sensed that something had to be done. He asked Carmack to move out of his own office and share space with him and Adrian in hopes of improving communication. The move only intimidated the other employees, who couldn't help but wonder what was going on with their owners behind closed doors. What was going on, in fact, was nothing much. Instead of talking, the co-owners worked in silence. The only sound came when Carmack left and Adrian and Kevin turned up their stereo.

By the end of the project, Graeme wasn't producing, he was programming. The bots were farmed out to a well-known mod maker in the Netherlands, who heroically brought them to life. The levels were stitched together in some sensible sequence. In November 1999, the game was close enough to completion that some members of the company went on a promotional bus tour for the release. The fun was cut short, however, when they discovered that their competitor, Epic, had one-upped them again, releasing Unreal Tournament just a week before Quake III hit shelves in early December.

At the wire, the question remained: Would players go with Carmack's—or Epic's—vision of a plot-free, deathmatch-only online world, or would they stand by Romero, the beleaguered designer who was hoping to prove that Daikatana, in all its wild ambition, would save the story after all? Romero weighed in on the matter in a business preview of Quake III that appeared in *Forbes*. "Online gaming is still a small segment of the market," he told the magazine. "And the people who play over the Web are the ones most likely to find sites where they can download the game for free." The magazine offered its own verdict of who would ultimately win the battle of the Two Johns. "It's quite possible," the story concluded, "that id's far less grandiose strategy is the better one."

"**Aaaaarrgggggggh!**" Shawn Green screamed as he thrashed his computer keyboard against the floor. It was midnight in the coders' cove of Ion Storm, and the cubes were as dark as the city below. Dressed in a black T-shirt, Romero's old friend hunched like an ape at the beginning of *2001: A Space Odyssey* as he whacked keys across the floor. A skinny programmer stretched his neck out of a nearby cube to observe the tantrum, then nonchalantly returned to his work. Shawn brushed his hair back as a smile crept across his face. "Nothing like a little stress relief," he said, tossing the battered keyboard down the hall.

Shawn, like the others on the Daikatana team, was deep into crunch mode. Despite Romero's pledge years before to Carmack that his death schedule days were over, he had upped the team's core hours to include weekends; the staff was now elbowing for bed space in the lounge. Brian "Squirrel" Eiserloh had recently spent eighty-five out of ninety days without leaving the office. Several others were crawling to sleep under their black-shrouded cubicles, nestling on floors covered in loose M&M's and pizza box pillows. Stevie Case was stuck home sick with a kidney infection. Romero had even taped a sign to the office's most popular arcade game that said, "No More Tekken 3 Until Daikatana Ships!"

Shawn himself was about to take his first and only break in weeks, heading off to an abandoned abortion clinic to unwind with his death metal band, Last Chapter. After staring at lines of code all day and sucking down a half case of Mountain Dew, he was always looking for new ways to blow off the steam and caffeine. He and Romero joked about making a life-size porcelain doll that would stand in the office holding a baseball bat. The punch line was that it held its own demise.

So did Ion Storm by the fall of 1999. Romero's ship wasn't just off course, it was perched on a rock in a violent sea with a steady flow of crew members leaping—or pushing each other—off board. Reeling from the Ion Eight departures, the *Dallas Observer* story, and the Columbine controversy, the company had suffered yet another blow as a result of that year's E3 convention. The pressure going into the convention had been enormous, especially with the game promised, this time, for a December release. Todd confronted Romero before the event. "Look," he said, "Eidos is significantly concerned, and we need to have some sort of oversight; I need to make sure that things are coming along the way they're supposed to come along." He would get the game ready and send it to them at E3.

Romero and Stevie showed up at E3 in May 1999 looking the part of gaming's rock-and-roll royalty. Romero was in black leather pants, mesh black shirt, long silver chain. Stevie's bleached blond hair spilled over a skintight baby blue shirt and black pants. Despite the bad press, they were besieged by the usual hordes of lustful boys and autograph-seeking Doom fanatics. When the disk of Daikatana's demo arrived, however, they didn't like what they saw. Bugs in the program were causing the game to chug slowly across the screen. Romero flew back to Dallas and stormed into the office of John Kavanaugh, the Eidos representative who had been stationed to keep an eye on the company.

"I'm fucking leaving," he told Kavanaugh. "If Todd's going to stay here, I'm fucking gone. I can't work with this guy, he's ruining everything." Kavanaugh told Romero a meeting would be called with Charles Cornwall, the owner of Eidos. "All you have to do," Kavanaugh said, "is nod your head."

In June, the Ion Storm partners—Romero, Tom Hall, Todd Porter, and Jerry O'Flaherty—flew to Los Angeles, ostensibly to talk with

Eidos about buying out the majority of the company to relieve the owners' $30 million debt. Todd and Jerry quickly learned otherwise. "I'm sick of all this bullshit!" Romero burst out. "Either Todd goes or I go."

Kavanaugh feigned incredulousness. "That's bullshit, John," he said. "You *are* Ion Storm. There's no decision here."

Jerry knew what this was all about: control. Romero wanted total control over his game. He tried haplessly to offer a solution: "If your problem is Todd working on your project," he said, "can we give Todd a project? Does anyone have a problem with that?"

"Look," Romero said, "this is not a fun place to work anymore, and I think we need to take a partnership and go in a different direction."

Before Jerry could suggest another option, to his surprise, Todd agreed. "Look," he said quietly, "you're right, John. It's no fun for me either. It's clearly no fun for Jerry." Jerry acquiesced. They would go. The four owners walked out into a flash of lightbulbs. But this time it wasn't for them. It was for actors Heather Graham and Rob Lowe, who were there for a photo shoot.

Ultimately, Todd and Jerry were happy to be getting what would surely be a healthy buyout for a company that seemed to be going down the tubes. Romero and Tom were relieved to have a new beginning. Maybe the company would be saved by the games, but either way they all still believed in their original vision: that design, that *the games* could be law. The problem, as Romero said, was that the design didn't take into account technology and it didn't take into account that the designer doesn't necessarily know how to manage.

In October, after reporting a loss of $44.8 million, Eidos announced that it was purchasing 51 percent of Ion Storm. Romero spent the fall buckling down on the game. The interview requests were turned away. Tekken 3 remained unplugged. Though the monsters, levels, sound, and art were nearing completion, there was a formidable task ahead: burning through the remaining bugs—all five hundred of them—in time for their promised December 17, 1999, release. But Eidos was confident enough to schedule a release party for that day, despite Romero's objections.

The party came, but without a finished Daikatana game. Not until April 21, 2000, would Romero finally feel ready to release it. The next day he sat down at his computer and typed a message for readers on the Internet. "My god, it's finally finished," he wrote. "And I thought working on a game for 1.5 years was long. . . . Wow. I wish everyone would take a nice, objective look at the game and not base their criticisms on hype, but on play value and what we've worked to achieve: a really fun single-player experience." Romero tried to dissuade the inevitable comparisons with his former company. "We did not," he wrote, "develop Daikatana to take on Quake 3." But the final score was out of his hands.

SIXTEEN

Persistent Worlds

By the end of 2000, Carmack didn't just have a new game release to celebrate, he had a marriage: his own. A couple of years earlier he had received an e-mail from a young businesswoman and Quake fan in California named Anna Kang. She wanted to start an all-female Quake tournament. Carmack said that'd be fine, but she'd probably get only twenty-five people. She got fifteen hundred. He respected anyone who could prove him wrong. *Who was Anna Kang?*

She was a strong-willed woman on a lifelong quest for respect. As an Asian American growing up in Los Angeles, Katherine Anna Kang was called a banana, a slur given to Asian American women who were thought to be white on the inside and yellow on the outside. Anna didn't let the insults sway her beliefs that, as she said, "women don't need to be subservient to males, that marrying outside their own race shouldn't be a sin, and that in general, capitalism isn't evil and socialism isn't ideal." One of her greatest role models was the author Ayn Rand; Anna wanted to be a powerful person like Gail Wynand, a character from *The Fountainhead*. She never felt as fierce as when she played Quake.

After successfully hosting the tournament, she stayed in correspondence with Carmack. He was intriguingly selfless—the way he shared his code and his knowledge. Even though she sometimes teasingly called him Spock, she believed he had a deep and generous soul. Carmack was equally impressed by her, talking at great length about Ayn Rand, philosophy, and games. He liked the way she challenged him.

They began a long-distance romance. Carmack ended up, with his staff's approval, offering Anna a job in business development so that she could have a reason to move to Dallas. She came, but the days at id wouldn't last. Her relationship with Carmack would. They wed in Hawaii in front of a small crowd of family and friends. It was one of the only vacations Carmack had taken in his life. And, like the other times, he brought his laptop. There was work to be done.

In Carmack's opinion, Quake III was—like all his other games—ancient history compared with what he was ready for now. Online games had become successful. The most ambitious existed as persistent worlds, which remained accessible over the Net around the clock for players to visit and explore. Medieval-themed titles like EverQuest and Ultima Online, based on Richard Garriott's early hits, had sold millions of copies, forging a genre called "massively multiplayer online role-playing games," which could support thousands of international players at a time. Players *lived* in these digital landscapes, spending dozens of hours per week exploring, battling, and building their game characters; EverQuest was nicknamed Evercrack. Some had even taken to selling coveted virtual objects—weapons and accessories—accumulated in the game for *real* money on auction sites like eBay.

For Carmack, this phenomenon fulfilled an ideology that harked back to the populist dreams of the Hacker Ethic. "It allows us to have virtual resource," he said. "Any of these digital resources allows us to create wealth from nothing, to be able to replicate wealth freely. . . . Unlike most fundamental physical objects, with the digital stuff there really is this possibility of wealth replication. The world can be a richer place."

Upon returning to Dallas, he decided to unveil his new direction to the rest of the team. "We should focus on doing a generalized infrastructure," he told them, "and doing a game as one element of this generalized infrastructure which can have a lot of the 3-D web environment that people always are thinking about and wishing about. We can do it now." This was it—the culmination of his work, his engineering, the dreams of science-fiction writers from Aldous Huxley to William Gibson. The Holodeck, Cyberspace, the Metaverse, the Virtual World, it had been called by many names, but the technology was never ready to bring a true glimpse of that place—however primordial—to life. That time, Carmack concluded, had come.

He looked around the conference room and waited for the response. All he got were blank stares. "But we're a game company," Adrian said, "we make *games.*" Carmack sighed. He knew that despite his power and prestige, he couldn't do this alone. He needed an experimenter who could use his technology to paint the new world. He needed a person who was so blown away he couldn't speak, someone who committed every cell of his body to bringing Carmack's visions to life, someone who understood that this was *the coolest fucking thing planet Earth had ever seen!* He needed Romero. The meeting was done.

The question of what id would do next remained unresolved. Though no one wanted to do the Metaverse, there was growing feeling in the company that they wanted to do something different. Graeme Devine came up with a proposal for a game called Quest: a multiplayer role-playing game, a far cry from a first-person shooter. Adrian and Kevin were excited about the possibility of a totally new kind of game. They weren't the only ones. With the community accusing id of going back to the well one too many times, this was a chance, it seemed, for a break. As Graeme proclaimed, "No more rocket launchers!" It was agreed. Quest would be id's next game.

But before long Carmack grew to hate it. It seemed murky, at best, like a three-year miasma waiting to happen. There was another idea, one that had surfaced again and again over the years: a new Doom. Carmack didn't exactly love the thought, but he didn't hate it either. Under id's supervision, another company, Gray Matter, was already working on a new PC game based on Wolfenstein 3-D called Return to Castle Wolfenstein, and the anticipation among gamers was high. For Doom III, Carmack could incorporate ideas he'd been kicking around for a next-generation graphics engine, something that could dynamically exploit the world of lights and shadows. Second-generation id guys like Tim Willits and Paul Steed, who got into the game business *because* of the original Doom, frothed at the opportunity to do a new installment. Carmack even kicked the idea around with Trent Reznor of Nine Inch Nails, who had done the Quake audio, to see if he would be interested in doing the sound for Doom III. Trent said yes. But others were less than intrigued.

Kevin, Graeme, and Adrian, in particular, disliked the idea. "It's like some old band going back and remaking their first album because they can do a better job now," Adrian said. "What the hell's the point in that? It's, like, make something new with your time! Instead of dedicating two years to making something you've already done, why not try and push this genre that we created further?"

To bide time, it was decided that the company would work on an add-on pack for Quake III called Team Arena. This game was a clear reaction to the success of Unreal Tournament and the criticism that id had not provided enough team play in their own title. The work on the mission pack, however, began to idle as people wondered what direction the company was going to take. While the prospect of Quest became all the more grim in Carmack's mind, he hatched a plan to get his way once and for all.

He walked into Paul's office one night and said, "Trent Reznor wants to do sounds for Doom."

"Doom?" Paul said. "We're not doing Doom, we're doing Quest."

"Well, I decided that I want to do Doom. Are you on board?"

"Fuck yeah!" Paul said. Tim agreed.

The next day Carmack walked into Kevin and Adrian's office and said, "I want to do Doom. Paul wants to do Doom. Tim wants to do Doom. If we don't do Doom, I'm leaving." Then he turned and walked out the door.

Kevin and Adrian couldn't believe it. But what could they do, fire Carmack? What was id without the Whiz Kid? They discussed the possibility of splitting the company in two teams or maybe, as Adrian thought, just throwing in the towel altogether. Carmack had threatened to quit before. And Adrian was beginning to feel like maybe the time had really come, maybe Carmack was through. Later he approached him and asked what was preventing him from just walking out the door once they started working on a new project. Carmack said, "Nothing." A decision was made. Carmack sat down at his computer the next day and told the world his plan.

"How's the Hummer?" *How's the Hummer? How's the Hummer?* That question again. At this moment in the summer of 2001, it was coming from a crew-cut teenage boy with a greasy face and a handful of Mexican menus at Temeraria's Restaurante and Club, the self-proclaimed "finest in Mexican Dining" in Lake Tawakoni, Texas; then again, it was the *only* Mexican dining here in this tiny strip of country thirty miles east of Dallas. Romero and Stevie Case had become regulars since escaping to the country a few months earlier. Now they were known around town less for their rock-star looks than for their fleet of expensive sports cars. After the hell of Daikatana, it was a welcome change.

The game was brutalized—critically and commercially, selling only 41,000 copies in the United States. With the exception of a few favorable reviews, the fans and media tore the game apart. *Entertainment Weekly* called it "a disaster of *Waterworld*-ian proportions," referring to the epic failure of Kevin Costner's notorious film. *PC Gamer* said the game "signals nothing more remarkable than the end of an era in fandom." *Computer Gaming World* was more succinct. "Yep," the headline declared, "it stinks."

Romero thought anyone who actually played the game would be hard pressed to not have a good time. But most people were hard pressed to play the game much at all. The opening level, with its swarm of mosquitoes and squishy stampede of robotic frogs, struck players as annoying. Many would not get past the pests. Romero was the first to say in interviews how much he enjoyed the game—despite its grueling development. He insisted that it broke even through all its license deals and foreign sales. In addition, Warren Spector's Deus Ex had proven a great success for Ion Storm, being voted computer game of the year by several publications. In his mind, no matter Daikatana's sales, Deus Ex had proven Romero's vision of a gaming empire with multiple titles right.

But Romero's enthusiasm, for once, couldn't stave off the inevitable. After Daikatana, he began sketching out ideas for a prototype of a follow-up game. Before long he had to help Tom Hall complete Anachronox after many on the team had departed in frustration. Tom's sci-fi role-playing game, which followed the trail of a down-and-out space detective who must thwart a mysterious alien oppressor, had become, like Daikatana, truly epic: employing hundreds of creatures, an arsenal of customizable weapons, and numerous games within games. But by early 2001, the work was near completion.

It wasn't the only thing coming to an end. One day, word spread that Eidos was going to be terminating some Ion Storm employees after Anachronox was complete. Curious, Romero walked over to the CFO's office to see who was on the list. He picked up the sheet of paper. It listed everyone's name in the Dallas office, including Tom's and his own. Warren Spector's team in Austin, however, would remain. Romero returned to his desk, sat in his chair with the highway behind him, and dialed Stevie. "That's it," he told her. "It's done." Romero was never one to mull, but this time it did actually stir his feelings. It was fucked up, he thought, that the vision, the dream design, didn't pan out like he had hoped. It was even . . . sad. But the sadness, as always, wouldn't stay long. He called Tom. It was like the clocks were rolling back and Romero was back at id, calling Tom at the end of one chapter and the beginning of the next.

Before long Romero, Tom, and Stevie hatched plans to start a new company. They sketched out ideas for games: maybe one about a ten-year-old kid, not unlike Commander Keen, who has to get through life, do his chores, and get along with his family, maybe an Old West shooter, or a game based on Madonna. They also talked about doing games specifically for mobile platforms — Pocket PCs, cell phones — an estimated $6 billion history by the year 2006. And Romero had an idea for a new game based on the Quake franchise. One afternoon he took the long drive to Mesquite to talk it over with id.

Id was no longer in its notorious black cube. The company had moved offices the year before to afford everyone more space. The new digs, Romero found, were even more plain than the last: just an ordinary office building across from a Hooters and an Olive Garden.

Though Romero had seen Carmack around town occasionally, it had been years since he had come to him with a business idea, a creative idea, a *game*, not since Quake, five years before. Carmack was at his computer, optimizing his new Doom engine, when Romero walked in. The office was bigger, cleaner, but minimalist as ever. Carmack sat before a large monitor angled in the corner. Through the blinds, he could keep a watchful eye on his Ferrari out back.

"Hey," Romero said.

"Hey," Carmack said.

Romero told him the reason for his visit and gave a brief pitch: "How would you feel about me licensing the Quake name to develop a game based on the franchise but set in a persistent world?"

Carmack nodded. "Sure, why not." He had already been kicking around the idea of getting the original team—Romero, Tom, Adrian, and himself—back together to do a version of Commander Keen for the Nintendo Game Boy, the handheld gaming device. Though he and Romero both knew they would probably not be in the same company again, that didn't mean they had to work apart.

Romero left and was on his way, on to the next thing, the flipped bit, the new vision. It all started with a house. Romero knew that he wanted a company like the early id, something intimate, something communal. And for that he needed just the right environment, like the lake house in Shreveport. Stevie saw something advertised online that she thought could fit the bill. They hopped in the Hummer and drove out past id, past Rockwall, down a long country road with strange country-road establishments: trading post, abandoned school buses, and a rusty flying saucer the size of a bus in the middle of a field. When they asked about the spaceship, locals joked that it had just appeared there a few years ago; now someone was trying to turn it into a hot-dog stand.

The house amazed them. It was down a rocky road behind a pond with a twenty-foot fountain, a log cabin, a lagoon pool, waterfalls, a hot tub, and a peacock farm. It was perfect. They bought it. Romero renamed the peacocks after video games—Pong, Pooyan, and Phoenix—and transformed the home into the ultimate kid's paradise: milk crates overflowing with games, crystal bowls of multicolored M&M's, video game music blasting from the speakers. It was the kind of house he had dreamed of when he was a boy. Now he would do what his own father never could—sit down and play games with his sons when they came to town. He could even play with his biological dad, Alfonso Antonio Romero, for whom, after he fell on hard times, Romero had bought a house not far away in town.

On the drive back from the Mexican restaurant, Romero and Stevie discussed the finishing touches for the estate: maybe a wooden sign on the gravel road with one board pointing to "The Cabin of Death" and the other to "Haunted Manor." Or, even better, a stone arrow leading to the woods with the words "For People We Don't Know or Trust." They considered constructing a stone arch over the driveway with the words "Castle Wolfenstein."

But these were all just grand designs, and their new company, Monkeystone Games, was going to be everything but. This time it would be something small, something personal, something fun. "It will be just good friends," Romero said, arriving home, "good friends making games."

For Carmack, the days of making games seemed like they might be numbered after all. The day after his contentious meeting with Kevin and Adrian, he uploaded his news. "It wasn't planned to announce this soon, but here it is," he wrote in his .plan. "We are working on a new Doom game, focusing on the single-player game experience, and using brand new technology in almost every aspect of it. That is all we are prepared to say about the game for quite some time, so don't push for interviews. We will talk about it when things are actually built, to avoid giving misleading comments. [The decision] went smoother than expected, but the other shoe dropped yesterday. Kevin and Adrian fired Paul Steed in retaliation, over my opposition."

Not long after the Doom III announcement hit, the rumor in Silicon Alamo started to spread: this would be Carmack's last game. And there seemed to be increasing evidence—tension between the owners and, more important, Carmack's new hobby, building rocket ships. *Real* rocket ships.

Carmack had rediscovered rocketry sometime during Quake III development. An interviewer had asked him about his childhood, and Carmack had related some stories about rockets, bombs, juvenile home, and being, as he now looked back, "an amoral little jerk." After the conversation, Carmack idly surfed the Net to see what had become of the model rocketry world. What he wandered into was the increasingly competitive and sophisticated world of hackers, engineers, and fry cooks who were trying to build giant high-powered rockets they could ride into outer space. Carmack was intrigued.

He ordered a few model rockets and shot them off at the end of his subdivision, moving up in power, week after week, until he got into the more impressive equipment. He began reading more about the amateur rocketry scene: the people who felt that NASA was nothing more than a trucking company, the ones who were competing for a $10 million "X Prize" to launch a ship into outer space with three people onboard. But what really appealed to him was the engineering.

The timing couldn't have been better. Despite the opportunities to innovate on Doom III, Carmack felt, as he said, "near the peak of the existing bodies of knowledge in graphics." Once he had made the leap into arbitrary 3-D with Quake, there wasn't much further to go beyond optimizations. It was like that time he had come to Softdisk and found Romero, someone who knew more than he did, someone who could help him learn more. Now Carmack saw a similar opportunity in the world of rockets. Rockets weren't just arbitrary things based on a market or a sanctioning body of rules or regulations. Here the goalposts were set by the way nature worked. It wasn't him against the computer, it was him against gravity.

Carmack bought thousands of dollars' worth of rocket science research books and got to work. He placed an ad on the local amateur rocketry website soliciting members who would be interested in building a manned rocket ship or, as he called it, a "vertical dragster." The group—a handful of low-key engineers—dubbed themselves Armadillo Aerospace. Bob Norwood volunteered his Ferarri shop for a work space. Before long they were meeting there every week.

While working on Doom III, Carmack began spending more and more time immersed in rockets. His house was covered in rocket parts.

His Ferrari trunk overflowed with motors. He was like the real-life manifestation of id's old game character Billy Blaze—the boy who built a rocket ship in his backyard. Carmack, the programmer who had once spent a hundred hours per week hunched over his computer, was now spending nearly half his time with grease and soldering irons. He would test-fire his high-powered rockets—complete with a bucket seat for someone his size—in abandoned parking lots. Sometimes, he would wait for events where he could launch his big ships with a few hundred other serious enthusiasts. Sometimes, he'd just grab a few small model rockets and head out to a field like when he was a kid—for fun.

On a gray afternoon in November 2001, Carmack loaded his car with a Day-Glo orange model rocket and headed east out of Mesquite until the buildings gave way to open pastures of grazing cows. He pulled in at Samuel Field, a browned patch of land that was used for radio-controlled planes and amateur rockets. A few picnic tables sat near a blue Porta Potti. An American flag fluttered on a rusty pole. A green garbage can spilled with debris; it looked like a can from Doom. "There are people who argue that you can just simulate reality," he said, "but I think there's value in coming out here and dealing with the wind."

Carmack set up his launch rod, a red-and-black frame that splayed on the ground with a long rod pointing toward the clouds. He laid out his rockets and assessed the wind. One of the first times he'd launched out here, the strong wind had lifted the ship until it disappeared. Carmack had since been working on a solution: a hot-wired global position system controlled by a radio modem and laptop. It would be, by all definitions, something of a hack—a piece of creative engineering that he'd invented to solve a problem. For now, he would be relying on an old-fashioned radio beacon that would beep a little distress signal when the rocket touched ground.

Carmack set up the first rocket, fitting it down on the metal pole, adjusting it for the wind. He clipped the wires to the bottom with rusty little clips. Stepping back, he pressed a small plastic button and—*swoooooooosh*—the rocket spiraled into the air with a trail of smoke. When it reached about three hundred feet, it arced down and the chamber popped open, so the clear plastic tube became a helicopter blade. Carmack jogged stiffly through the field to retrieve it.

"Okay," he said, "now let's try this one." He twisted open the base of the orange rocket. He'd made this rocket himself, starting with the main tube, scaling the fins in the slots, fixing the right epoxy, painting the body Day-Glo orange. He put in a G-80 engine, sixteen times more powerful than that of the last rocket. Carmack opened the cone and pushed in the purple-and-white parachute and the audio beacon, mashing the stuff down with a three-foot dowel.

These rocket motors were kids' stuff, he said. His high-powered rockets, by contrast, required high-grade hydrogen peroxide—something difficult to acquire. To get the dangerous stuff, an inspector has to make sure a rocketeer has enough room to house it. Also, it cost about twelve hundred bucks for a drum. Rather than deal with these hassles, Carmack and his rocket group started making moonshine rocket fuel, buying 70 percent grade hydrogen peroxide and distilling it to 90 percent. It was a dangerous brew; a mistake could shatter nearby glass or cause explosions. Carmack soon nixed the plan.

"We'll need to step a little further back for this one," he said, once the orange rocket was ready. Carmack rolled out the wires, attached them to the base, and hit the button. This time there was a *boomswoosh-boom* at blastoff, a puff of light and smoke. But the rocket was too low. It was heading off into the horizon over the trees. "Oh boy," he said, "hope we can find it." Carmack jogged off toward the woods. Down the path were broken propellers, loose bits of plastic hanging from trees like the membranes of robot intestines. Carmack stopped cold, hearing the shrill squeal of the beacon. The rocket was safe.

Though the cold wind was picking up, Carmack was not about to head home. He was just starting to have fun. He was talking a lot. Smiling. Ready for more. It was time to try a new engine, something with a little more oomph: an engine that was twice as powerful as what was meant for this size ship. He twisted off the old engine, dumped it out, and reached for the new one. He adjusted the rod, aimed straight for the clouds.

Carmack disdained talk of highfalutin things like legacies but when pressed would allow at least one thought on his own. "In the information age, the barriers just aren't there," he said. "The barriers are self-imposed. If you want to set off and go develop some grand new thing, you don't need millions of dollars of capitalization. You need enough pizza and Diet Coke to stick in your refrigerator, a cheap PC to work on, and the dedication to go through with it. We slept on floors. We waded across rivers."

Without warning he pressed the launch button, unleashing a thick black trail of smoke with a bang. High above the cows, the rocket soared.

EPILOGUE

I took a decade after the Two Johns met for their industry to come of age. Video game sales hit a record $10.8 billion in the United States, once again surpassing box-office receipts. With the emerging multibillion-dollar market for games on cell phones, games would outsell music too.

Gamers were also growing up. Far from being pimply boys, their average age was twenty-eight. Their diversity reflected the new range of game themes: from baseball to bridge, ancient Rome to future Japan, Mickey Mouse to David Bowie. An estimated 60 percent of all Americans—145 million people, including 62 million women *and* the U.S. president (who admitted to daily rounds of computer solitaire)— played. In countries such as Japan, Germany, and South Korea, games were already national pastimes.

As games seized the mainstream, some of the tremors over first-person shooters began to subside. Senator Lieberman praised the game companies' efforts in informing parents about mature content. And while there were continued efforts by politicians to legislate violent games, the courts sent a message by throwing out the multimillion-dollar lawsuits that alleged the teenage shooters at Columbine and Paducah were influenced by Doom. "This was a tragic situation," a U.S. district judge declared, "but tragedies such as this simply defy rational explanation and the courts should not pretend otherwise."

The time also proved the end of an era, particularly for the extended family of Silicon Alamo. Dallas, once home to at least a half dozen game companies, saw some of its most ambitious start-ups— including Romero's Ion Storm and Mike Wilson's Gathering of Developers—close their doors. A golden age seemed to have passed, when rebellious outsiders could independently rule a multibillion-dollar industry. But the spirit remained. Even the largest companies now emulated the innovations of id (such as online play, giving away demos, and encouraging game modification), but they called it viral marketing. And with new platforms like mobile phones emerging, maybe the next great gamers were waiting to rise from the swamps. The world would always be ready for the next great games.

As for id, the company's decision to revisit its former hits met with mixed results. The id-developed mission pack Quake III Team Arena was both a critical and a commercial disappointment, viewed by many as a lackluster attempt to answer the success of Unreal Tournament. A Game Boy Advance version of Commander Keen, produced but not developed by id, met a similar reception. Return to Castle Wolfenstein, however, proved to be both a critical and a commercial smash even though the title bore little resemblance to its predecessor (aside from a few turkey dinners on the tables).

This period saw John Carmack elevated to legendary status. His innovations in graphics programming were among the reasons why, as MIT's *Technology Review* magazine put it, "video games drive the evolution of computing." And his philanthropy—including the source code he continued to give away for free online—was surpassed by none. At an annual Game Developers Conference in San Jose, a twenty-nine-year-old Carmack became the third and youngest person ever inducted into the Academy of Interactive Arts and Sciences' Hall of Fame—the Oscars of the gaming business. After a videotaped congratulations from Bill Gates (who joked, "I just want you to know that I can write slicker and tighter code than John"), Carmack took the stage and endured a standing ovation from peers—comparable to that received by the industry's first inductee, Nintendo's Shigeru Miyamoto, creator of the very Mario game Carmack had replicated on the PC that fateful night at Softdisk.

The question on many gamers' minds was whether Carmack would be done with games after Doom III. Carmack himself wasn't sure. Between game and engine license sales, he felt he had more than enough money and, in fact, was giving frequently to charities. Plus, after so many years immersed in the science of graphics, he had achieved an almost Zen-like understanding of his craft. In the shower, he would see a few bars of light on the wall and think, Hey, that's a diffuse specular reflection from the overhead lights reflected off the faucet. Rather than detaching him from the natural world, this viewpoint only made him appreciate it more deeply. "These are things I find enchanting and miraculous," he said. "I don't have to be at the Grand Canyon to appreciate the way the world works, I can see that in reflections of light in my bathroom."

He immersed himself more deeply in a new source of learning: his rockets. On Saturdays he met with his team of rocketeers, including Ferrari whiz Bob Norwood, to work on what he called his vertical-landing hydrogen peroxide rocket vehicles. Carmack fashioned a Lunar Lander–style craft complete with a bucket seat in the middle for him or his wife, Anna. Next up: maybe a shot at the $10 million X Prize, which required the winner to launch three people into orbit and back two times within fourteen days. Those who knew Carmack expected him to have a decent shot.

John Romero, meanwhile, was happy to set his sights closer to home. Living with Stevie Case in their sprawling house in the Dallas countryside, he decided to get back, as he said, to his roots: designing and programming games. After some brief attempts at a traditional publishing deal, Romero, Stevie, and Tom Hall—despite good reviews of Anachronox—decided to forgo the route of ambitious computer games for the uncharted territory of games for pocket computers, cell phones, and other handheld devices. As the first well-known developer to embrace this new area of gaming, Romero became a cheerleader for mobile games much the way he once was for PC games.

EPILOGUE

True to their original vision of a small team turning out small games with short development cycles, Monkeystone completed their first title, Hyperspace Delivery Boy, in a matter of months. Working with three other developers late into the night at Romero's country house, Tom and Romero designed and programmed the entire game—just like the old days. The game cast players as Guy Carrington, an interstellar courier whose job was "to deliver the universe's most important parcels!" One reviewer called Hyperspace Delivery Boy one of the few pocket PC games worth buying. Next up: maybe a new version of Commander Keen, thanks to a license purchased from id. Tom was happy to have his boy, Billy Blaze, back home.

For Romero, the fun at Monkeystone wasn't just a new beginning, it was a break from the past. Shortly after his thirty-fourth birthday, he followed Tom's lead and cut off the notorious hair he'd been growing since 1991, leaving him with a close-cropped coif that was as easy to manage as his new company. Never one to let things go to waste, Romero wrapped the long black mane in a package and donated it to Locks of Love, a nonprofit group that supplies hairpieces for sick and needy children. His trademark hair wasn't the only thing to go. Now that he was living amid the trucks and dirt roads of the country, Romero found little use for his once prized possession: the Ferrari that Doom bought.

He lovingly photographed the car from a variety of angles in his front yard and uploaded the pictures with a description to eBay, the popular online auction depot, with the headline "Brutal Luxury." His opening price of $65,000 was well worth it, he explained, considering the more than $100,000 of modifications he'd installed, from the turbo system to the custom engine. "The sound that comes out of this car is completely amazing and destructive," he wrote. "Going down the street, you will sound like an Indy car when you hit the gas. . . . All you can do is laugh, it's so awesome." "It was," he promised, "the most awesome Ferrari Testarossa you'll ever see." The buyer who drove it away for $82,500 agreed.

Another Ferrari would bring Romero and Carmack back together. It happened outside a Quake III tournament in Mesquite. In previous years, the Two Johns all but ignored each other here. But this time was different. The games had been played. The scores had been settled. And a friend was in need. Carmack was in the parking lot having trouble starting his engine. Hearing a rumble, he looked up into the headlights of a fly yellow Hummer. Romero stepped from the car, jumper cables at the ready. There was work to be done.

AUTHOR'S NOTE

Like a lot of people in their thirties, I grew up in the same nascent gamer culture as the Two Johns. My favorite birthday present was a paper bag filled with tokens from Wizards, my neighborhood arcade. Wizards was *the* place: dark and windowless like a casino, lined with all the latest games flashing and beeping along the walls. I dumped a sizable portion of my lawn mowing money there. I owned the high score on Crazy Climber. And, after a challenging night with a bottle of Boone's Farm apple wine, I triumphantly vomited on a game called Omega Race. I was only a kid, but I sure felt free.

With video games came other explorations of fantasy, control, and rebellion. One time my friends and I chucked a smoke bomb into a creek, only to see a six-foot tongue of flames lick the sky. I never ran so fast in my life. We played Dungeons and Dragons. We launched lizards high above the suburbs in tiny model rockets. My first attempt at hacking occurred at Chuck E. Cheese—the pizza parlor arcade chain launched by Atari's Nolan Bushnell. This was in the early 1980s, and "the Cheese" had just gotten in a few primordial computers. For a token, we could type in any kind of message and the computer would speak it back in its robotic voice. Of course we immediately tried to type profanities, but the machine was programmed not to accept them. So we typed "phuck the manager" instead, taping down the keys so the message looped.

I was in my twenties working at an online bulletin board service in New York City when I first heard about Doom. One night late after work, a friend of mine booted it up and I jumped in for a round. Several hours later, we stumbled out into the darkness. *This* was a game. A couple years later, in 1996, I managed to convince an editor to assign me an article about the subculture of Quake: the latest from id Software. The next thing I knew I was tripping over wires in a University of Kansas flophouse where the two top clans, Impulse 9 and the Ruthless Bastards, had convened for a marathon deathmatch. These people were sacrificing everything to inhabit, modify, and create alternate realities. This wasn't just a game, this was a world—a relatively (and alluringly) undocumented world—filled with characters and stories and dreams and rivalries. That world led me to the Two Johns.

I spent the next six years exploring and chronicling the lives and industry of gamers. It was both amazing and frustrating to me that this multibillion-dollar business and culture remained such a mystery to so many people, and that mystery was breeding confusion and misperceptions everywhere I turned. To me, the story of John Carmack and John Romero was a classic American adventure that captured the birth of a new medium and the coming of age of two compelling and gifted young people. By telling it, I hoped to give gamers the respect and understanding they deserved. And I wanted the reader to have a good time.

ACKNOWLEDGMENTS

A BFT (Big Fucking Thanks, if you need to know) goes to everyone I interviewed while living in Dallas, traveling the country, and phoning or e-mailing from Brooklyn. Your recollections brought the past to life.

I'd like especially to thank the Two Johns. I had no idea how they would feel about answering all my questions, but they remained nothing less than gracious throughout our many late nights. John Carmack was as generous with his thoughts and memories as he is with his code. He also took me out to launch rockets and let me experience the turbo Ferrari firsthand; thanks for the ride. John Romero was always willing to dig into his vast archives of *everything*: games, art, comics, Burger King receipts, et cetera, et cetera, et cetera. He and Stevie even let me crash at their ranch to dig for myself; I'm grateful.

Thanks to all my magazine editors who believed in (and assigned) stories over the years.

I'm-not-worthy bows for my unbeatable clan: my agent, Mary Ann Naples at the Creative Culture, Inc., my editors, Jonathan Karp and Timothy Farrell, Jon's assistant, Jake Greenberg, my production editor, Benjamin Dreyer, and everyone else at Random House.

And thanks to my family and friends, for help and inspiration along the way.

BIBLIOGRAPHY

These books were helpful in my research.

ab Hugh, Dafydd, and Brad Linaweaver. *Doom: Hell on Earth.* New York: Penguin, 1995.

Campbell-Kelly, Martin, and William Aspray. *Computer: A History of the Information Machine.* New York: Basic Books, 1996.

Dear, William. *Dungeon Master: The Disappearance of James Dallas Egbert III.* Boston: Houghton Mifflin, 1984.

Dungeon Master Guide: Advanced Dungeons and Dragons. Renton, Wash.: TSR, 1995.

Freiberger, Paul, and Michael Swaine. *Fire in the Valley: The Making of the Personal Computer.* New York: McGraw-Hill, 2000.

Gibson, William. *Neuromancer.* New York: Berkeley, 1984.

Grossman, Dave, and Gloria DeGaetano. *Stop Teaching Our Kids to Kill: A Call to Action Against TV, Movie, and Video Game Violence.* New York: Crown, 1995.

Hafner, Katie, and Matthew Lyon. *Where Wizards Stay Up Late: The Origins of the Internet.* New York: Simon and Schuster, 1996.

Herman, Leonard. *Phoenix: The Rise and Fall of VideoGames.* Union, Nev.: Rolenta Press, 1997.

Herz, J. C. *Joystick Nation: How Video Games Ate Our Quarters, Won Our Hearts, and Rewired Our Minds.* New York: Little, Brown, 1995.

BIBLIOGRAPHY

Huizinga, Johan. *Homo Ludens: A Study of the Play Element in Culture*. Boston: Beacon, 1955.

Huxley, Aldous. *Brave New World*. New York: Harper and Row, 1946.

Id anthology. id Software, 1996. (Specifically, the story about id that accompanied this boxed set of games.)

Jones, Gerard. *Killing Monsters: Why Children Need Fantasy, Super Heroes, and Make-Believe Violence*. New York: Basic Books, 2002.

Kent, Steven L. *The First Quarter*. Bothell, Wash.: BWD Press, 2000.

Kidder, Tracy. *The Soul of a New Machine*. Boston: Little, Brown, 1981.

Leukart, Hank. *The Doom Hacker's Guide*. New York: MIS Press, 1995.

Levy, Steven. *Hackers: Heroes of the Computer Revolution*. New York: Bantam Doubleday Dell, 1984.

———. *Insanely Great: The Life and Times of the Macintosh, the Computer That Changed Everything*. New York: Penguin, 2000.

McLuhan, Marshall. *Understand Media: The Extensions of Man*. New York: McGraw-Hill, 1964.

Mendoza, John. *The Official Doom Survivor's Strategies and Secrets*. Alameda, Calif.: SYBEX, 1994.

Packer, Randall, and Ken Jordan. *Multimedia: From Wagner to Virtual Reality*. New York: W. W. Norton, 2001.

Player Handbook: Advanced Dungeons and Dragons. Renton, Wash.: TSR, 1995.

Poole, Steven. *Trigger Happy: Video Games and the Entertainment Revolution*. New York: Arcade, 2000.

Quake Authorized Strategy Guide. Indianapolis: Brady, 1995.

Rheingold, Howard. *The Virtual Community: Homesteading on the Electronic Frontier*. New York: HarperCollins, 1993.

Rucker, Rudy, R. U. Sirius, and Queen Mu. *Mondo 2000: User's Guide to the New Edge*. New York: HarperCollins, 1992.

Salzman, Marc. *Game Design: Secrets of the Sages*. Indianapolis: Brady, 1999.

Sheff, David. *Game Over: Press Start to Continue*. Wilton, Conn.: GamePress, 1999.

Stephenson, Neal. *Snow Crash*. New York: Bantam Spectra, 1993.

Turkle, Sherry. *Life on Screen: Identity in the Age of the Internet*. New York: Touchstone, 1995.

White, Michael. *Acid Tongues and Tranquil Dreams: Tales of Bitter Rivalry That Fueled the Advancement of Science and Technology*. New York: HarperCollins, 2001.

NOTES

The greatest challenge of telling a story I didn't experience firsthand was precisely that. With the exception of about a half dozen scenes I witnessed—such as the gaming conventions, the University of Kansas deathmatch, Carmack's rocket launch—most of this book relies upon the memories of others.

To re-create the story of the Two Johns, I conducted hundreds of interviews over six years, often with each person on multiple occasions. After moving to Dallas in the fall of 2000 for research, I became known in offices, barbecue joints, and bars around town as "the guy writing the Book." John Romero and John Carmack each spent dozens of hours in person answering my most picayune questions: how they were feeling, what they were thinking, what they were saying, hearing, seeing, playing. What they and others couldn't recall, I unearthed from websites, newsgroups, e-mails, chat transcripts, and magazines (though I drew from some of these articles, I made a point of getting the gamers' *own* versions of what happened as well). I also played a delirious amount of games: at home, online, and at a couple tournaments (yeah, I lost).

I spent six months transcribing all my taped interviews. From this material, I assembled a narrative of dialogue and description that re-creates the events as faithfully and accurately as possible. As often as appropriate, I told the story from each person's point of view to give readers the different perspectives.

Among the people I interviewed are, in no particular order, John Carmack, John Romero, Tom Hall, Adrian Carmack, Al Vekovius, Alex St. Johns, American McGee, Angel Munoz, Barrett Alexander, Robert Kotick, Brandon James, Christian Ankow, David Grossman, David Datta, Gabe Newell, Graeme Devine, Inga Carmack, Stan Carmack, Jan Paul van Waveren, Jay Wilbur, Jerry O'Flaherty, Eric Smith, Jim Dose, Kenneth Scott, Kevin Cloud, Lane Roathe, Larry Goldberg, Larry Herring, Michael Abrash, Mike Breslin, Mike Wilson, Paul Steed, Robert Atkins, Rob Dyer, Robert Duffy, John Schuneman, Ginny Schuneman, Ron Chaimowitz, Sandy Petersen, Scott Miller, Sean Martin, Shawn Green, Brian Eiserloh, Steve "Blue" Heaslip, Stevie Case, Sverre Kvernmo, Dennis "Thresh" Fong, Trent Reznor, Tim Sweeney, Mark Rein, Tim Willits, Todd Hollenshead, Todd Porter, Tom Mustaine, Warren Spector, William Haskins, "DWANGO" Bob Huntley, Harry Miller, Audrey Mann, Lori Mezoff, Andrea Schneider, Cliff Bleszinski, Matt Firme, Rob Smith, Richard "Levelord" Gray, Katherine Anna Kang, Donna Jackson, Paul Jaquays, Will Wright, Sid Meier, Doug Lowenstein, Seneca Menard, Noel Stephens, Luke "Weasl" Whiteside, Bobby Pavlock, Doug Myres, Mark Dochtermann, Steve Maines, Brian Raffel, Steven Raffel, Joost Schuur, Will Loconto, Jeff Hartman, Stan Nuevo, Chad Barron, Kelly Hoerner, Robert Westmoreland, Pam Wolford, Dave Taylor, Drew Markham, Hank Leukart, Jim Perkins, Roman Ribaric, Arthur Pober, Bob Norwood, Chris Roberts, Rick Brenner, Gene Lipkin, Vince Desiderio, Max Schaefer, David Brevik, Gary Gygax, Clint "_fo0k" Richards, Tom "Entropy" Kizmey, Larry Muller, Frans P. de Vries, Dan Hammond, Alex Quintana, Billy Browning, Jay Franke . . . Sorry to anyone I neglected to list.

Portions of this book are drawn from articles of mine that originally appeared in publications including *Spin, Salon, Rolling Stone, Wired News, Feed, Spectrum, POV,* and *Popular Science.*

The notes here reflect the supplementary resources cited. Some of the articles are from magazines that no longer exist beyond some old photocopies in gamers' archives; as a result, some page numbers and dates were unavailable as noted.

INTRODUCTION: THE TWO JOHNS

ix   one afternoon in April 2000: I attended this conference and observed the events described, including the meeting of Carmack and Romero.

x   more money . . . than on movie tickets: According to the Motion Picture Association of America, moviegoers spent $8.4 billion at U.S. box offices in 2001, while, according to the NPD Group, Americans spent $10.8 billion on video games.

xi   "Romero wants an empire": E-mail interview with Chris Spencer on January 8, 1997, posted on onenet.quake newsgroup.

ONE: THE ROCK STAR

6   James Dallas Egbert III disappeared: William Dear, *Dungeon Master: The Disappearance of James Dallas Egbert III* (Boston: Houghton Mifflin, 1984).

6   $25 million in annual sales: Interview, Gary Gygax.

7   the D&D rule book: *Player Handbook: Advanced Dungeons and Dragons* (Renton, Wash.: TSR, 1995).

8   sales reaching over $7 billion: Martin Campbell-Kelly and William Aspray, *Computer: A History of the Information Machine* (New York: Basic Books, 1996), pp. 131–153.

8   Three years later in 1961: Steven Levy, *Hackers: Heroes of the Computer Revolution* (New York: Bantam Doubleday Dell, 1984), pp. 50–69.

8   Ten years later . . . Will Crowther: Ibid., pp. 140–141.

9   the language of the priests: Ibid., p. 19.

9   arcade games bringing in $5 billion a year: "Games That People Play," *Time*, January 18, 1982, p. 51.

9   In one, a dog named Chewy: John Romero's personal archives.

9   a homemade comic book called *Weird:* Ibid.

10   Apple had become the darling: Paul Freiberger and Michael Swaine, *Fire in the Valley: The Making of the Personal Computer* (New York: McGraw-Hill, 2000), p. 118.

10   the Two Steves: Ibid., pp. 253–263.

10   hacked Spacewar: Steven L. Kent, *The First Quarter* (Bothell, Wash.: BWD Press, 2000), pp. 25–28.

10   Woz was equal parts: Freiberger and Swaine, *Fire in the Valley*, pp. 261–262.

11   But the Apple II . . . was mass market: Ibid., p. 267.

12   Ken and Roberta Williams: Levy, *Hackers*, pp. 280–302.

12   Silas Warner: Personal homepage, http://pwp.value.net/penomee/silas.html.

13   "Machine of the Year": "Machine of the Year: The Computer Moves In," *Time*, January 3, 1982.

13   $536 million in losses: Kent, *First Quarter,* p. 198.

13   $1 billion in sales: Ibid., p. 214.

13   comics he called "Melvin": John Romero's personal archives.

14   the good news came: Ibid.

14   "When I win": Ibid.

14   "I've been learning computers": Ibid.

TWO: THE ROCKET SCIENTIST

19   In second grade, only seven years old: School report letter in Inga Car-
      mack's personal archives.

19   his top five problems: Inga Carmack's archives.

19   when he refused to do extracredit homework: Ibid.

20   The game was so compelling: Herman, *Phoenix,* p. 51.

20   a letter to his teacher: Inga Carmack's archives.

21   *WarGames:* Ibid.

22   "Though some in the field": Levy, *Hackers,* pp. 6–7.

22   Bulletin board systems came about: Freiberger and Swaine, *Fire in the
      Valley,* p. 142.

23   The WELL: The WELL, www.thewell.com; Howard Rheingold, *The
      Virtual Community: Homesteading on the Electronic Frontier* (New York:
      HarperCollins, 1993), pp. 17–37.

25   new television series, *Star Trek: The Next Generation:* "Encounter at Far-
      point," airdate: September 28, 1987.

26   "Why can't you realise": Inga Carmack archives.

26   Wraith: Nite Owl Productions, 1990.

THREE: DANGEROUS DAVE IN COPYRIGHT
INFRINGEMENT

29   In 1864, Confederate soldiers: John Andrew Prime, *Shreveport's Civil
      War Defenses,* http://www.shreve.net/~japrime/lagenweb/defenses.htm.

30   its burgeoning clones: Freiberger and Swaine, *Fire in the Valley,* p. 349.

32   Softdisk occupied two buildings: I saw the buildings during a visit in
      November 2000.

33   By refusing to incorporate: Freiberger and Swaine, *Fire in the Valley,* pp.
      357–365.

46   Defender: Kent, *First Quarter,* p. 118.

51   Nintendo was on the way: David Sheff, *Game Over: Press Start to Continue*
      (Wilton, Conn.: GamePress, 1999), p. 3.

FOUR: PIZZA MONEY

57   "Dear John . . . Loved your game": John Romero archives.

58   "Dear John . . . loved your game": Ibid.

58 a brief article: "Into the Depths," *PC Games Magazine,* 1990 [photocopy from Romero's archives; month and page number missing].

58 "Scott: You, sir, have serious psychological problems": Romero's archives.

59 "Dear Mr. Miller": Ibid.

60 Andrew Fluegelman: "Try It, You'll Like It," *Forbes,* November 28, 1988, p. 227.

68 Warren Robinett: Herman, *Phoenix,* p. 44.

69 "*The Fight for Justice*": Text from "Previews!" screen of Commander Keen: Marooned on Mars, Apogee Software Productions, 1990.

71 "Superlative alert!": Unidentified shareware catalog, 1991 [photocopy from Scott Miller's archives; month and page number missing].

71 "sets a new standard for shareware games": "Games That Are More Than Keen," *BBS Caller's Digest,* 1991 [photocopy from Scott Miller's archives; month and page number missing].

71 "For stimulating": "Commander Keen: Invasion of the Vorticons," *PC Magazine,* December 1991, p. 69.

FIVE: MORE FUN THAN REAL LIFE

79 Violent fantasy . . . had an ancient history: Many such examples appear in Gerard Jones, *Killing Monsters: Why Children* Need *Fantasy, Super Heroes, and Make-Believe Violence* (New York: Basic Books, 2002).

79 first video game to be banned: Kent, *First Quarter,* pp. 73–74.

80 primal desire: Randall Packer and Ken Jordan, *Multimedia: From Wagner to Virtual Reality* (New York: W. W. Norton, 2001), p. xx.

80 cave paintings in Lascaux: Ibid.

80 "dazzling and incomparably more solid": Aldous Huxley, *Brave New World* (New York: Harper and Row, 1946), p. 113.

80 Morton Heilig: Morton Heilig, "El Cin del Futuro," *Espacios* (Mexico), no. 23–24, January–June 1955, as cited by Packer and Jordan, *Multimedia,* p. 227.

80 "The environments . . . suggest a new art medium": Myron Krueger, "Responsive Environments," *American Federation of Information Processing Systems* 46, June 13–16, 1977, pp. 423–433, as cited by Packer and Jordan, *Multimedia,* p. 115.

81 Scott Fisher: Scott Fisher, *Virtual Interface Environments: The Art of Human-Computer Interface Design,* edited by Brenda Laurel (Reading, Mass.: Addison-Wesley, 1989), as cited by Packer and Jordan, *Multimedia,* pp. 237–251.

81 "kind of electronic persona": Ibid., p. 246.

NOTES

SIX: GREEN AND PISSED

89 Someone siphoned gasoline . . . Adrian was particularly miserable: Id anthology, id Software, 1996.

90 "WANTED: CLERIC and/or THIEF!": Tom Hall's archives.

93 On a cold winter day: Id anthology.

93 a NeXT computer: Freiberger and Swaine, *Fire in the Valley*, p. 372.

SEVEN: SPEAR OF DESTINY

105 They wanted the games banned: "Games That People Play," p. 52.

110 "Id software is brought to you": Audiotape from Romero's archives.

113 "There's no surprise": Ron Dippold, "Wolfenstein 3-D Reviewed," *Game Bytes* [photocopy from Romero's archives; date and page number missing].

114 "how popular Wolf 3-D is": Romero's archives.

114 "more like an interactive movie": Wolfenstein Review, *Shareware Update* [photocopy from Romero's archives; date and page number missing].

114 "single-handedly justifying the existence of shareware": "Wolfenstein 3-D," *Video Games and Computer Entertainment,* September 1992, p. 113.

114 Even *Computer Gaming World:* "The Third Reich in the Third Dimension," *Computer Gaming World,* 1992, pp. 50, 52.

114 A Kentucky entrepreneur hooked up a version: "Reality Rocket Enables You to Really Get into Video Game," *Courier-Journal* (Louisville, KY), September 19, 1992, p. 2S.

114 Some players thought: Wolfenstein 3-D Frequently Asked Questions, ftp://ftp.gamers.org/pub/games/wolf3d/docs/Wolfenstein-3D.faq.

114 "This game certainly goes heavy": "Revived Game Is Heavy on the Gore," *Toronto Star,* November 21, 1992, p. J4.

115 "Wolfenstein 3-D may have no socially redeeming value": *PC Computing,* December 1992, p. 176.

115 "Nazis in Cyberspace": *BBS Callers Digest,* August 1992, pp. 30–34.

118 Tom documented: Romero's archives.

EIGHT: SUMMON THE DEMONS

125 one of "the most remarkable . . . success stories": "Apogee: The Height of Shareware," *Electronic Games,* 1992, p. 45 [photocopy from Scott Miller's archives; date missing].

134 Fuzzy Pumper Palette Shop: John Mendoza, *The Official Doom Survivor's Strategies and Secrets* (Alameda, Calif.: SYBEX, 1994), p. 257.

134 "The overall effect is distorted": Ibid.

136 "We don't know what nasty sludge": "They're Going to Hell for This One," *Computer Gaming World,* June 1993, p. 102.

NINE: THE COOLEST GAME

144 selling more than 4 million copies: *PC Data,* 2000.

145 "Its brilliantly designed and rendered 3-D images": "Surrealistic Puzzle Paradise," *Wired,* January 1994; www.wired.com/wired/archive/2.01/streetered.html?pg=3.

146 A community television program did a piece: *Nightly Business Report,* November 2, 1992.

151 "You started posting hype": comp.sys.ibm.pc.games.action, August 19, 1993.

151 "I was firing the shotgun": Ibid., November 2, 1993.

151 "The Night Before Doom": Hank Leukart, comp.sys.ibm.pc.games .action, December 9, 1993.

151 "A Parent's Nightmare": Douglas Adler, *Computer Paper,* December 1993, as cited in comp.sys.ibm.pc.games.action.

TEN: THE DOOM GENERATION

154 Like a lot of parents: Kent, *First Quarter,* p. 373.

154 By choosing to release the blood-and-guts version: Sheff, *Game Over,* p. 460.

155 Senator Lieberman was also joined: Cited in J. C. Herz, *Joystick Nation: How Video Games Ate Our Quarters, Won Our Hearts, and Rewired Our Minds* (New York: Little, Brown, 1995), p. 189.

155 "Satan's efficient agents"; media-effects research: Jones, *Killing Monsters,* pp. 134–137.

156 New York City mayor Fiorello La Guardia: Kent, *First Quarter,* p. 4.

156 a $6 billion industry: "Games People Play," p. 51.

156 "The PTA is concerned": "Video Games: Help or Hazard to Children's Health?" UPI, November 16, 1982.

156 "Children are putting their book fees": "Video Games — Fun or Serious Threat?" *U.S. News & World Report,* February 22, 1982, p. 7.

156 shut down arcades: "Video Games Assailed in Asia," *Facts on File World News Digest,* December 31, 1982.

156 "Video Games — Fun or Serious Threat?": *U.S. News & World Report,* February 22, 1982, p. 7.

NOTES

157 "Video Game Fever—Peril or Payoff for the Computer Generation," *Children's Health*, September 1983, pp. 24–25.

157 "The video game craze": "Pac-Man Perils," *MacNeil/Lehrer Report*, December 29, 1982.

157 C. Everett Koop: Sheff, *Game Over*, p. 189; Herz, *Joystick Nation*, p. 184.

157 "Dr. Nicholas Pott": "Invasion of the Video Creatures," *Newsweek*, November 16, 1981, p. 90.

157 "There is no evidence": "Personality Differences Between High and Low Electronic Video Game Users," *Journal of Psychology* 114, 1983, pp. 159–165. Cited in Herz, *Joystick Nation*, p. 184.

157 "A lot of kids who are good": "Invasion of the Video Creatures," p. 90.

157 The hearings were filled with impassioned statements: Joint Hearings Before the Subcommittee on Juvenile Justice, One Hundred Third Congress, Serial No. J-103-37, December 9, 1993.

159 Though a global network of computers had been around: Freiberger and Swaine, *Fire in the Valley*, pp. 409–411.

160 "It was a mob scene": "A Doom Boom," *Dallas Morning News*, May 17, 1994, p. 15A.

160 "Since today's release of Doom": "'Doom' Bursts onto College Computer Networks," *Houston Chronicle*, December 15, 1993, Business, p. 1.

160 Intel . . . Texas A&M: "'Doom' Bursts onto College Computer Networks," p. 1.

160 "People sprint in here": "Lovers of Guts and Gore Should Meet This Doom," *Courier-Journal* (Louisville, Ky.), May 7, 1994, p. 2S.

160 "3-D tour de force": "3-D Applications Can Add New Dimension to Business World," *PC Week*, January 31, 1994, p. 59.

161 "The once-dull PC": "The Best in Arcade Game Software," *Compute*, January 1994, p. S1.

161 "The follow-up to Wolfenstein 3-D": "Games," *The Guardian* (London), January 13, 1994, p. 17.

161 "This game is so intense": "Doom Awaits Fun-Seeking PC Owners," *Arizona Republic*, March 6, 1994, p. E1.

162 "You know . . . I do have a battle-ax": "A Visit to the id Office," *Electronic Games*, January 1995, p. 39.

164 They were philanthropic: "Doom's Day Afternoon: id's Hell on Earth," *Computer Player*, October 1994, p. 28.

164 "I wanted to buy them things": "Former Student Repays School with Computer Equipment," *Kansas City Star*, April 21, 1994, p. C4.

170 "Microsoft is committed to delivering": "Microsoft Gets Serious About Fun in Windows," *Business Wire*, April 26, 1994.

NOTES

170 "heroinware": "Hit Game Sequel Spells 'Doom' Again," *San Francisco Chronicle,* October 8, 1994, p. E1.

170 "Privately held id Software": "Profits from the Underground," *Forbes,* May 9, 1994, p. 176.

170 *The New York Times:* "Wallowing in Doom," *New York Times,* May 15, 1994, Styles, p. 8.

170 *USA Today:* "'Doom' Brings a New Dimension to 3-D Games," *USA Today,* May 25, 1994, p. 3D.

170 *Variety:* "It's Doomsday in Hollywood," *Daily Variety,* July 5, 1994, p. 7.

171 "Everyone is talking": "A Doom Boom; Software Firm Creates a Monster Hit via the Information Superhighway," *Dallas Morning News,* May 17, 1994, p. 15A.

171 China was considering banning Doom: "Good, Strong Guidelines Needed; 'Gory' Game Gives Cause for Concern," *South China Morning Post,* March 22, 1994, p. 1.

171 Brazil . . . would later outlaw the game: "Duke Nukem Banned in Brazil," Reuters, December 21, 1999.

171 Night Trap . . . Mortal Kombat II: Kent, *First Quarter,* pp. 382–384.

171 Austin Virtual Gaming: "Virtual Addiction," *Austin American-Statesman,* April 2, 1994, p. F1.

174 "So we can beat everybody": "Players Get Virtual Kicks in Doom Tournament," *Austin American-Statesman,* May 8, 1994, p. B1.

ELEVEN: QUAKES

178 "Every man and woman should play": Cited in Johan Huizinga, *Homo Ludens: A Study of the Play Element in Culture* (Boston: Beacon, 1955), pp. 18–19.

178 "play . . . is a *significant* function": Ibid., p. 1.

178 "a society without games": Marshall McLuhan, *Understand Media: The Extensions of Man* (New York: McGraw-Hill, 1964), pp. 208–211.

179 "Quake won't be just a game": "Doom's Day Afternoon: id's Hell on Earth," *Computer Player,* October 1994, p. 28.

182 "It's as close to virtual reality": "Doom and Links 3.6 Pro Give Hours of Fun," *Chicago Sun-Times,* October 17, 1994, Financial, p. 54.

182 "Virtual Mayhem and Real Profits": *New York Times,* September 3, 1994, sec. 1, p. 35.

182 "Doomonomics": "Doomonomics," *Economist,* May 25, 1996, pp. 12–14.

182 "an entire file": "Power Finance or Boot Strap?" *Red Herring,* December 1994, p. 81.

193 In Quantico, Virginia: "Doom Goes to War," *Wired*, April 1997, pp. 114–118.

194 D!Zone . . . surpassed Doom II: "Top Software," *Entertainment Weekly*, June 9, 1995.

TWELVE: JUDGMENT DAY

200 The party was in full swing: "Microsoft Shows Games at Halloween Bash," UPI International, October 30, 1995.

210 Sales for Doom II: *PC Data*, 2000.

210 GTI's sales; "[GTI] came out of nowhere": "GT Masters Software Universe with New-Fangled Sales Smarts," *Crain's New York Business*, July 1, 1996, News, p. 4.

217 a cover story on id: "The Egos at Id," *Wired*, August 1996, pp. 122–127.

THIRTEEN: DEATHMATCH

221 In a dark room: The story of this tournament originally appeared in different form in my article "Blood Sport," *Spin*, June 1997, pp. 104–107.

222 "bloody amazing": " 'Quake': Bloody Amazing," *USA Today*, June 27, 1996, p. 5D.

222 "a towering programming feat": "10 on the Richter Scale: id Software Quake Action Game Software Review," *Computer Gaming World*, October 1996, p. 174.

222 "Quake delivers the most carnage": "Multimedia: The Best and Worst of 1996," *Entertainment Weekly*, December 27, 1996.

222 "Electronic games": *Spin*, June 1997, p. 106.

228 "Lots of people will read": E-mail interview with Chris Spencer on January 8, 1997, posted on onenet.quake newsgroup.

228 *Time* magazine estimated: "Cyber Elite: Inside the Top Fifty Time Digital Cyber Elite," *Time Digital*, October 5, 1998, http://www.time.com/time/digital/cyberelite/36.html.

233 "the Willy Wonka Chocolate Factory of Gaming!": "Game Designers Take Penthouse; Programmers of 'Doom' Create Culture Clash at Texas Commerce Tower," *Dallas Business Journal*, July 25, 1997, p. 1.

234 "cyber elite": *Time Digital*, October 5, 1998.

234 "cool companies": "Cool Companies," *Fortune*, July 7, 1997, p. 84.

234 "Id is a technology-oriented company": "Connected: There Is Another Way to Achieve the Sort of Financial Security That Brings the Freedom to Throw TVs out of Hotel Windows and Drive Rolls-Royces into Swimming Pools," *Daily Telegraph*, April 29, 1997, p. 15.

234 "After I left": "Braindrain at id: Mood 'Dark and Gloomy,'" *Wired News*, January 18, 1997, http://www.wired.com/news/culture/0,1284,1539,00. html.

234 "It's going to happen": "Merchant of Doom Is Reborn as the Ion Man," *The Times*, April 16, 1997, features section.

235 "the creative talent behind [id]": Ibid.

235 "the man responsible": "Connected," p. 15.

236 "After he got rich and famous": "Beyond Doom and Quake: Everything That Game Designer John Romero Touches Turns to Gore. And to Gold," *Time*, June 23, 1997, p. 56.

238 "I always flip my hair": Dear Romero! PlanetQuake, June 9, 1999, http://www.planetquake.com/features/mynx/dearromero.shtm.

241 "I bought my first Ferrari": "Intergraph, id Software, Rendition, and ClanRing to Sponsor QUAKE Tournament," *Business Wire*, March 7, 1997.

FOURTEEN: SILICON ALAMO

Note: Though parts of this chapter draw from an article that appeared in the *Dallas Observer* about Ion Storm ("Stormy Weather," *Dallas Observer*, January 14–28, 1999, pp. 34–46), I chose not to include here the internal e-mails published in the *Observer* piece.

243 "New Cowboys": "Greetings from America's Secret Capitols," *Time*, July 13, 1998, www.time.com/time/magazine/archives.

243 "Doom babies": "Legions of Doom," *Wired*, March 1998, p. 157.

243 "the new Hollywood": "Why the New Hollywood Is in Texas," *Boston Globe*, November 23, 1997, p. N5.

244 Of the $3.7 billion generated: "Gamemakers Feeding Growing Appetite for Fun," *USA Today*, June 19, 1997, p. 4D.

244 "The PC gaming boom": Ibid.

257 "You can't keep up with Carmack": "Knee Deep in a Dream: The Story of Daikatana," *GameSpot*, May 2000, http://www.gamespot.com/features/btg-daikatana/index.html.

259 "Hi . . . I'm here to tell you": "John Romero—Artiste," *Penny Arcade*, November 25, 1998, http://www.penny-arcade.com/view.php3?date=1998-11-25.

259 But when a gaming magazine: "John Romero Killed at Age 30," *Adrenaline Vault*, August 28, 1998, www.avault.com.

260 "Either people who are no longer": "Stormy Weather," *Dallas Observer*, January 14–28, 1999, p. 45.

NOTES

FIFTEEN: STRAIGHT OUT OF DOOM

262 He made amateurish mods: I downloaded and played Eric Harris's mods.

262 "Whatsup all you doomers": Text included with Eric Harris's U.A.C. Labs mod posted online.

262 "It's going to be like fucking Doom": "The Columbine Tapes," *Time*, December 20, 1999, pp. 40–51.

263 "Several readers have written in": "Doom in the School," *Blue's News*, April 21, 1999, www.bluesnews.com archives.

263 The Simon Wiesenthal Center: "Doom Level a 'Dry Run,' Rabbi Suggests," *Denver Post*, May 4, 1999, p. A10.

263 "dark, dangerous place": "Social Outcasts Built Fantasy World of Violence," Washington Post News Service, April 22, 1999.

263 "widen the hole in any kid's soul": "Sow Cultural Violence and Reap Death," *Newsday*, April 22, 1999, p. A57.

263 "murder simulators": "Who's to Blame?" *60 Minutes*, April 25, 1999.

263 Even President Clinton chimed in: Cited in "Clinton Sees Violent Influence in Three Video Games," *Los Angeles Times*, April 25, 1999, p. A12.

263 Marilyn Manson: "The Trouble with Looking for Signs of Trouble," *New York Times*, April 25, 1999, Week in Review, p. 1.

263 banned trench coats: "Dress Rehearsal for Death," *Daily Record*, April 23, 1999, p. 8.

263 Disney World and Disneyland: "Disneyland Disarms Some Video Games," *Los Angeles Times*, May 14, 1999, p. 1A.

264 In an April 28 statement: Statement of Senator Joseph Lieberman Calling for a White House Summit on Media Violence, April 28, 1999.

264 "How many of us accept": "Violence Engendered by the War," *Baltimore Sun*, May 23, 1999, p. 3D.

264 "There's more to learn": "Harris and Klebold," *Good Morning America*, May 24, 1999.

264 As Jones noted: Jones, *Killing Monsters*, pp. 37–38.

265 Researchers since the 1980s: "Personality, Psychopathology, and Development Issues in Male Adolescent Video Game Use," *Journal of American Academic Child Psychiatry* 24, 1988, pp. 329–333, as cited in Herz, *Joystick Nation*, p. 184.

265 An academic study in England: "Cyber-Games Make Children Brighter," *Sunday Times*, July 22, 2001, http://www.sunday-times.co.uk.

265 In Finland, researchers used computer games: "Computer Game Helps Dyslexics," BBC News Online, August 20, 2001, http://news.bbc.co.uk/hi/english/sci/tech/newsid_1496000/1496709.stm.

265 "Violence in film": Stuart Fischoff, "Psychology's Quixotic Quest for the Media-Violence Connection," American Psychological Association Convention, Boston, 1999; as cited in Jones, *Killing Monsters*, p. 28.

265 "This is so crazy and hysterical": "Video Games, Net Unfairly Blamed for Kids' Violence," *San Francisco Chronicle*, May 5, 1999, p. B1.

266 "Violence has always been": "A Room Full of Doom," *Time*, May 24, 1999, p. 65.

266 "The video game 'Quake'": "The Violent World of Video Games," *Insight on the News*, June 28, 1999, p. 14.

266 "more fun than shooting": "Do Kids Buy Into Violence? Clinton Orders Inquiry into Marketing Practices," Gannett News Service, June 2, 1999.

268 a $130 million lawsuit: "A Game Boy in the Crosshairs," *New York Times*, May 23, 1999, sec. 6, p. 36.

271 "come hell or high water": *PC Games*, February 1999, as cited in "Knee Deep in a Dream."

271 "the place where the 'designer's vision'": "Stormy Weather," *Dallas Observer*, January 14–28, 1999, p. 38.

272 "Shut up and finish the game": "Knee Deep in a Dream."

273 "For those of you": Source, Interactive Digital Software Association.

277 "Online gaming is still a small segment": "Don't Shoot While I'm Talking," *Forbes*, October 18, 1999, p. 158.

277 "Aaaaarrgggggggggh!": This and other scenes at Ion Storm are drawn from my two-part article "Hearts of Darkness" and "How Do Game Developers Hack It?" *Salon*, March 7, 2000, http://www.salon.com/tech/feature/2000/03/07/romero/index.html and http://www.salon.com/tech/feature/2000/03/08/ion_two/index.html.

SIXTEEN: PERSISTENT WORLDS

281 Katherine Anna Kang was called a banana: "Interview with Anna Kang," *Domain of Games*, November 9, 2000, http://www.domainofgames.com/?display=interviews&id=annakang&page=index.html.

285 selling only 41,000 copies: NPD Group, 2002.

285 "a disaster": "Sworded Affair," *Entertainment Weekly*, June 13, 2000, accessed online at www.ew.com.

285 "signals nothing more remarkable": Daikatana Review, *PC Gamer*, August 9, 2000, accessed online at http://www.pcgamer.com/reviews/archives/review_2000-08-09am.html.

285 "Yep . . . it stinks": "Yep It Stinks," *Computer Gaming World*, November 2000, accessed online at http://www.zdnet.com/products/stories/reviews/0,4161,2667023,00.html.

NOTES

286 an estimated $6 billion history: Datamonitor, 2002.

289 "an amoral little jerk": Interview with John Carmack, *Slashdot*, October
     15, 1999, www.slashdot.org.

EPILOGUE

293 $10.8 billion in the United States: NPD Group, 2002. This number re-
     flects sales of video game console hardware, video game console soft-
     ware, and PC software.

293 surpassing box-office receipts . . . music: According to the Motion Pic-
     ture Association of America, moviegoers spent $8.4 billion at U.S. box
     offices in 2001, and the Recording Industry of America put music sales at
     $13.7 billion in 2001.

293 An estimated 60 percent of all Americans: NPD Group and Interactive
     Digital Software Association.

294 "This was a tragic situation": "Parents of Students Killed in Kentucky
     Lose Lawsuit," Associated Press, April 7, 2000.

294 "video games drive the evolution": *Technology Review*, March 2002 cover.

296 one of the few pocket PC games: "Hyperspace Delivery Boy," *Pocket-
     gamer*, January 8, 2002, http://www.pocketgamer.org/reviews/action/hdb/.

INDEX

INDEX

INDEX

INDEX

INDEX

INDEX

INDEX

DAVID KUSHNER has written for numerous publications, including *The New York Times*, *Rolling Stone*, *Wired*, *The Village Voice*, and *Spin*. He has also worked as a senior writer and producer for the music website SonicNet. He lives in New York City.

This book was set in Cochin, named for Charles Nicolas Cochin the younger, an eighteenth-century French engraver. Henry Johnson first arranged for the cutting of the Cochin type in America, to be used in *Harper's Bazaar*.

Cochin type is a commendable effort to reproduce the work of the French copperplate engravers of the eighteenth century.